PRAEGER LIBRARY OF U.S. GOVERNMENT DEPARTMENTS
AND AGENCIES

The Department of Health, Education, and Welfare

PRAEGER LIBRARY OF U.S. GOVERNMENT DEPARTMENTS
AND AGENCIES

Consulting Editors

ERNEST S. GRIFFITH

Former University Professor and Dean Emeritus, School of International Service, American University; former Director, Legislative Reference Service, Library of Congress; and author of *The American System of Government* and *The Modern Government in Action*

HUGH LANGDON ELSBREE

Former Chairman, Department of Political Science, Dartmouth College; former Managing Editor, *American Political Science Review;* former Director, Legislative Reference Service, Library of Congress

THE U.S. GOVERNMENT today is a maze of departments and agencies engaged in a worldwide range of programs and activities. Some departments are as old as the government itself; others are newly created or have been expanded or redirected by recent legislation. The books in this series describe the origin, development, function, methods, and structure of specific departments or agencies and explain how far their activities extend and how they relate to other branches of the government and to the public. All are written by authors with firsthand knowledge of their subjects.

The *Praeger Library of U.S. Government Departments and Agencies* is the only comprehensive, detailed source of such information. A list of those titles already published appears at the back of this volume.—THE EDITORS

The Department of Health, Education, and Welfare

Rufus E. Miles, Jr.

PRAEGER PUBLISHERS
New York · Washington

To the
UNSUNG CAREER EMPLOYEES
OF **HEW**

RA
5
M 54

Published in the United States of America in 1974
by Praeger Publishers, Inc.
111 Fourth Avenue, New York, N.Y. 10003

© 1974 by Praeger Publishers, Inc.

This book is No. 39 in the series
Praeger Library of U.S. Government Departments and Agencies

Library of Congress Cataloging in Publication Data

Miles, Rufus E
The Department of Health, Education, and Welfare.

(The Praeger library of U.S. Government departments and agencies, no. 39)
Bibliography: p. 317
1. United States. Dept. of Health, Education, and Welfare. [DNLM: 1. Education—U.S. 2. Public health administration—U.S. 3. Social welfare—U.S. WA540 A
D4M 1974]
RA5.M54   353.84   72-88986

Printed in the United States of America

Preface

It is impossible to pack into three hundred pages an adequate
characterization of the Department of Health, Education, and
Welfare. To anyone who has lived in it and with it and seen it
grow from a loose conglomeration of modest-sized bureaus to the
largest department in the world—in expenditure terms—in a
mere two decades, it seems especially frustrating to try to tell so
large a saga in so short a space. The best among difficult alternatives
would seem to be to capture some sense of its historical roots,
some feel for its mode of operation, some evaluation of its successes and failures, some idea as to what its leaders have been
like, and a guess as to what the future holds for HEW. Above
all, the purpose of this book is to try to catch its spirit and help
enable people to understand what makes it tick.

As will be apparent to the reader, the only source for some
of the information upon which the book is based is the memory
of the author. Fortunately, most of this material has had the
benefit of corroboration from one or more others who shared
the unforgettable experiences.

It has also seemed important to try to put the dynamics of
HEW into the context of the corresponding dynamics of the
larger society. This could only be done within the space constraints by paring to the bone and even omitting descriptions of
many of HEW's smaller activities. A listing of its nearly 200
programs is contained in Appendix A, which gives the source of
additional information about each.

The book deliberately emphasizes the perspective of the Secretary and his office, and is, therefore, unduly brief in treating the program agencies. Even so, the amount of space that could be allocated to the stewardship of each of the ten Secretaries is painfully brief.

For various kinds and degrees of help and kindly criticism, I am deeply indebted to the following people, most of whom have seen a great deal of HEW from the inside: Stuart Clarke, Joel Cohen, Kathryn Heath, James Isbister, Wallace Janssen, Dorothy Jones, James Kelly, John Kelso, Charles Kidd, Samuel and Helen Martz, Charles Miller, S. McKee Rosen, Mary Ross, Sidney Saperstein, Richard Seggel, Joseph Weikel, Alanson and Marjorie Willcox, and Edward Yourman. I am also indebted to Janet Embry for typing the manuscript, and especially to Malinda Elliott for numerous helpful editorial improvements. For any errors that remain, I take full responsibility.

To the scores of people whose names I would have liked to include but could not, I offer my thanks. It is ever thus. The unsung are those who make an organization more than its laws and its policies and its leadership, more even than the sum of its parts. It is they who make an institution into a living organism and at its best give it the feeling of an extended family, committed both to helping its members and the larger society. To them this book is dedicated.

RUFUS E. MILES, JR.

September, 1973
Washington, D.C.

Contents

TABLES

CHARTS

A section of photographs follows page 104.

Prologue

The Department of Health, Education, and Welfare is the foremost institutional expression of five social revolutions that have, within a single generation, completely altered the relationship between U.S. citizens and their national government.

• *The New Deal* was the first of these revolutions. Franklin Roosevelt's New Deal brought U.S. domestic policy out of the nineteenth century and into the twentieth with a degree of suddenness that utterly shocked the establishment of his time. Bolstered by the iconoclastic economics of John Maynard Keynes, the New Deal made it respectable and eventually indispensable to use all the fiscal and budgetary powers of the federal government—including deficit financing on a scale previously unthinkable—to fight depressions, recessions, and even "rolling readjustments." Simultaneously, it began the process of establishing systems to protect citizens from the economic hazards of a complex industrial society—hazards against which they could not reasonably be expected to protect themselves. Social Security became Roosevelt's proudest monument.

The other four revolutions came after World War II, and were partially generated by that war. None has run its full course.

• *The education revolution* was the second revolution. It resulted from urbanization, technology, specialization, the baby boom, and rising educational aspirations. The financial burdens on local communities skyrocketed and eventually the demands for federal

1

aid, despite the strong traditions of local control, became irresistible. By 1972, HEW had over 100 educational programs, which in 1973 were consolidated into sixty-five programs.

• *The civil rights revolution,* long in coming, finally burst forth in the 1960's, nearly a decade after the Supreme Court's landmark opinion of 1954. After the boycotts and protest marches led by Martin Luther King, the assassination of President Kennedy, and the enactment of the Civil Rights Act of 1964, HEW was thrust into the center of governmental efforts to achieve the desegregation of schools. Before 1960, HEW had not one single full-time employee concerned with civil rights or nondiscrimination. By the end of the decade, it had more than 700. Changing the mores of a society comes hard.

• *The health revolution,* which has a long way to go, is a revolution of rising expectations for better health care and for federal intervention and action to assure its delivery to all citizens without regard to their economic status. Its most active salients in the two decades after World War II were reflected in the explosive growth in federal funds for medical research and in the great build-up in voluntary health insurance, followed by the enactment of "Medicare" and "Medicaid" legislation. The medical research boom was undoubtedly engendered by the sudden and naive confidence on the part of the public that if scientists could produce penicillin, radar, atomic bombs, television, computers, and polio vaccine in a few short years, there was no limit to what they might do in overcoming cancer, heart disease, and other scourges of mankind. Even though confidence in science later dropped off, public interest in good health remains undiminished. The decades of the 1970's and 1980's seem clearly set for a major struggle and some fundamental changes in the way health services are financed and delivered to people. Both political parties have endorsed the principle of guaranteeing to all citizens medical care that meets prescribed standards. HEW would be the guarantor. Nobody yet knows how best to do it.

• *The consumer rights revolution* is the most recent of all the basic shifts in public expectation toward their government. Ralph Nader did not do it singlehandedly, but he has been its foremost symbol. In a mere 5-year period, the American public has swung from being a docile consumer herd to becoming hundreds of platoons of self-appointed and self-organized defenders of "consumer rights," demanding that the government protect them from all manner of preventable hazards. Presidential budget requests for HEW's Food and Drug Administration were quadrupled in only nine years, and the expansion has not yet run its course.

When HEW first came into being as a Cabinet department in 1953, it did not occur to any of its many midwives that it would grow so rapidly that within two decades it would have a budget that would exceed in size the total national budget of any other nation except, possibly, that of the Soviet Union. In this period, HEW annual expenditures have skyrocketed from $5.4 billion in 1953 to some $84 billion in 1973, and will reach $94 billion in 1974 and $102 billion in 1975, according to the budget estimates which President Nixon presented to Congress in January, 1973.

That a single department of government should continue to be assigned what has become the gigantic responsibility of presiding over and helping to guide the major social, legal, and institutional changes engendered by these five revolutions seems to some people astonishing. But to others, including President Nixon and his organizational advisers who seek to narrow the President's very broad span of control, it seems both desirable and necessary to enlarge the Department still further. They would give to a re-organized Department of HEW—to be called the Department of Human Resources—responsibility for the manpower and training, employment service, and unemployment insurance programs now in the Department of Labor; the food stamp, nutrition, and meat and poultry inspection programs of the Department of Agriculture; and a number of other programs. The proposed Department of Human Resources would be charged with the government's share of initiative and action to enable all citizens to develop their fullest potential.

This laudable objective is unexceptionable but difficult to convert into an organizing principle since this is presumably the fundamental purpose of the totality of government in a democratic society. All other functions could be subsumed under it. Logic would lead to the consolidation of all domestic functions into a single department. The effort to create a super Department of Human Resources represents an intuitive compromise between the extreme of a single domestic department and the asserted need to interrelate, within a few very large departments, most of the numerous and intertwined federal activities concerned with promoting the general welfare.

To what extent either the existing Department of HEW, or an enlarged Department of Human Resources, represents a workable, wise, and durable organizational arrangement is difficult for even the best-informed to judge. People who have had extensive experience within the Department or have observed it closely for long periods from the outside seem to come to quite opposite conclusions about it. As in all major issues of organization and public administration, there is no such thing as complete objectivity on this matter. And, as in all political issues, those charged with the responsibility of governing must make judgments, no matter how difficult an approach to objectivity may be. Whatever the future course of Presidential and congressional deliberations and negotiations, the outcome will be of no little interest and consequence to the American people.

I

HEW: Large Offspring of a Social Revolution

The Department of Health, Education, and Welfare (HEW), was officially born on April 11, 1953, but it had a long gestation period. It was conceived and brought far along toward delivery by the economic and social revolution ushered in by Franklin D. Roosevelt's New Deal.

To many of America's senior citizens, the New Deal was a revolution that seems to have started "only yesterday," but to the younger generation, the striking contrast between the way things are said to have been before the Great Depression and the way they are now is not easily comprehensible. The overwhelming change seems to have a peculiarly unreal quality about it. Perhaps an understanding of the manner in which the Department of Health, Education, and Welfare came into being may help make both the revolution and the Department more understandable.

Although most Americans were unaware of it at the time, the United States had, prior to the Great Depression, an under-developed national government. The frontier psychology of the nineteenth century and the early twentieth century has shaped the attitudes of the nation's lawmakers. Congressmen and senators from rural districts dominated key congressional committees. Both the nation's laws and the way in which the laws were in-terpreted reflected the point of view of farmers and small-town residents much more than that of industrial workers and other

5

urban dwellers. The Supreme Court had interpreted the Constitution as intending that the principal domestic powers and responsibilities of government should be exercised by states and their subdivisions. "The powers not delegated to the United States by the Constitution, nor prohibited by it to the States, are reserved to the States respectively, or to the people," the Tenth Amendment had said, and for nearly a century and a half, the courts did not search very hard for ways of interpreting the Constitution liberally.

American political institutions and social structure were based on the unique availability, throughout the whole of the nineteenth century, of farmable land open to anybody with a strong back and a will and capacity for hard work. These were the qualities that made the nineteenth-century refugees from Europe's political upheavals turn into the settlers of America's heartlands and develop a fierce pride in their own qualities of self-reliance and independence from government. Men and women with such backgrounds believed that somewhere within the fast-growing nation there was work for all who genuinely wanted to work years beyond the time when such thinking was demonstrably false. Only the handicapped and other conspicuous unfortunates had adequate excuse, they thought, for staying unemployed for very long, even during recurrent periods of recession.

The antigovernment attitude of farmers was reinforced by that of the new industrial magnates, some of whom were not far removed from farm backgrounds. Labor unions existed, but they were few and had little power during the entire nineteenth century. They had almost no influence on legislation in behalf of urban industrial workers, victims of industrial accidents, the unemployed, or the destitute. With little organized opposition to provide counterbalance, therefore, the power of the large coalition of rural rugged individualists and wealthy, industrial free-enterprisers was the dominant negative influence over federal domestic legislation until the Great Depression. This was true even in the face of very substantial poverty and other conditions that seemed to cry out for some type of governmental action.

So far as the federal government was concerned, the President and Congress had a double excuse for looking the other way when conditions of the poor were brought to their attention. First, poverty was considered an inevitable condition of life among the improvident, and second, there was an accepted public attitude that dealing with the poor was clearly a matter for private charity and for local and state government, in that order. Except in times of extreme national emergency, which hardly anybody was brash or silly enough to forecast in the euphoric "chicken in every pot" years preceding 1929, there was no reason why the federal government should become involved in "socialistic practices" such as publicly operated insurance against the hazards of unemployment, old age, or disability, or extending welfare benefits to the destitute. There were, of course, liberal journalists and reformers —people like Upton Sinclair, Lincoln Steffens, Jane Addams, Lillian Wald, Paul Kellogg, Grace and Edith Abbott, and many others—who exposed and sought to correct the shocking and pitiful conditions of life among the urban poor, but they could muster all too little support where it counted—in the halls of Congress. Despite the fact that Theodore Roosevelt and Woodrow Wilson were progressive Presidents, the legislative resistance to federal government initiatives in the field of social legislation was overwhelming.

In Europe, meanwhile, governmental actions to protect workers against the hazards of the industrial age had begun developing in the late nineteenth century and had progressed far beyond anything acceptable to either the lawmakers or the public in the United States. Bismarck had initiated the social insurance concept in 1884, and by the early part of the twentieth century most of the European nations had some form of social insurance. England established workmen's compensation in 1897 and adopted health and unemployment insurance in 1911. With few exceptions, the Western European nations were more highly industrialized than the United States, and none had to contend with the passionately individualist psychology so pervasive and influential in the United States.

At the outset of the Great Depression, therefore, the United States lagged far behind Europe in social legislation. This country had no social insurance whatsoever, either at the federal or the state level, except for workmen's compensation for industrial accidents (against which most states had provided limited insurance protection). There was no insurance against unemployment, old age, disability, or illness, no nationwide system of public employment offices, and no accepted federal responsibility for aiding the poor, no matter how great their numbers or extreme their condition. There was hardly any federal concern for the health of the total citizenry except for provision of a quarantine service to prevent the introduction of communicable diseases into this country, or their spread from state to state if they should break out, and federal support of a relatively tiny medical research program.

Education was almost totally a private, local, or state matter. Apart from its farsighted land grants of the eighteenth and nineteenth centuries, the creation of a tiny Bureau of Education after the Civil War, and its stimulatory program of aid for vocational education beginning at the time of World War I, the federal government accepted almost no responsibility for the education of its citizenry.

The 1930 budget of the United States, prepared and acted upon before the 1929 stock market crash, showed no category labeled "welfare" or any roughly equivalent synonym. The estimated requirement for "the promotion of public health" was $19 million, most of which was to be spent on limited special groups, such as merchant seamen and American Indians. The expenditure plan for education called for $11,866,000 (including $565,000 for educating Alaskan natives). The combined expenditures for health and education, with nothing for welfare or social security, thus amounted to only $31 million, less than two-thirds of 1 per cent of the federal budget.

This is not to say that the federal government was totally impotent in domestic affairs. It gave, sold, and leased land and allocated franchises for the development of the nation's railroads; it determined freight rates; it granted patents; it took decennial censuses; it promoted agricultural research; it managed public lands and forests and leased mineral rights; and it regulated commerce in a variety of ways. But in the fiscal year 1930, the U.S. Government's total domestic budget (that is, excluding interest and debt retirement and veterans' pensions, as well as national defense) totaled $729 million—hardly more than 1 per cent of the gross national product. The public had not yet learned to regard the federal government as the source of financial aid to state and local governments or as the insurer against numerous economic hazards.

Then came the Crash. Like the explosion of the great volcano

Krakatoa in 1883 (which blew a cubic mile of basaltic dust into the air where it stayed, circling the globe, for two years), the stock market crash of 1929 touched off a worldwide depression that affected the nations of every continent for most of the 1930's. At first it appeared to be primarily an unforgettable lesson to hordes of greedy speculators who had propelled the Bull Market up and up in the spring of 1929. The suicides of the speculators who had lost everything and found themselves in such deep debt that they could never dig out were but a prelude to much more profound effects on the whole of society. The stock market collapse turned out to be the first great rumble of an economic and social earthquake.

Buying slowed to a crawl. Big inventories meant few new orders, and mass layoffs resulted. Rising unemployment without either unemployment insurance or any general system of relief gradually overstrained private charity and then began to overwhelm local resources. Public confidence in the ability of the economic system to work out self-corrections without excessive hardship on labor or business was deeply shaken. Bread lines grew longer and soup kitchens more numerous, but still the bottom had not been reached.

President Herbert Hoover, one of the great apostles of free enterprise, did not allow his ideology to keep him from beginning the process of using the power of the federal government to fight the Depression, but he was cautious in his application. He used his Presidential prestige to discourage the precipitous lowering of wages; he urged the building of new public works by all levels of government; and, in 1931, he got Congress to approve the creation of the Reconstruction Finance Corporation (RFC) to stimulate new building and investment. If worst came to worst, as it did, the RFC was authorized to make loans to cities to help them meet their desperate relief needs. But it was like applying band-aids to third-degree body burns. It did not begin to suffice.

Apple vendors appeared on thousands of street corners, engaged in a form of begging that enabled the supplicant-salesmen to maintain a tiny modicum of self-respect. Hundreds of thousands of people took to the highways as hitchhikers, or to riding the rods of the trains, thinking that things might be better elsewhere. They rarely were. Banks became more and more precarious as savings were exhausted, and millions of real estate and commercial loans were in default. Bankruptcies generated more bankruptcies, like a row of dominoes going down. Finally the banks started toppling too.

This was the nightmare in which Herbert Hoover lived during the three years from the stock market collapse of 1929 to his defeat in the election of 1932. In retrospect, it is hard to understand why he should have wished to run for re-election. It is an incredibly hard thing for a President to admit failure. Hoover probably did not allow himself to face the fact that the condition of the country was far more precarious in terms of public confidence than it had been since the Civil War. The desperate American electorate clearly felt that bolder action than Hoover was capable of providing was required.

THE BIRTH OF SOCIAL REVOLUTION

This was the social, economic, and psychological stage onto which Franklin Roosevelt walked with withered legs but with enormous self-confidence on March 4, 1933. He had almost a *tabula rasa* on which to begin to draw his conception of a "New Deal." And he had both a Congress and a public that were ready and waiting for it. Roosevelt was not a philosopher but a supreme pragmatist. He believed in doing what needed to be done. He was more a jerry-builder than a Frank Lloyd Wright. His aides found an economist of some note, John Maynard Keynes, to provide theoretical underpinning for his deficit financing, but he would have done what he did with no theory to support it other than sheer necessity. Necessity dictated that the U.S. Government be converted from a nineteenth- to a twentieth-century model.

After his memorable inaugural on March 4, 1933, with its stirring reassurance that "the only thing we have to fear is fear itself," and after his week-long bank holiday had quelled the panic, Roosevelt embarked on his 100-day honeymoon with the U.S. Congress. Following the Emergency Banking Act and the Economy Act, it produced a series of emergency relief and work programs. The first was the Civilian Conservation Corps (CCC), a program that was especially close to the heart of the amateur forester, Franklin Roosevelt. The alacrity with which the government moved reflected the bounce back from the depths of despair to the enthusiasm of renewed confidence. It took only eighteen days to establish the first CCC camp. Next Congress passed the

Federal Emergency Relief Act (FERA) and the Agricultural Adjustment Act on May 12, followed on May 18 by the creation of the Tennessee Valley Authority (TVA). A month later it authorized the Home Owners' Loan Corporation and the Farm Credit Administration to stave off bankruptcy for millions whose principal equity was in their homes and farms. Congress then enacted the National Industrial Recovery Act, authorizing a system of industrial self-government and also providing for a $3.3 billion public works program.

These measures were by no means all, but they meant the birth of the New Deal and the beginning of a far-reaching social revolution. In certain respects, it seemed more like the restoration of the *status quo ante* and the salvation of the existing system. Walter Lippmann's words convey this feeling: "At the end of February we were a congeries of disorderly, panic-stricken mobs and factions. In the hundred days from March to June we became again an organized nation, confident of our power to provide for our own security and to control our own destiny." Not many months were to pass, however, before those who had controlled the economic system throughout the 1920's would turn on their rescuer and complain bitterly about the President's betrayal of his own class and kind.

The National Recovery Administration, with its blue eagle, administered by the salty "Ironpants" Hugh Johnson, was supposed to create millions of new jobs in short order and regenerate the nation's sputtering economy. Nobody could ever determine just how many jobs it did create in its short-lived existence before the Supreme Court struck it down as unconstitutional in 1935. But, whatever the number, it was not enough. Even as early as November of 1933, it became apparent that something more drastic had to be done. President Roosevelt was a deep believer in the work ethic and felt that it was seriously demoralizing for the breadwinner in millions of families to receive relief in the form of food and cash while sitting idle and discouraged at home. He was determined to see that as many as possible of the unemployed should be afforded the dignity of earning wages while performing useful work.

As the first winter of his Presidency approached, therefore, Roosevelt used his executive power to create the Civil Works Administration, designed to employ primarily heads of families who had been reduced to applying for emergency relief. It was the forerunner of the WPA—the Works Progress Administration—and the beginning of the idea that the government should be the "employer of last resort." It was particularly offensive to conservatives who saw in it the seeds of a socialistic welfare state.

LEGISLATING SOCIAL SECURITY

By the spring of 1934, Roosevelt could see that his temporary relief and work programs were having good effect, but he could also see that no permanent structure was being built to protect the working man and his family against the hazards of unemployment, destitution in old age, poverty arising from disability, and the death of the family breadwinner. The aged were in particularly desperate shape and were organizing to make themselves felt politically. The Townsend Movement, named after its founder, was demanding a national, noncontributory pension program that would provide $100 a month and, later, "$30 every Thursday"—a tremendous sum in those days—for every retired couple over sixty-five. Roosevelt made one of the most important decisions of his Presidency. He decided not to wait until the Great Depression was over to begin building the permanent structure of protection against the hazards of the economic system. He started immediately.

On June 29, 1934, Roosevelt created a Committee on Economic Security to make a careful study and recommend to him a program of social legislation. The committee was headed by Frances Perkins, Secretary of Labor, and was supported by an Advisory Council (twenty-three members) and a Technical Board, chaired by Arthur Altmeyer, with Edwin E. Witte as executive director. Both men were from Wisconsin and were disciples of the famous labor-law scholar and reformer, John R. Commons. They went to work immediately and moved with typical New Deal speed. The study was begun in the summer of 1934 and completed in December of the same year.

The timing of the Social Security legislation was all-important. Astute political leaders have an uncanny and intuitive sense of timing. Roosevelt knew that if he waited until the Depression was over, he would have an uphill fight getting it. As he sized matters up, 1935 would be an ideal year for the enactment of a broad program of social insurance and related welfare benefits. And so it turned out.

The Committee on Economic Security rendered its report to the President on January 15, 1935, and Roosevelt found its recommendations to his liking. The committee's plan would later become the most enduring institution of the New Deal and by far the largest component of what was later to be the Department of Health, Education, and Welfare.

The central feature of the Social Security Act of 1935 was the plan for two types of social insurance. The first was a program of old-age insurance for persons who were over sixty-five and had retired from the labor force. It was to be operated entirely by the federal government and was based on a payroll tax borne in equal proportions by the employer and the employee. The second was a program of unemployment insurance that would be operated by the states, supported by state payroll taxes payable by employers, with minimum standards set by federal law but with opportunity for the states to improve upon those standards if they wished. In addition to these two social insurance systems, the committee recommended and the President agreed that the federal government should create a program of grants-in-aid to states to help them give financial aid to the destitute aged and dependent children, and the Senate added the blind to those to be assisted. The committee also considered the desirability of recommending health insurance but decided that this would be too big a step to take at one time. Instead, they settled on several lesser measures: grants-in-aid to states for maternal and child health services, for crippled children's services, and for the building up of state and local health departments, and grants to state welfare departments for child welfare services.

Both the committee and Roosevelt were confident that as the social insurance system matured, the public assistance program for the needy, based on a "means test," would gradually phase down and out. Nothing that originated in his terms of office would have dismayed Roosevelt more, if he had lived to see the latter-day results of his handiwork, than the ballooning public assistance rolls of the 1960's.

Congressional debate over the far-reaching Social Security Act was heated. Cries of anguish emanated from the National Association of Manufacturers, the United States Chamber of Commerce, and sundry other protectors of the "American way of life." The Act was attacked as socialistic, even communistic. But it was the product of an idea whose time had come and nothing could stop it. The Social Security Act became law on August 14, 1935, and was to be administered by a 3-man Social Security Board appointed by the President. It was the beginning of the social welfare era.

Before the Social Security Board had paid out a single dollar in old-age benefits, both unemployment compensation and old-age insurance were challenged in the courts as violating the expenditure powers of Congress under the general welfare clause of the Constitution, or the Tenth Amendment, or both. To young lawyers studying the powers of Congress today, it seems amazing that as recently as the mid-1930's, U.S. courts might possibly have construed the Constitution so narrowly as to outlaw the social insurance systems of the Social Security Act. In 1937, however, when the Supreme Court was called upon to render its opinion on the merits of this argument, the nation was just emerging from the era when the best government was the least government, and the conservative justices whose opinions provoked Roosevelt into his ill-fated court-packing plan still had significant power on the Court. The cases on the constitutionality of the Social Security Act were, in fact, decided in the shadow of the court-packing controversy, only a few months after Roosevelt proposed the plan to Congress.

Justice Benjamin N. Cardozo wrote the opinion for the majority, holding the Act within the powers of Congress. One paragraph is particularly noteworthy:

> Whether wisdom or unwisdom resides in the scheme of benefits set forth in Title II, it is not for us to say. The answer to such inquiries must come from Congress, not the courts. Our concern here, as often, is with power, not with wisdom. Counsel for respondent has recalled to us the virtues of self-reliance and frugality. There is a possibility, he says, that aid from a paternal government may sap those sturdy virtues and breed a race of weaklings. If Massachusetts so believes and shapes her laws in that conviction, must her breed of sons be changed, he asks, because some other philosophy finds favor in the halls of Congress? But the answer is not doubtful. One might ask with equal reason whether the system of protective tariffs is to be set aside at will in one state or another whenever local policy prefers the rule of *laissez faire*. The issue is a closed one. It was fought out long ago. When money is spent to promote the general

welfare, the concept of welfare or the opposite is shaped by Congress, not the states. So the concept be not arbitrary, the locality must yield. Constitution, Art. VI, Par. 2. [*Helvering, Welch, and the Edison Electric Illuminating Co.* v. *George P. Davis,* May 24, 1937.]

Even though Cardozo's opinion was not sweeping, it was a major landmark. The tracks were being cleared for Congress to spend what it thought necessary for the general welfare. Some would rephrase it to say the floodgates were opened. However the Court's ruling was phrased, it began an era when federal expenditures for health, education, and welfare were to move from about $2.5 billion in 1937 (most of it for temporary work relief) to about $84 billion in 1972–73, thirty-six years later.

In 1939, two years after the constitutionality of the Social Security Act was assured, Congress enlarged its scope by adding survivors' insurance to protect widows and minor children of workers who died. Life insurance companies were apprehensive at the time that this legislation might seriously undercut their business. As it turned out, it stimulated their sales by calling attention to the need for such insurance while providing such a small amount that persons who could afford to were encouraged to supplement it with private insurance.

One provision of the Social Security Act that received little notice at the time and has received all too little attention since is the requirement that participating states establish merit systems for staffing the federal-state programs financed through Social Security Act funds. This applied to the public assistance, unemployment compensation, maternal and child health, and child welfare titles of the Act, and to grants to state departments of health for the improvement of general health services, administered by the Public Health Service.

Prior to this provision of the Social Security Act (1939), only a few states had, on their own initiative, developed merit systems worthy of the name. The new systems established in response to the requirements of the Social Security Act were the beginnings of the personnel systems now existing in the majority of the states. Some of these new organizations and personnel policies left much to be desired, and the Social Security Board (later the functions were administered by the Office of the Secretary of HEW and in 1970 were transferred to the Civil Service Commission) was limited in the extent to which it could require the states to meet standards that now seem basic. Nevertheless, the whole concept was unprecedented and, when viewed in retrospect, was a significant step in the direction of upgrading the personnel standards of state governments. For almost three decades the program was quietly administered by one man, the late Albert Henry Aronson.

As in so many other cases, the atmosphere of the times had laid the groundwork for this provision of the Act. Relief funds in state after state had been manipulated by the governors in their efforts to assure re-election. In Ohio, the situation grew so bad that Harry Hopkins, the FERA administrator, decided to take the whole relief program out of the governor's hands. In so doing, Hopkins made some unusually candid remarks about Governor Martin L. Davey, to which Davey responded with a warrant for Hopkins's arrest on charges of libel. Since libel was not an extraditable offense, Harry Hopkins could lean back in his big leather chair in Washington, smiling his famous wry and angular smile.

In 1934 a number of congressmen and senators, led by Senator Robert Wagner of New York, would have liked to see a national health insurance program added to the social insurance program, but Roosevelt knew that the time was not yet ripe for such a move. Despite his realization that it could not pass, Wagner introduced the first national health insurance bill in that year and hoped that it would gradually acquire support.

Roosevelt was not unconcerned with education and health, but made them secondary to his primary goal of conquering the Depression and giving people jobs and economic security. His interest in education and culture was manifested in a variety of ways. The Civilian Conservation Corps had an education program in every one of its 1,500 camps, employing 300,000 young men and war veterans. The National Youth Administration laid great emphasis on vocational training. The WPA developed a variety of educational and cultural programs, ranging from adult literacy training to public works of art projects, employing impoverished artists. Federal aid for education and culture was substantial but temporary. The Office of Education remained a small bureau of less than a hundred people located in the Department of the Interior throughout the Depression years. The revolution in governmental support for education was not destined to arrive until after World War II had come and gone.

Health, too, was put on the back burner until after the war. The United States Public Health Service had a devoted staff and a proud tradition dating back to 1798, with important responsibilities for the control of communicable diseases, but it had never been asked to concern itself with such fundamental problems as the health-care delivery system of the nation, the inequalities in the availability of hospital and medical services, and problems of social insurance to cover hospitalization and medical care costs. As mentioned, the Social Security Act did represent a small breakthrough in the assumption by the federal government of responsibility for building up state and local health departments and the provision of specific health services, primarily for the poor. The health programs created by the Social Security Act had been divided between the Public Health Service, then located in the Treasury Department, and the Children's Bureau, then located in the Department of Labor, a peculiar fragmentation of functions that stimulated thoughts in Franklin Roosevelt's mind about improving the organization of these and other related functions of the federal government.

REORGANIZING THE GOVERNMENT

Following his landslide re-election in 1936, Roosevelt was increasingly concerned about the outmoded organization of the government, not only in the health field, but in a number of areas. His organizational problems had been compounded by the creation of dozens of temporary agencies, many answerable directly to him, but for which he had no time for supervision. The numerous human resource programs and the various public works agencies especially seemed to demand consolidation. He appointed a committee of three able men to examine the organization of the government. They were Louis Brownlow, Luther Gulick, and Charles Merriam. The group, called the President's Committee on Administrative Management (also called the Brownlow Committee), moved with dispatch to study the major organization problems and make its recommendations. Its report, made in 1937, stands to this day as one of the great documents in the field of public administration.

One of the innovative concepts of the Brownlow report was the idea of permitting the President to submit reorganization plans to the Congress, which would automatically be approved unless specifically turned down by Congress within sixty days. This would give the President greater control over the executive branch of the government than ever before. It was a bold idea and one that could only have been approved under a popular President with a supportive Congress. Roosevelt was enthusiastic and recommended that the Congress adopt such a law. They did so on April 3, 1939, paving the way for a series of important reorganizations of the federal government, including the eventual creation of the Department of Health, Education, and Welfare.

Roosevelt was so impressed with the Brownlow report that he asked the three men to develop specific reorganization plans to implement their report. Among their recommendations was the creation of a Department of Social Welfare. Unfortunately, the law passed by Congress precluded the creation of new Cabinet-level departments, but it did not prevent accomplishing the same purpose in other ways.

Brownlow and his associates went to work on what was to become the most important reorganization plan ever written. Brownlow was ensconced at the Hay-Adams House, across Lafayette Square from the White House, but as word got around in the higher circles of government about his purpose, he was so swamped with calls from special pleaders that his telephone rang without let-up. He went into hiding, with no forwarding address, until the reorganization plan was complete and had been sent to Capitol Hill. It was a blockbuster, especially for Labor Secretary Frances Perkins, who had had no advance notice that the U.S. Employment Service was to be removed from her department.

Part One of the plan created a new Executive Office of the President and moved the Bureau of the Budget out of the Treasury Department into the new Executive Office, to become the President's principal institutional staff arm.

Part Two created what its authors would have liked to call the "Department of Social Welfare," but were forced to name the Federal Security Agency (FSA). Today it seems like an odd name, illustrating the rapidity with which circumstances can change the connotation of words. At that time, "security" meant economic security. It was a clear, strong word, with nothing but good overtones for most of the American public—for all but the die-hard conservatives who inveighed against excessive security as a demoralizing influence. This was before World War II. Later the meaning of the word "security" changed to connote FBI investigations, cryptography, and counterespionage. Eventually, the name Federal Security Agency would have to be changed.

Part Three of the plan created a Federal Works Agency and consolidated the New Deal public works programs into the new agency.

In his memoirs, *A Passion for Anonymity* (1958), Louis Brownlow describes the creation of the new organization that was destined to become, in 1953, the Department of Health, Education, and Welfare:

> Part II of Plan I set up a Federal Security Agency. This was to take the place of the department of social welfare that had been a feature of our original recommendations. Forbidden to create a department, "F. D. R." created an agency. Forbidden to call its head a "secretary," he called him an "administrator." Forbidden to give a salary of $10,000 a year, equal to that of members of the Cabinet and incidentally to that of members of the two houses of Congress, he provided for the administrator a salary of $9,000 a year. Actually, the Federal Security Agency became in everything but words a major department of the government, although it was not until the early days of the Eisenhower administration that it was set up as the Department of Health, Education, and Welfare and its administrator blessed with the title of "Secretary."
>
> The Federal Security Agency was named "security" instead of "welfare" because the vice-president, John Nance Garner, told the President that there was a great objection to the terms "welfare," "social welfare," "public welfare," etc., in Congress, that its use could only lead to a continuation of the welfare activities of the government, which should be stopped as soon as possible, but there was no objection to the word "security" because it looked as if the Social Security Board might be a pretty good thing.

Roosevelt put the principal divisions of government concerned with health, education, and welfare into the new Federal Security Agency. These were three independent agencies—the Social Security Board, the National Youth Administration, and the Civilian Conservation Corps—plus three bureaus from other departments —the Public Health Service, transferred from the Treasury Department, the Office of Education, transferred from the Interior

Department, and the United States Employment Service, moved from the Labor Department. General supervision over the American Printing House for the Blind, a government-aided corporation producing Braille books, was also shifted from Treasury to the new FSA. Even though HEW's official birth did not occur until 1953, when FSA's name was changed and its head became a Cabinet officer, this was the real beginning of the Department of Health, Education, and Welfare.

The Federal Security Agency had three administrators: Paul V. McNutt (1939–45), the extraordinarily handsome, prematurely white-haired, former governor of Indiana, who had Presidential aspirations; Watson B. Miller (1945–47), past national official of the American Legion, who had served as McNutt's deputy before being elevated to the post of administrator; and Oscar R. Ewing (1947–53), a well-to-do, public-spirited corporation lawyer, who had served as vice-chairman of the Democratic National Committee and who had itched to move into a top administrative post in the government. Whether by coincidence or otherwise, all three of these men were natives of Indiana, a state that would be astonished, even today, to have itself identified as the "cradle of the welfare state."

McNutt's service as FSA administrator coincided with the years of World War II, during which time the need for all but war-related activities in the fields of health, education, and welfare slackened off as millions of young men went into uniform, and millions of women, as well as previously unemployed men, responded to the call and the good wages of war industry. McNutt was named chairman of the War Manpower Commission in addition to his post as FSA administrator. This new and theoretically part-time assignment had such heavy responsibilities that it left McNutt little time to oversee the agencies that he had acquired under the 1939 reorganization plan and the additional agencies handed to him under other reorganizations in 1940. The new additions included the Food and Drug Administration, transferred from the Department of Agriculture, two federally operated hospitals in the District of Columbia—Saint Elizabeth's and Freedmens—moved from Interior, and the federal functions relating to Howard University and Columbia Institution for the Deaf (later renamed Gallaudet College), also shifted from Interior.

None of these received much attention during the war years or for some time thereafter.

REORGANIZING AND CREATING NEW AGENCIES

The war rapidly erased the need for temporary work-relief agencies. The whole nation soon became a labor-shortage area. No longer was there a need or a place for the Civilian Conservation Corps. Most of its young enrollees either enlisted or were drafted into the armed forces. The National Youth Administration was able to make a contribution for a time by converting some of its vocational training centers into war-industry training programs. But before the war had proceeded very far, both organizations were phased out of existence.

As these agencies faded away, the national manpower shortage and the increasing number of industrial accidents involving inexperienced workers in war industry generated a spurt of interest in enlarging the vocational rehabilitation program, which was then in the Office of Education, and in emphasizing the physical rehabilitation component, which had theretofore been neglected. A new law was passed in 1943, creating an operating agency separate from the Office of Education, answerable directly to the administrator and named the Office of Vocational Rehabilitation. It was to conduct a grant-in-aid program under which each state would establish a single state agency to sponsor vocational rehabilitation of the handicapped, a program that later became one of the most successful of all HEW activities.

The tight job market also put heavy new responsibilities on the Office of Education for the conduct of short-term training courses for war-industry workers. And the war placed new responsibilities on the young Federal Security Agency to aid in relieving community strains and crises generated by military bases and new concentrations of war industry. An Office of Defense, Health, and Welfare Services was created in 1941. It was charged with several responsibilities: adjusting the distribution of professional personnel, particularly health-care personnel, to meet the requirements of the rapidly shifting population; relieving the shortages of health, education, and recreation facilities and services in areas adjacent to military camps and war industry; and attempting to minimize the conditions that were causing rapid spread of venereal disease. After the war, this agency was, of course, abolished.

A year after the war's end, President Harry S. Truman issued his Reorganization Plan Number 2 of 1946, abolishing the 3-man Social Security Board and transferring its powers and duties to the Federal Security Administrator. The transfer of the powers and duties belonging to subordinate units of departments and agencies to the heads of those departments was one of the original recommendations of the Brownlow Committee on Government Organization, and became a continuing theme of reorganization plans for the next thirty years. The philosophy, supported actively by the first Hoover Commission (1948–50), was that the heads of departments and agencies should be in a position to reorganize their departments to take account of changing conditions without limitation by either Congress or even the President. They felt that Congress could not—and should not try to—acquire either the information or the perspective needed to make wise judgments about the internal organization of departments and agencies. They also felt that if the President is to hold his principal subordinates responsible for good administration, he must also give them the latitude to organize the functions of agencies as they see fit. Transferring all subordinate legal powers to the head of the agency was a prerequisite to such latitude of decision.

By the same reorganization plan, the Children's Bureau, except for those functions concerned with child labor, was transferred from the Department of Labor to the Federal Security Agency and placed within the Social Security Administration. Also, the National Office of Vital Statistics was moved from the Census Bureau in the Commerce Department to the FSA and assigned to the Public Health Service to administer. Dividing the Children's Bureau was traumatic. It left deep scars for a long time. In some ways, even worse than the indignity of splitting the Children's Bureau and moving it to a non-Cabinet agency was the fact that this proud bureau was subordinated to an official who did not report directly to the President. This was a demotion that was very hard for the women who dominated the bureau to swallow.*

The year 1946 was also an uncommonly productive legislative

---

* Some sense of the depth of feeling engendered by this reorganization can be gained from a case study about it contained in Harold Stein's *Public Administration and Policy Development: A Casebook* (1952).

year for the FSA. With a cutback in defense spending and a major backlog of unsatisfied needs in the fields of health, education, and welfare, Congress enacted a number of important new laws: the Mental Health Act, the Hospital Survey and Construction Act, authorization for a huge new clinical research center at the National Institute of Health in Bethesda, Maryland, major amendments to the Social Security Act, and a variety of other laws.

The Truman years witnessed a running controversy with Congress over health insurance, with a deep effect on the Federal Security Agency. People were spending more on hospital and medical services than before the war, but they were dissatisfied with what they were getting, and not getting, for their money. The time seemed to some people to be propitious for a dramatic new approach to the provision of health service. President Truman proposed such an approach—national health insurance—to Congress and the nation, and Senators Robert Wagner of New York and Thomas Murray of Montana, and Congressman John Dingell of Detroit, introduced what became widely known as the Wagner-Murray-Dingell Bill. It was an ill-starred effort to enact the President's program. Oscar Ewing became the Administration's spokesman for the bill and the chief scapegoat of the vocal critics of "socialized medicine."

An important event that weakened the case for national health insurance was a 1949 decision by the National Labor Relations Board, subsequently affirmed by the U.S. Court of Appeals, that the inclusion of industry-financed health insurance as a fringe benefit was a proper subject for collective bargaining. This was the start of a great boom in voluntary health insurance. The opponents of national health insurance argued effectively that voluntary health insurance should be allowed its chance before resorting to governmental intervention.

Truman, Ewing, Wagner, and their associates seem to have been twenty-five or thirty years ahead of their time. By the early 1970's, both political parties would agree that some form of national health insurance, or nationally mandated health insurance, was needed.

Twice during the Truman years, the President sought to elevate the Federal Security Agency to Cabinet status, but opponents of health insurance made sure it did not happen. At the time, there was considerable separatist inclination on the part of some of the components of the FSA, which contributed to the failure of the effort. But the lack of support for departmental status did not impede the rapid development of the agency. It had reached what growth economists refer to as the "take-off point," and nothing could stop it from sailing into the wild blue yonder.

II

The First Twenty Years

The conversion of the Federal Security Agency into the Department of Health, Education, and Welfare, and its explosive growth thereafter, might be recounted in several ways. To the author (who observed and assisted in the creation of the new Department and shared its growing pains and feeling of mission), the most interesting way is to provide some insight into the contrasting styles of HEW's ten Secretaries.

OVETA CULP HOBBY

Newly elected Presidents like to take dramatic actions soon after their inauguration. Dwight D. Eisenhower looked for such actions in November and December of 1952 and found the object for what turned out to be his first bold stroke in the Hoover Commission's recommendations of 1950—the creation of a Cabinet "Department of Social Welfare." It seems ironic in retrospect that after the Democrats had tried twice to create such a department and failed, the first important action taken by the incoming Republican President was to do the very thing his party had opposed prior to his election.

Eisenhower appointed a woman, Oveta Culp Hobby, to head the Federal Security Agency, giving her the initial assignment of leading the effort to elevate the agency to a Cabinet department. Mrs. Hobby, former commander of the Women's Army Corps who had served under him in the European theater during World

War II, and who was editor and publisher of the *Houston Post* at the time of her appointment, had been a lifelong Democrat. (She was parliamentarian of the Texas House of Representatives at the age of twenty-one.) However, she had been an ardent supporter of General Eisenhower during the 1952 Presidential campaign.

With the aid of the White House, the Bureau of the Budget, her own meager staff, and Senator Robert A. Taft—to whom Eisenhower paid great deference after defeating him for the Republican Presidential nomination—Mrs. Hobby went to work on the preparation of a reorganization plan to create the new Department. During that particular period, Cabinet departments could be created by a reorganization plan, subject to veto by either house of Congress. The decision was made very early to make the plan as simple as possible in order not to jeopardize its approval. Nothing new would be added to the Department by transfer from other parts of the government. The President would not even ask Congress to transfer the various legal authorities vested in the surgeon general of the Public Health Service and the commissioner of Education to the Secretary for fear of provoking a fight. Everything would remain the same except that the name would be changed, the Secretary would automatically become a member of the Cabinet, and the President would be authorized to appoint the under secretary, three new officials with the rank of assistant secretary, and a general counsel, all subject to Senate confirmation.

The question of the name of the new Department and the roles to be assigned to the new assistant secretaries turned out to be more difficult than had been foreseen. There was a strong preference for short names, as was the custom among all the other departments. At first there was some support for the name "Department of Welfare," but Senator Taft quickly vetoed that with an assertion reminiscent of Vice-President John N. Garner's comment in 1939. Taft said that the Republican Party had just won an election proclaiming the evils of the welfare state, and it would be an affront to those who elected President Eisenhower to begin his new administration by creating a Department of Welfare.

For a brief time there was some discussion of "Department of the General Welfare," taking a phrase from the preamble of the

Constitution. Senator Taft and others thought this was so broad in its implication as to be presumptuous for the most junior of the departments.

The third name to gain some support was the "Department of Human Resources." The reason for its rejection is interesting in the light of the recent popularity of the name at state and city levels, and perhaps even at the federal level. It was asserted by one participant in the discussions that the name sounded as if U.S. citizens were to be regarded as resources for the use of the state rather than entities for whose benefit the state was created. If we wished to give our government a totalitarian cast, he said, we could do no better than name the new agency the "Department of Human Resources." That finished the discussion.

The fourth name to wind up in the wastebasket was the "Department of Health, Education, and Social Security." As soon as a career man alert to acronyms pointed out that its initials spelled HESS—Hitler's deputy to whom *Mein Kampf* was dedicated—the proposal was dead. In the end, after a few more names were tried, the current name was accepted by everyone despite its length. It did not take long for the awkwardness of its multiword title to be forgotten. It became simply "HEW."

The problem of the assistant secretaries' role brought out the differing perspectives of pressure groups and Presidential advisers. Senator Taft, although by no means a spokesman for the pressure groups, unwittingly adopted their point of view. He recommended to Mrs. Hobby that there should be three assistant secretaries—one for health, one for education, and one for welfare. Each should be a line officer in charge of those functions. He thought this was a logical division of responsibilities and would be conducive to good management. For quite different reasons, the American Medical Association and the various national education associations also recommended separate assistant secretaries for health, education, and welfare. Each interest group thought that if it had an assistant secretary to concern himself with its specific functions, he would become an effective spokesman within the Administration for the group's interests. Both Taft and the professional associations argued that this form of organization was both logical in its division, clearly understandable to the public, and would give a Presidential appointee the necessary line authority over agencies that had traditionally been managed by professional educators, in the case of the Office of Education, and career medical officers in the case of the Public Health Service.

The Bureau of the Budget was opposed to the idea of giving line authority to the three assistant secretaries. It was concerned that these three appointees might become captives of the pressure groups and the bureaucracy, working in league with one another, and told Mrs. Hobby that she needed some top-level assistants to aid her in her job—a significant part of which was fighting off the pleas of special-interest groups. She had become aware of the fact that she had an unbelievably small staff to oversee a large Department and that she surely did need some assistant secretaries who would help her look at the problems of the organization from a comprehensive point of view rather than a parochial perspective. She persuaded Senator Taft of the wisdom of such an arrangement.

But Senator Taft did not have the last word, at least not until the American Medical Association had brought up all its guns to have one of those assistant secretaries designated assistant secretary for Health. The result of their efforts was a compromise. One of the positions was changed to what was clearly a staff position but was equally clearly concerned with health affairs. That position, "Special Assistant to the Secretary for Health and Medical Affairs," had the rank of assistant secretary (and was so designated in the law). The other two assistant secretaryships were unlabeled in law but given titles by the Secretary. One later became the assistant secretary for Legislation—an extremely important and powerful post during most of the Department's two decades of existence—and the other assistant secretary for Federal-State Relations—a portfolio that allowed the Secretary a great deal of latitude in assigning functions.

Secretary Hobby had a tiny staff of her own choosing and an unusually small number of supporting civil servants. She and Under Secretary Nelson Rockefeller looked with envy upon the staffs of the well-established departments. Unfortunately, it was part of the reorganization plan testimony that the new department status would not require any substantial build-up in the Secretary's staff. It was years before a reasonably adequate staff was authorized.

The conversion of the Federal Security Agency to a Cabinet

department had a dramatic effect on journalists, the media, writers of civics and political science texts, and consequently on the general public. People who had never paid any attention to the Federal Security Agency thought that this new Department had sprung from almost nothing and was accomplishing great things in a short time. Although no new powers had been added when HEW was created, the press, in both its news columns and its social columns, suddenly started to give much attention to the comings and goings of the new Secretary. The fact that Mrs. Hobby was the lone woman Cabinet member provided a glamour not shared by the other departments and undoubtedly contributed to the increased press coverage, but that fact provides only a partial explanation of the rising interest in the Department. Cabinet status is a matter of high importance to the American public, and persons who occupy positions involving vastly greater responsibility but lacking anointment as a Cabinet member are downgraded by the news media.

At the time HEW officially came into being in 1953, the organization was no infant. It had over 34,000 employees with total expenditures of $5.4 billion, including $2.0 billion in general funds and $3.4 billion in Social Security trust funds. It was clear that the Social Security program would grow steadily and rapidly for many years, assuming the system was preserved in its form at that time. What was far less clear was how the other components of the Department would change. Nobody really realized how forces and events during the next twenty years would throw one responsibility after another on the shoulders of the young Department, straining its capacity to cope with all its functions.

Despite its seeming popularity, Social Security came under attack in the early days of Secretary Hobby's regime. There were jibes calling it a noninsurance system, too much concerned with urban labor and failing miserably to deal with those who were not attached as regular employees of industrial and commercial enterprises. There was even an effort to convert Social Security into a pension-type program, eliminating the wage-related foundation of the system. Secretary Hobby decided to appoint Roswell B. Perkins, who later became HEW's youngest assistant secretary, and also a committee of expert consultants to examine the issues carefully. The upshot of the examination was confirmation of the essential soundness of the old-age and survivors' insurance program and a recommendation for broadening and liberalizing the coverage requirements for farm and domestic workers and extending coverage to farm operators. These recommendations were subsequently forwarded to Congress and enacted into law on September 1, 1954, adding 10 million persons to the Social Security rolls. Social Security was clearly given a bipartisan blessing—a matter that had been in some doubt until the Republican Party gained control of both the Presidency and the Congress.

Some components of the new Department soon seemed to Secretary Hobby to have responsibilities that exceeded their capacity to handle them. She had had no realization that many operating-type decisions that she thought ought to be handled at lower levels would come to her desk for resolution. This was especially true for the regulatory responsibilities of the Department involving control over the safety and efficacy of drugs and vaccines, the cleanliness of foods, and other such matters. She had hardly taken her oath as Secretary of HEW when she found herself involved in a controversy between the Food and Drug Administration (FDA) and the Department of Agriculture over the issue of standards for the cleanliness of wheat. The FDA had issued administrative guidelines to go into effect on July 30, 1953, which directed its field force to seize wheat sold to millers for human consumption that contained rat excreta in excess of one pellet per average pint of wheat and similar guidelines concerning insect contamination. The Department of Agriculture, on behalf of owners of large stocks of grain, asserted that this standard would cause the loss of huge quantities of wheat and asked for deferral of the effective date. The FDA replied that they had already deferred the date twice and were not going to do so again. At this point, Secretary of Agriculture Ezra Taft Benson thought it time to consult directly with Secretary Hobby.

A joint meeting was held, bringing together the top technical and policy staffs of the Food and Drug Administration and the Department of Agriculture, with the two Secretaries listening to the cases presented by both sides. Then the staffs withdrew and only the two Secretaries remained to settle the case. It was Mrs. Hobby's first experience in such a situation, and she found the arguments or the pressures so persuasive that she agreed to a further postponement.

No more compelling example could be adduced of the conflict

of interest that the Secretary of Agriculture had prior to 1940 and the reason President Franklin Roosevelt decided to use his reorganization power to transfer the FDA from the Agriculture Department to the Federal Security Agency, as the Brownlow Committee and the Bureau of the Budget had recommended.

Mrs. Hobby's introduction to the decision-making process in the regulatory field came as a rude shock. No new Secretary without previous background in regulatory work is fully prepared for it. (More will be said in Chapter IX about this little understood and extremely difficult role of weighing competing equities —economic loss against public safety—when the factors are basically imcomparable.) It convinced Mrs. Hobby that she needed a trusted lieutenant on her immediate staff who knew something about this field. In due course, she oppointed Bradshaw Mintener, a progressive lawyer from the food industry, as assistant secretary. He was known favorably to the Food and Drug Administration, and quickly set out to strengthen that organization.

The FDA staff level had been almost constant for a number of years while the problems with which it was confronted had mounted steadily. On the advice of two successive commissioners —Charles Crawford and George Larrick—supported by Assistant Secretary Mintener, Secretary Hobby appointed a Citizen's Committee on Food and Drugs to make a careful study of the policies and the adequacy of the staff and facilities of the FDA. The committee took five months to complete its study and came up with findings that the Food and Drug Administration was urgently in need of enlarged and strengthened staff, particularly in the area of drug safety. The report, made public in July, 1955, recommended increasing the staff three- to fourfold in five to ten years. This became the basis for overcoming or overriding the attitudes of some strategically placed congressmen who felt that the FDA was a group of zealots who were unnecessarily and unjustifiably interfering with the free enterprise system.

During the early years of the Eisenhower Administration, especially during the first two years when the Republicans controlled the Congress, the Democrats sought to make political hay from the reluctance of the President to expand programs in the fields of health, education, and welfare. They sought to press more money and more programs on HEW than the Administration was prepared to accept. They tried to get federal aid for education (they failed) and greatly increased appropriations for medical research (they succeeded) as well as enlarging various other HEW programs. By virtue of her position as Secretary of HEW, Mrs. Hobby was the Administration's principal spokesman in presenting the case for a more modest approach. She was cartooned in the liberal press as the "Secretary of Not-Too-Much Health, Education, and Welfare." Cabinet officers must expect to take criticism for policies set by the President, but few in recent decades have had to bear as much heat as Mrs. Hobby. The popularity of President Eisenhower rendered him particularly immune to direct criticism, and the brunt fell on her.

Nevertheless, Mrs. Hobby was able, with the aid of her Under Secretary Nelson Rockefeller, to pilot through the Congress several significant legislative advances. Particularly noteworthy during her administration were major rewriting and improvement of legislation in the fields of hospital construction and vocational rehabilitation. Emphasis in the hospital construction field was shifted from building general hospitals in rural and other areas having little or poor hospital service, to the construction of chronic disease hospitals, diagnostic and treatment centers, nursing homes, and rehabilitation centers. The popular and demonstrably successful program of aid to states for the vocational rehabilitation of the handicapped was revamped and a four-fold increase in five years was authorized.

In the spring of 1955, toward the end of her stint as Secretary of HEW, Mrs. Hobby had thrust upon her a dramatic event that created headlines and high waves for weeks—even months. Dr. Jonas Salk succeeded in producing a vaccine that was apparently safe and effective against poliomyelitis. From the moment the announcement was made, worried parents clamored for the vaccine. Many sought to use their wealth or their political influence to obtain vaccine for their children at the earliest possible moment. There was simply not enough to go around, and some system had to be devised for equitable distribution. While the system was being devised, drug manufacturers were licensed to produce the "magic" safeguard. Finally, when the early batches of the vaccine were released, the product of one of the manufacturers was found to be contaminated. A number of children contracted paralytic polio. The high hopes and faith of millions of parents momentarily turned to panic. The source of the contamination was eventually located and corrected, but additional time was required to restore public confidence. The strain placed on Secretary Hobby as a result of this unfortunate chain of events was extraordinarily acute. She bore more than her share of the pressure without complaint.

MARION B. FOLSOM

In the summer of 1955, Oveta Culp Hobby resigned as Secretary of HEW and was succeeded by Marion B. Folsom, then under secretary of the Treasury. Folsom had been one of the national leaders in the development of social insurance in the United States. He had served as treasurer of the Eastman Kodak Company for many years and, from that base, had been a pioneer in persuading business and government to accept unemployment insurance, old-age and survivors' insurance, and other progressive changes.

Marion Folsom brought to the Department a carefully worked out philosophy against which he could test most issues as they came to him for consideration. The core of that philosophy was that the primary roles of government in the social field should be, first, to provide a framework of social insurance protection from the hazards of an industrial society against which most people could not be expected to fully protect themselves, second, to find and apply methods of preventing people from becoming dependent or ill so as to minimize the trauma and cost of cures, and, third, to provide early and total rehabilitation service to disabled people who had prospects of regaining the capacity for self-support. The second of these components caused him to stress programs of medical research and education. His philosophy was later picked up, amplified, and further articulated by his assistant secretary, Elliot Richardson.

Shortly after Mr. Folsom became Secretary, a White House Conference on Education, which had been initiated under Mrs. Hobby, met and hammered out seventy-two recommendations for improving elementary and secondary schools, including broad federal aid to states and through states to local school systems. Up to this time, President Eisenhower had steadfastly opposed federal aid for education, and Mr. Folsom feared that the recommendation of the White House Conference would not be sufficient to induce the President to change his mind. Being firmly convinced himself of the need for federal aid, Folsom carefully planned a strategy that he thought might persuade the President to change his stand. He went to see his former chief, Secretary of the Treasury George Humphrey, the most articulate member of the Cabinet and the man whose judgment President Eisenhower seemed to trust above all others. He explained his reasons for supporting federal aid to education. Humphrey was impressed but not convinced. Folsom had anticipated this and was ready with a fall-back position. He said he planned to make a presentation of the issue to the President and his Cabinet and would greatly appreciate it if Secretary Humphrey would defer any comments he might have until Folsom had completed his presentation and one or two other Cabinet officers had spoken. Humphrey agreed to this.

Folsom made his chart presentation to the Cabinet, showing how the baby boom had resulted in severe overcrowding of the nation's schools. Over 2 million students in excess of normal school capacity were enrolled and 80,000 new classrooms were needed to meet the overflow. The fiscal burdens on the school districts in many parts of the nation were unprecedented. Taxpayers were understandably pleading for financial help not only from the states but also from the federal government. The President seemed impressed and began to view the idea with some degree of sympathy. Two or three other Cabinet members supported Folsom. George Humphrey's negative comments, when they came, were relatively mild. The President decided to give the program the green light, but his heart was never really behind his decision or the idea of federal aid for education.

In the years 1956 and 1957, Folsom spent a significant share of his energy trying to work out with the Congress a bill for federal aid to education that would be acceptable. But the religious issue, more than any other, defeated him. The Catholic hierarchy was steadfastly opposed to any form of federal aid that did not provide aid for hard-pressed parochial schools. The high probability that such a provision would be declared unconstitutional by the courts made no dent in their position. His efforts did, however, lay a groundwork for an unexpected breakthrough that occurred during the last year of his service as Secretary.

In September, 1957, the Russians startled the world with their Sputnik, which was rocketed out of the earth's atmosphere and circled the globe every hour and a half at a speed of 18,000 miles per hour. Americans were shocked that Russian science and technology had outdone what they had confidently believed to be their superior scientific competence. What had happened? Why were the Russians ahead of us? What should be done about it? Secretary Folsom consulted with his Assistant Secretary for Legislation Elliot Richardson and others and concluded that the sudden change in the national psychology made the time ripe for a new educational emphasis. Richardson, who was to become Secretary of HEW thirteen years later, was given the important leadership role of developing the National Defense Education Act, a major breakthrough in the long struggle for federal aid to education.

A survey by the Office of Education showed that of the 2,776,000 students enrolled in the eleventh and twelfth grades of public schools in 1956, only 830,000 were studying science and 659,000 were studying mathematics. In many schools no advanced mathematics of any kind was offered. Furthermore, United States schools were found to be weaker than those of any other major country in teaching foreign languages. A shortage of 130,000 qualified elementary and secondary school teachers was found to exist, and the classroom shortage was estimated at 142,000. These facts formed the basis for a renewed effort to provide selective support for public schools and to encourage high school graduates to continue their education, especially in subject matter areas where the United States educational system seemed conspicuously weak.

The National Defense Education Act, approved a month after Folsom left office, on September 2, 1958, provided for expanded and improved teaching in science, mathematics, and foreign languages, area vocational training centers, training of college teachers and language specialists, guidance counseling and testing, research in the educational uses of television and other media, and loans to needy college students. It authorized aid in the amount of about $900 million—the largest educational aid program ever enacted up to that time. It pushed open the door of federal aid to education sufficiently so as to make the final breakthrough (which came seven years later with the enactment of the Elementary and Secondary Education Act) much easier.

Folsom also sought to recapture the initiative that Congress had snatched from HEW and the President in determining the appropriate level of funding for medical research. Each year the Congress was outbidding the President by adding millions to his budget for this purpose. Folsom appointed a high-level advisory committee chaired by Dr. Stanhope Bayne-Jones, and on the basis of its expert assessment of opportunities, Folsom recommended a substantial increase in the 1957 budget for biomedical research. But Congress was still not satisfied that the President's budget was large enough. They increased it still further and continued for a decade thereafter to add more millions, year after year, to the National Institutes of Health budget, always exceeding the President's recommendations.

ARTHUR S. FLEMMING

Marion Folsom had agreed to serve as Secretary of HEW for only two years, but at the urging of the White House stretched it to three. He was succeeded by Arthur S. Flemming, a man who had spent much time in top positions under both Republican and Democratic administrations, but who was, at the time of his appointment, president of Ohio Wesleyan University. He had been a member of the Civil Service Commission under Roosevelt, a member of the War Manpower Commission during World War II, and director of the Office of Defense Mobilization during and after the Korean War, serving under both President Truman and President Eisenhower.

Flemming's 30-month service as Secretary (up to the inauguration of John F. Kennedy) was marked less by spectacular legislative developments than by steady growth of the Department and increasing complexities of administration. The National Defense Education Act was being carried out; the National Institutes of Health continued to have its appropriations greatly increased by Congress each year; the Social Security program expanded inexorably; and preparations were made for the sixth decennial White House Conference on Children and Youth. These typified the scores of developments that preoccupied the Secretary. The Flemming regime can probably be best understood from brief accounts of two cases with which he was confronted and on which he took action. They are not atypical of the administrative fare of HEW Secretaries. One had to do with cranberries and the other with illegitimate children.

Just as the Thanksgiving season was approaching in 1959, Secretary Flemming returned from a trip to the Pacific Northwest, where he had learned of cranberry crops being plowed under by bulldozers because the cranberries were contaminated with a weed-killing chemical called aminotriazole. The compound was authorized for use after cranberry harvests, but not after the new cranberries were formed. Tests on laboratory rats had shown that consumption of aminotriazole in abnormally large amounts could cause cancer. Under the Delaney clause of the Food Additive Amendment, enacted the year before, a food containing any amount of such a substance, however small, was illegal.

In a press conference on November 9, two weeks before Thanksgiving, Flemming informed the public of the existence of the tainted cranberries and the intent of the Food and Drug Administration to seize any and all shipments that showed evidence of aminotriazole residue. He was asked how the public could tell whether the cranberries they bought in the stores were "safe" or not. Neither Flemming nor the FDA had an answer to this crucial question. The contaminated cranberries had been mixed with others from many sources and only laboratory tests could determine which cranberries had spray residue and which ones did not. Something had to be done quickly, for at the first word of the alleged danger, the public panicked.

Flemming quickly convened a large public hearing to review the alternatives. The cranberry producers association stressed the low degree of danger, and one witness testified that a person would have to consume something like a ton of cranberries to run any danger. But no matter how small the danger, according to HEW Assistant General Counsel William Goodrich, the Secretary had no choice under the Delaney clause but to do his best to prevent all cranberries with any trace of aminotriazole spray from reaching the public. Needless to say, there was chaos in the cranberry business.

Working day and night, Flemming and the FDA worked out a plan for testing cranberries, using both FDA's own laboratories and approved contract laboratories, and certifying those that were found to be free of residual spray. But it was too slow a process to cover anything like the total supply of cranberries prior to the holiday. Press reports were issued daily on batches of berries cleared during the remaining few days before Thanksgiving, but public confidence had been shattered. A large part of the 1959 crop went unsold with consequent heavy financial losses not only to the growers guilty of the infraction, but to all growers, and of course to the distributors. The losses were somewhat reduced the following spring by Department of Agriculture purchases of some $10 million worth of surplus cranberries.

Flemming was both warmly praised and bitterly criticized. The decision was clearly that of a single, responsible official—the Secretary of Health, Education, and Welfare. Such a one-man regulatory decision illustrated both the strength and the hazard of vesting in the Secretary of HEW all the legal power to administer food and drug laws. Regulatory decisions are often complex, difficult, and close. Criticism is inevitable. Someone must take the heat. Is it best to share that heat through the group decision of a commission, as is done in the conduct of most regulatory functions of the U.S. Government, or is it best to have a single administrator able to make quick decisions? Will the decisions be more likely to be wise and judicious if made by the group process after carefully hearing, sifting, and weighing the issues? Flemming used to say that he believed in "quick, sound decisions," an objective devoutly to be sought, but the key to this administrative nirvana has never been discovered.

In this instance, if a commission had been faced with the problem, it would almost certainly have been still considering what position to take while people were eating their Thanksgiving dinners. On the other hand, if a Secretary of HEW must keep himself sufficiently well informed about all the regulatory activities of the Food and Drug Administration so as to be able to make even moderately quick and moderately sound decisions, he may have little time left for his numerous other important duties. It is a dilemma with big horns.

A second case that arose during Flemming's last year in office illuminates a part of the evolution of the rights of welfare children and their mothers. In the spring of 1960, Louisiana passed a law that summarily cut off assistance payments to children and their mothers if the mothers bore additional children determined to be illegitimate. The law established the presumption that the homes into which such children were born were unsuitable unless declared otherwise by the local parish board. The law took effect on July 1, 1960.

Although Bureau of Public Assistance officials and their parent organization, the Social Security Administration, were disturbed by the law, the commissioner of Social Security and the Office of the General Counsel of HEW did not feel that they had grounds for declaring it out of conformity with the Social Security Act. To compound the difficulty, the law was quite similar to one that had been in effect for some time in Mississippi without objection from the SSA. The principle of excluding children who lived in unsuitable homes from eligibility for public assistance had been well-established by the nonobjection to such state laws by the Social Security Administration, acting on the opinion of HEW's general counsel that Congress had not intended to forbid such exclusion.

But the course of events in Louisiana was startlingly different. In other states, the application of the law had been on a case-by-case basis, and had been inconspicuous. In Louisiana, aid to a large group of poor children and their mothers was cut off abruptly. No substitute method of caring for the children was provided. Their condition became serious and in some cases desperate. Someone thought of sending a telegram to the United Nations asking emergency aid from UNICEF and publicizing it. A prominent story in the *Washington Post* dramatized the condition of the children and the apparently timid acquiescence of the Washington bureaucracy to the Louisiana law.

Arthur Flemming, acutely sensitive to press criticism since he held regular and frequent press conferences (more frequent than any other Secretary, before or since), strongly urged the commissioner of Social Security, William Mitchell, to find some way to make Louisiana deal in a more humane way with the children of "sinful" or careless mothers. Mitchell found two bases for action and called a conformity hearing under the Social Security Act. During the hearing, held in mid-November, 1960, Louisiana agreed to change its procedures and correct the practices that the Social Security Administration had belatedly determined to be in violation of the law: summarily cutting off children and their mothers without a case-by-case review as to whether the home was, or was not, suitable, and failure to provide an appeal mechanism for aggrieved persons. But this did not satisfy Flemming. He wanted to declare all those state laws that cut off public assistance to children on the ground that the home in which they lived was unsuitable to be out of conformity with the Social Security Act.

Meanwhile, by virtue of the election of President John F. Kennedy and the prompt announcement of his intention to appoint Abraham Ribicoff to succeed Flemming as Secretary of HEW, Flemming had become a lame duck. This status did not dampen his desire to take a bold step and issue a regulation saying that no state could outlaw public assistance payments to destitute children because the home in which they lived was unsuitable. He convened a meeting with his general counsel and supporting legal staff, the commissioner of Social Security and his key staff, and several other advisers. He told them what he proposed to do. The general counsel strongly demurred, saying such action by the Secretary would be illegal. As the meeting proceeded, the atmosphere became extremely tense. Flemming finally told the general counsel in the strongest possible terms that he—the general counsel—did not understand his proper role. He was not a judge of the U.S. court system, and the Secretary had not asked him to pretend that he was. The Secretary was asking him to be an advocate who sought to put forward the strongest possible case in support of a position that the Secretary wished to take. "Suppose I take this action," the Secretary said, in effect, "what kind of a defense could you put forward for me if someone takes me to court?"

Although it was repugnant to him to do so, the general counsel, Parke Banta, finally acceded and agreed to carry out the Secretary's request. Flemming was satisfied that he had a case with a good chance of being upheld in court. On January 17, 1961, just three days before he left office, Flemming issued an order that was to take effect the following July 1. It was nationwide in application and said that no state could outlaw payments to needy children on the grounds that they lived in unsuitable homes (meaning, particularly, that the "legitimacy" of birth could never be used as a *prima facie* disqualification). Flemming intuitively felt that the courts would find some ground for supporting a position that seemed to him so morally and rationally right. As matters turned out, Congress later enacted a law that gave support to Flemming's position. Thereafter the sins of the parents could not be visited upon the children, as far as the Social Security Act was concerned, even unto the first generation.

Flemming reveled in his job and hated to give it up. He kept right on making decisions until the final hour of his secretaryship and even asked for office space after his successor was sworn in to finish a number of pending items.

ABRAHAM RIBICOFF

Following John F. Kennedy's victory over Richard Nixon in the election of 1960, Abraham Ribicoff, then governor of Connecticut, was Kennedy's first appointment to the Cabinet. An early supporter of Kennedy, Ribicoff had been a municipal judge and a congressman before being elected governor. Ribicoff was offered his choice among a number of Cabinet posts and promptly chose HEW. After less than a year and a half, he was to question the wisdom of his choice and decide that being a senator from Connecticut more nearly fitted his talents, his interests, and his disposition.

Ribicoff's most important sub-Cabinet choice was that of assistant secretary for Legislation. Kennedy and Ribicoff agreed that the man for the key spot was Wilbur Cohen, who was then a professor at the University of Michigan but was also a 20-year veteran of the Social Security Administration. Cohen had assisted in writing the original Social Security Act. He had also served as an informal legislative adviser to Kennedy when he was senator and, after the 1960 Presidential election, had chaired a special task force to recommend new legislative initiatives in the field of health and social security.

Ribicoff and Cohen began by seeking prompt modification of the Social Security Act to overcome some glaring faults that had become increasingly evident. The law had authorized grants to states for "aid to dependent children," including funds for support of one caretaker of the children, usually the mother, but no funds for the support of two parents when the father was unemployed and destitute. Thus the only way a family could become eligible for public aid in some states was for the father to abandon his family. The law actually created a powerful pressure toward family breakup. (Some states did have programs financed entirely with their own funds to take care of whole families.) Secretary Ribicoff had seen these pressures at work when he served as a municipal court judge. He was determined to do something about it.

At the urging of President Kennedy and Secretary Ribicoff, and with Assistant Secretary Cohen spearheading the change on Capitol Hill, Congress enacted a temporary measure in the spring of 1961, which included funds for unemployed parents in its coverage and which became the forerunner of more extensive amendments the following year. These Public Welfare Amendments of 1962 permanently enlarged the scope of the law to include unemployed parents, but did not require states to amend their own laws to include unemployed fathers if they did not wish to. A decade later, there were still twenty-eight states that had not taken advantage of the broader federal offer and were providing no support to whole families where there was an able-bodied, unemployed father. This became, understandably, a major impetus toward welfare reform when President Nixon took office in 1969.

One of the most difficult legal and political issues to face any of the HEW Secretaries was whether the Department should leave the interpretation of what constituted "all deliberate speed" in the desegregation of public schools, as stated in the famous Brown decision of the Supreme Court in 1954, to the courts and Congress. HEW was paying out substantial sums of money to schools that were still segregated after more than seven years. Had they acted with "all deliberate speed," and, if not, what ground rules should the Department apply to the question of when it should withhold funds and when it should not? Did HEW have the legal authority to issue such ground rules to supplement and make more specific the ruling of the courts, especially if such ground rules were contrary to laws of Congress enacted prior to the 1954 decision? Clearly, Congress had the power to deal with the problem but had not exercised it.

Prior to President Kennedy's election the issue did not arise. Under no circumstances would President Eisenhower have wished to have his Cabinet officers take into their own hands, without specific legislative authorization, the responsibility for interpreting the Constitution in such a way as to carry out what they believed to be the broad intent of the Supreme Court in the succession of decisions beginning with *Brown* v. *the Board of Education*. But after Kennedy's election and the beginning of a new era, it was cause for a great deal of internal discussion and soul-searching. Secretaries and their general counsel had been trained to interpret laws enacted by Congress and not to assume the judicial authority to apply the Constitution directly to the manner of administering the laws of Congress.

The controversy over this issue was heightened by Congressman Adam Clayton Powell's ascendancy to the chairmanship of the House Committee on Education and Labor and his appointment of an *ad hoc* Subcommittee on Integration in Federally Assisted Education with the specific purpose of attempting to force HEW to use the power he was convinced it had. Senator Jacob Javits asserted that the whole matter could be taken care of by an executive order of the President. But the Justice Department and the HEW legal staff counseled otherwise. In view of Kennedy's narrow victory in 1960, he certainly had no intention of taking the onus of withholding massive federal funds from segregated Southern school systems on very questionable legal grounds.

It was not until the mood of the country changed sharply as a result of the events of the spring of 1963—the Birmingham protest meetings with fire hoses and police dogs and state troopers "controlling" peaceful demonstrators before a hundred million television viewers, followed by the brutal murder of Medgar Evers and other shocking events—that the Administration decided to seek a federal civil rights statute that would eventually give federal agencies the power the President and the Secretary of HEW were reluctant to assert in contravention of specific statutory authority. This major issue ran through the administration of Secretary Ribicoff, and later of Secretary Anthony Celebrezze, like the recurring theme of a dissonant tone poem.

How much this seemingly insoluble dilemma contributed to Ribicoff's decision to leave the secretaryship of HEW might be difficult for even Ribicoff himself to tell. That it was a contributing factor seems very likely although it was only one of many "no win" situations with which he was involved. In his final press conference, Ribicoff was more pessimistic in his appraisal of the job of Secretary than any of his predecessors or successors and very candid in his comments. He said that the Department was so big and diverse as to be unmanageable. Although he did not say how he would divide it, his later bills to dismember the Department were foreshadowed by his departure statement.

ANTHONY J. CELEBREZZE

Anthony Celebrezze was a surprised man when he was called out of the woods of Ontario by special messenger to respond at the nearest telephone to a call from President Kennedy. Kennedy asked him to leave his post as mayor of Cleveland—to which he had been elected five times—and come to Washington to succeed Abraham Ribicoff as Secretary of Health, Education, and Welfare. He was so taken aback that he said he would have to consult his wife first. After she concurred, Mayor Celebrezze quickly made his way to Washington to be sworn in as the fifth Secretary of HEW.

The reforms of the Public Assistance Program, initiated by Secretary Ribicoff and Assistant Secretary Cohen, which had become effective just before Celebrezze took office, highlighted the magnitude and difficulty of welfare problems and the smallness of the welfare organization within the Department of HEW assigned to cope with these problems. The Bureau of Public Assistance, responsible for the administration of more than $4 billion in annual welfare grants to states, had a total employment of about 375, including a very small research arm. The more Secretary Celebrezze thought about the magnitude of the problems in the welfare field, the more he thought it was desirable to strengthen and enlarge the federal unit responsible for overseeing the programs. On January 25, 1963, he ordered an important reorganization that separated the social insurance functions of the Social Security Administration from the public assistance and child health and welfare functions. The Social Security Administration name then became associated explicitly with the social insurance function—something accomplished years earlier in the minds and speech of most of the American public.

A new Welfare Administration was established with an implicit but impossible assignment of doing something about the seemingly inexorable growth in the number of abandoned mothers and children on welfare rolls. The Welfare Administration also had other concerns—the programs of the Children's Bureau, the Cuban Refugee Program, the Office of Juvenile Delinquency, and later the Administration on Aging—but by far the most important one, in terms of public concern, was the problem of dependent children and their parents. The ensuing years only proved the adage that difficult problems are rarely, if ever, solved by reorganization.

The second half of Secretary Celebrezze's three years at the helm of HEW coincided with one of the greatest spurts of activity in American legislative history. Following the assassination of President Kennedy in November, 1963, the remorse of the nation and the natural inclination of Lyndon B. Johnson to model his domestic strategy in the pattern of his hero and mentor, Franklin D. Roosevelt, combined to produce new legislation wholesale from the same Congress that had been reluctant to enact the recommendations of President Kennedy. After Johnson's overwhelming victory over Republican Barry Goldwater in 1964 and the simultaneous election of a very liberal Congress, ready and eager to support the President's recently declared War on Poverty, legislation seemed to roll out by the bushel basketful, not only in respect to the national crusade against poverty, but in the fields of health and education as well. Probably the most important legislative landmarks of 1964 and the first seven months of 1965, so far as HEW was concerned, were the Civil Rights Act of 1964, the Elementary and Secondary Education Act of 1965, the Higher Education Act of 1965, (following after only two years the Higher Education Facilities Act of 1963), and the Medicare and Medicaid amendments to the Social Security Act of 1965. The Economic Opportunity Act of 1964 also had important spillover effects on HEW, even though its principal functions were vested in an independent agency.

Other laws that the Eighty-eighth and Eighty-ninth Congresses added to HEW's responsibilities included:

- The Clean Air Act
- The Mental Retardation Facilities and Community Mental Health Construction Act of 1963
- The Vocational Education Act of 1963
- The Maternal and Child Health and Mental Retardation Planning Amendments of 1963
- Drug Abuse Control Amendments of 1965
- Federal Cigarette Labelling and Advertising Act
- Manpower Act of 1965 (including experimental and demonstration projects for professional employees)
- National Technical Institute for the Deaf

- Medical Library Assistance Act
- Solid Waste Disposal Act of 1965
- Vocational Rehabilitation Act Amendments

This is only a partial list. The lack of such listing for previous or subsequent Congresses should not be construed as implying that they were not also active in giving HEW new responsibilities. But this was the most prolific production of social legislation in U.S. history. Much more will be said in subsequent chapters about the major components of this legislative outpouring.

A disproportionately high share of HEW programs was the product of the Eighty-ninth Congress. (See Appendix A for a list of HEW programs up to the year 1973.) Assistant Secretary Cohen was in charge of the legislative arm of HEW during those years, and although he had phenomenal talent in handling great numbers of policy issues at one time, even he had difficulty in keeping up with the eager beavers in the White House and on Capitol Hill. To Secretary Celebrezze, who had come to the secretaryship without any special background in the numerous and complex programs of HEW, or in the strange ways of the Washington legislative process, it seemed like a madhouse at times. At the end of three tough years—he set an endurance record by a few days—he accepted President Johnson's offer to return to his home state (Ohio) as a judge of the circuit court of appeals with alacrity and few misgivings. He made no public statement about HEW's manageability, but there could be no mistaking his private views. Having lived through a period when at least 60 new programs were added to the 150 or so that were there when he arrived, it is not surprising that he felt the Department's appetite exceeded its capacity.

JOHN W. GARDNER

On August 18, 1965, Secretary Celebrezze turned the reins of office over to John W. Gardner, a highly respected educator, psychologist, author of a number of widely read books, and foundation executive. At the time of his appointment, Gardner was in his twelfth year as president of the Carnegie Corporation, a foundation primarily concerned with educational innovation.

Gardner had served several months prior to his HEW appointment as the chairman of an advisory group appointed by President Johnson to counsel him on educational matters. In this capacity, he had supported a recommendation to the President for the creation of a separate Department of Education. The magnitude of the government's educational responsibilites had seemed to the group to have reached a point calling for an organization with Cabinet status and with the added leverage, funds, and access to the public media that have commonly been the automatic accompaniments of Cabinet rank. It was particularly interesting to newsmen and scholars to note, however, that Gardner made a lightning reversal of judgment after his appointment as HEW Secretary. When asked by a journalist, shortly after he took his oath of office, whether he still advocated a separate Department of Education, he replied firmly in the negative. He thus became one of the more prominent victims of Miles's Law (the author's widely quoted maxim): "Where you stand depends on where you sit."

To those who have never been faced with a remotely similar situation, this switch in position may seem to indicate disingenuousness. To those who know John Gardner and to those who have been faced with even partially comparable embarrassments, Gardner's quick change of view was both responsible and sincere. Gardner had spent his life being concerned with educational matters. He was suddenly assigned a broader portfolio of responsibility. When he turned his mind to the relationships between health, education, and welfare activities, and the opportunities that he might have to facilitate those relationships under a single department, he concluded that a separation of educational activities was not such a good idea as he had thought.

In fact, the more John Gardner thought about it, the more he realized that the combination of health, education, and welfare functions for which his Department was responsible gave him one of the finest podiums in the country from which to articulate his overarching philosophy of human fulfillment. His greatest talent was for moral leadership, and HEW offered incredibly wide scope for that talent, especially since HEW had by then become the principal instrument of government in desegregating public schools. There was no pussyfooting about where he stood on that subject. "I consider civil rights to be *the* most important issue before our society today," he told the Capital Press Club in June, 1966. And in every aspect of HEW's activity, he found important ethical issues in which he could help to set high goals and standards of performance.

Holding the Department together, rather than splitting it up, became one of Gardner's strong motivations. More than any of his predecessors, he became a philosopher-spokesman on behalf of services to people as whole human beings, and of HEW as the logical and proper instrument of government to provide such services. This was a theme that would later be picked up and given added meaning by Elliot Richardson. As Gardner came to recognize, it is far more difficult to put this particular idea into practice than to expound the philosophy.

So great became Gardner's conviction of the desirability of a strong Department of Health, Education, and Welfare that he consulted with Robert McNamara about using the Department of Defense model. Shortly thereafter, during a visit with President Johnson at his Texas ranch in November, 1965, Gardner unveiled his preliminary thinking on this subject. There was not much news that day, and the reporters were hounding the President for something to write about. Without endorsing Gardner's plan, Johnson led the Secretary to the microphone and asked him to outline his proposal. Gardner said that he thought the time had come to convert HEW into a superdepartment that resembled the structure of the Department of Defense. All existing functions of HEW would be grouped under three sub-Cabinet departments: a Department of Health, a Department of Education, and a Department of Individual and Family Services. The Secretary expressed the conviction that this form of organization would help the federal government cope with the nation's extraordinarily difficult social problems.

Gardner's plan had not been discussed with the then Bureau of the Budget, which had the duty of passing on all reorganization proposals. The idea had been released prematurely and unintentionally. One of its purposes was tactical—to head off the creation of a separate Department of Education—but Gardner sincerely felt that the plan had basic merit and would upgrade both the management and the prestige of the entire enterprise. But when Bureau of the Budget officials read the idea on the press "ticker," they were less than impressed with its merit, besides being a bit annoyed. They felt that sub-Cabinet departments would only increase the Secretary's difficulties in administration. Each sub-Cabinet department would become an empire unto itself and would be far more difficult to manage than the then existing operating agencies. The heads of the sub-Cabinet departments would outrank anyone in the Secretary's office except the Secretary and the deputy secretary. The Secretary would then be left without high-ranking officials to coordinate the crosscutting functions within the Department. Counterargument that Secretary McNamara had been successful in using assistant secretaries to deal with sub-Cabinet secretaries of the army, navy, and air force, who outranked them, was unpersuasive to Bureau of the Budget officials. McNamara's problem was to make the most of an organizational design that he inherited. The secretaries of the army, navy, and air force had already been demoted once since World War II, and it would have been most impolitic to demote them again. Instead, he developed his famous "planning, programming, and budgeting system" and other procedural devices that had the effect of strengthening the staff offices in the Office of the Secretary. He demoted the service secretaries in relative power without doing so in protocol terms. Gardner's plan would have elevated the "service secretaries" in both protocol and power terms and, relatively, "demoted" the assistant secretaries—just opposite of what Mc-Namara did.

No reorganization proposal ever dropped out of sight faster than Gardner's. It might have had some chance of survival if it had followed the concept advocated by Marion Folsom. Folsom had proposed line under secretaries for health, education, and welfare. He felt that under secretaries could be made to feel and behave as part of the Secretary's staff, working as a team to carry out agreed-upon purposes, while sub-Cabinet secretaries were certain to be separatists and probably empire builders. Even that proposal, however, might have made coordination of HEW's components more difficult in the absence of officials with the capacity and power to coordinate the work of the three under secretaries.

New legislation was pouring at full force from the cornucopia of the Eighty-ninth Congress when Gardner took office. He concluded that his greatest challenge would be in the field of administration rather than in formulating more bills authorizing still more programs. Putting his administrative house in order and finding top-flight people to fill the unusually large number of vacancies in key leadership positions within the Department became, therefore, the top items on his agenda.

President Johnson's government-wide push toward "PPBS" (planning, programming, and budgeting system) was newly under way when Gardner came into office, and it gave him an added reason for doing what he probably would have done anyway— building up a capability within his office for program evaluation and planning. This had been a neglected area during the first twenty-five years of FSA-HEW, partially because Congress did not want a strong Office of the Secretary and did not look with favor on requests for substantial increases in funds for planning and related activities. To the more conservative members of Congress, requests for a planning staff seemed to imply movement toward social planning, the welfare state, and socialism. To more liberal members, such as Congressman John Fogarty, the powerful chairman of the House subcommittee on HEW appropriations, a strong planning staff could only mean that his own opportunity to exercise initiative and gain credit for innovative action would be seriously jeopardized. It was a question of comparative power and credit. But even as Gardner entered on his first year as Secretary, John Fogarty had begun to relent. The log jam was broken, and a competent planning staff was finally brought into being.

Another of Gardner's early decisions was to separate financial and nonfinancial management. Under the pattern adopted by most government departments following the recommendations of the first Hoover Commission, the assistant secretary for Administration (the one assistant secretary who had traditionally come from the career ranks) had been charged with both financial and nonfinancial management. In HEW, his deputy served as comptroller and carried a great deal of the responsibility and authority for financial management. Gardner decided that the magnitude of the functions had become so great that it would be better to have separate and coequal officials, each answerable directly to the Secretary and under secretary. In a Department whose budget was then about $30 billion, and heading upward at an almost fantastic pace, with some 200 different programs to manage and oversee, the concentration of responsibility and power in a single official for both administrative and financial types of management seemed to be more than any one man could be expected to handle.

Secretary Gardner felt that the foremost key to good administration was the combination of good organizational patterns and first-rate leadership personnel, and to these concepts he devoted a higher proportion of his time than had most of his predecessors. He fended off and delegated to others testimony before Congress and direct personal contact with congressmen and senators whenever he reasonably could, so that he could concentrate on improving administration and personnel. Even with his extraordinary attractiveness to first-rate people, he discovered that it was not always easy to recruit and retain the people he wanted to carry some of the key responsibilities of the Department. In some cases, it could almost be said that persons with the combination of skill and character traits that would make them suitable for some of the most demanding jobs of HEW were nonexistent.

As mentioned, civil rights was a special concern of Gardner's. He established a position titled "Special Assistant to the Secretary for Civil Rights" and gave that official power and staff to conduct a far more vigorous program than had occurred prior to his arrival. He reprogrammed funds intended for other purposes and directed that they be used for civil rights enforcement. His first budget called for an increase of 348 new positions for civil rights work.

In the field of welfare, the costs of supporting dependent children and their mothers were rising at an inexplicably rapid rate in a period when unemployment was comparatively low. Neither Gardner nor anyone else had any sure solution to this problem but it occurred to Gardner that it might be of some avail to combine the highly successful vocational rehabilitation program with the welfare program and place both of them under the leadership of Mary Switzer, who had had a long and distinguished career at the helm of the Vocational Rehabilitation Administration. The new agency thus created was named the Social and Rehabilitation Service. (Chapter V is devoted to its programs and problems.) Nothing that occurred later led Gardner to the conclusion that this was an unwise reorganization, but it could not stem the upward surge in the welfare rolls. This was too profound a problem to be dealt with by mere reorganization.

With hardly any explanation, Gardner submitted his resignation to President Johnson at the end of December, 1967, to take effect a month later. The two men had obviously clashed, both philosophically and temperamentally, but the full story will have to await Gardner's memoirs—if he ever writes them. If and when he does, his unhappiness over Johnson's policies on the Vietnam war seems likely to loom larger than it did in either public or private statements while he was serving as a Cabinet officer.

WILBUR J. COHEN

Following Gardner's departure at the end of January, 1968, Wilbur Cohen, the under secretary, became the Acting Secretary, and two months later President Johnson nominated him to become the Department's seventh Secretary. Cohen was probably the nation's foremost expert on Social Security policy, and in his seven years of service under Presidents Kennedy and Johnson as HEW's assistant secretary for Legislation and as under secretary, he had become well versed in problems of health and education.

By the time of Cohen's swearing-in on May 16, 1968, President Johnson had declared himself to be a noncandidate for the fall election. The President's attention had drifted away from the legislative marathon, and congressional attention turned sharply toward the conventions and the later campaigns. It was apparent that the legislative boom was over. It had been an unprecedented period of legislative activity both for HEW and the nation. Probably no departmental official ever participated in formulating and guiding through the Congress more bills in an 8-year period—possibly any period—than did Wilbur Cohen.

Well before Cohen became Secretary, he had participated with Gardner and Philip R. Lee, the assistant secretary for Health and Scientific Affairs, in many discussions about the organization of the health activities of the Department. Medicare and Medicaid were in their infancy, but they were evidences of the growing expectation of the American people that good medical care should become a right guaranteed by the government, not a privilege for those who could afford it. The manner of financing and delivering medical care was moving into the political arena, requiring more and more top-policy leadership from the Office of the Secretary.

Gardner, Cohen, and Lee concluded that it was unrealistic to expect innovative policy leadership in the delivery and financing of medical care and the training of adequate medical and paramedical manpower to evolve among the commissioned officer corps of the Public Health Service (PHS), which had been created and designed for a much more limited purpose. That role would have to be performed, they concluded, by a strong assistant secretary for Health and Scientific Affairs, named by the President and serving at his pleasure, in contrast to a surgeon general, who was required by law to be chosen from among PHS commissioned officers for a term of four years. In 1968, however, the surgeon general had most of the financial resources and the staff positions needed by the assistant secretary to perform the needed functions of policy leadership. A basic reorganization seemed to be the only way to deal with this situation.

Effective March 13, 1968, Cohen issued a reorganization order transferring all functions of the Public Health Service and the Food and Drug Administration to the supervision of the assistant secretary for Health and Scientific Affairs, Dr. Philip Lee, who had participated actively in the design of the plan. In addition, Lee was given responsibility for policy analysis, coordination, and guidance over the other health programs of HEW, such as Medicare, Medicaid, and the health programs of the Children's Bureau, a difficult staff role to perform, which was never successfully achieved. The former Office of the Surgeon General was abolished, and its functions and personnel were divided between the Office of the Secretary and the former operating components of the Public Health Service. The surgeon general himself was made a deputy assistant secretary while also retaining, and preferring, his historic and more glamorous military-sounding title.

On the heels of this major step—and a traumatic one it was for the commissioned officers of the Public Health Service—came the reorganization of the bureau structure of the PHS. The National Institutes of Health (NIH) was revamped by transferring to it the National Library of Medicine—already physically located on its Bethesda campus—and the Bureau of Health Manpower Education. All other operating functions of the former Public Health Service were consolidated under a new agency to be called the Health Services and Mental Health Administration. (This title resulted in the most unpronounceable acronym in Washington—HSMHA.) As its name implies, the new organization acquired all the mental health activities of the Department, which had been vested in the National Institute of Mental Health (NIMH), which had earlier been one of the largest of the NIH institutes, and which now had supervisory responsibility over St. Elizabeths Hospital, one of the largest mental hospitals in the United States, located in the District of Columbia. NIMH was a hybrid organization, combining research, service, and professional training programs. The magnitude of the service programs had become so great that it seemed logical to place the NIMH in the new service-oriented HSMHA. And finally, the Regional Medical Programs—a jerry-built product of the legislation-mad 1960's, intermixing research and service functions—was transferred from NIH to the new HSMHA.

However logical this reorganization may have seemed to Secretary Cohen and his advisers, it seemed more like a disaster to many career officers of the Public Health Service who had spent their professional lives with the organization. Although the name Public Health Service was legally retained, nobody quite knew what it meant any more. It could have been used to refer generally to the three organizations: the Food and Drug Administration, the Health Services and Mental Health Administration, and the National Institutes of Health, but it was almost never used that way. It did not describe a cohesive organization, and it was no longer a title to conjure up a proud tradition extending back to 1798. The least the Secretary could have done, thought many, was to preserve the name in a meaningful way by assigning it to the organization that now had the awkward and easily forgettable name of Health Services and Mental Health Administration.

As the hot and acrimonious summer of conventions and demonstrations yielded to the speech-making of the fall campaigns, Cohen's attention shifted toward the future. He decided to put all his ideas for the improvement of the nation's social programs into one package and print it as "The Secretary's Introduction" to the HEW *Annual Report* of 1968. In it he expressed his views on all manner of subjects, from his confidence in the manageability of HEW—about which discussion seems never-ending—to the creation of a Selective Service lottery. It was a remarkable document, one that could only have been written, in all probability, as a "swan song."

Like Flemming, Cohen hugely enjoyed being Secretary and was frustrated by the brevity of his term of service. He was just getting warmed up for all kinds of action when the political wheel turned him out of office.

ROBERT H. FINCH

Following President Richard Nixon's election in November, 1968, Robert Finch, then lieutenant governor of California and one of Nixon's closest political advisers, found himself in much the same position as Abraham Ribicoff had been in eight years earlier. He was permitted to express a preference among Cabinet posts, and, like Ribicoff, he chose HEW. Both came to believe that HEW is probably the hardest place in Washington in which to enhance one's reputation.

It took only days after Finch was sworn into office on January 20, 1969, for him to begin to realize he had been put into the jaws of a giant nutcracker. President Nixon had given the very strong impression to Southerners during the campaign that he would begin promptly after his inauguration to ease the pressure on Southern school districts to desegregate. South Carolina's Senator Strom Thurmond felt that he had been given solid assurances that this would occur, and he fully expected the President, his Secretary of HEW, and his Attorney General to deliver on the commitment. Other powerful Southerners interpreted Mr. Nixon's ambiguous public statements as being more than the usual campaign promises. They were waiting to see what would happen.

On the other side were the civil rights activists who had struggled hard and seemingly gained much in the four and a half years since the enactment of the Civil Rights Act of 1964. Also on the other side were the dedicated staff of 350 civil service people who constituted the Office of Civil Rights. And watching both were the *New York Times,* the *Washington Post,* and other newspapers with wide circulation and intense interest in the issues.

On December 30, 1968, Secretary Wilbur Cohen had signed an order, as required by law, that five school districts in North Carolina, South Carolina, and Mississippi would lose their federal funds in thirty days because of noncompliance with Title VI of the Civil Rights Act. The cutoff date was nine days after the inauguration of the new President. Inevitably, the pressure to defer deadlines and soften enforcement was applied to both the White House and HEW almost within hours after the Cabinet officers had taken their oaths of office.

After days of jockeying, the decision that was finally reached was characteristic of the uncertainty surrounding civil rights decisions for fourteen of Secretary Finch's seventeen months in office. It tried to satisfy both sides and satisfied nobody. There was to be a brief delay and a further review before the order took final effect. Both sides recognized it as a temporizing action, and it gained respect for the Administration in neither quarter.

It is hard to conceive of a more trying set of circumstances into which a Secretary could be put: a change of party, and a change of policy—in terms of Presidential rhetoric, but without Presidential guidelines—relating to the deepest schism of American society in the twentieth century. There was a Supreme Court, a civil rights activists' movement, a liberal press, and a dedicated bureaucracy all pointing in one direction, and a President, a White House staff, and a strong Southern bloc of both parties pointing in the other. The Secretary of HEW, long a loyal friend and supporter of the President, but essentially more liberal than the President, with the explicit responsibility for enforcing Title VI of the Civil Rights Act—the principal legal instrument for desegregating public schools—stood somewhere in the middle. It was a conflict of responsibilities and loyalties of the first order, played out during much of Finch's term of office.

The civil rights issue did not settle down into a pattern of consistent decisions and actions until March of 1970, fourteen months after Finch took office. During all this time there was much pulling and hauling going on with all the contending parties, with the Justice Department playing an increasingly important role. Finally, in March, 1970, the Administration decided that temporizing with the problem was worse than taking a firm stand, however temporarily unpopular it might be within the South. It decided that all segregated school districts had to take major steps to desegregate by the following fall or face court action.

Civil rights was the foremost example of the difficulties confronting a new Secretary of HEW when administration changes from one party to another. The problems are not different in kind, but they are different in degree from those of other departments. Any new Administration is understandably concerned to gain prompt control over the policy-making machinery and personnel of the government. It comes, however, equipped with rhetoric about change but not with carefully worked out policy positions. The new appointees who are asked to help develop the specifics of the new policies are, more frequently than not, distrustful of civil service personnel who are left over from the previous administration. Yet, they themselves are not sufficiently informed about the issues to make intelligent judgments or analyses until they have been there for some time. In a small department or agency—or even a large one like the Veterans' Administration where the issues are less numerous and complex—this shifting of personnel and policy positions may not become an overwhelming burden, but in a department like HEW, which had more than 200 programs and a budget of more than $50 billion when Finch took office, the challenge of determining whether these programs are heading in the right direction and are being properly administered, in the eyes of the new administration, is of incredible magnitude and complexity.

Several organizational changes were made in 1969 by Secretary Finch to strengthen the Department's program affecting children. He created an Office of Child Development in the Office of the Secretary, concerned particularly with the needs of preschool children. The Head Start Program was transferred to it from the Office of Economic Opportunity, as was, subsequently, what remained of the Children's Bureau—mainly research and demonstration functions—after its health programs had been transferred to HSMHA.

The most dramatic proposal, and probably the most controversial in many years of HEW growth and change, was formally launched in the fall of 1969. President Nixon recommended a complete revamping of the welfare structure and program. The new Family Assistance Program, as it was called, would place a floor of uniform federal welfare payments under the existing federal-state-local payments and, for the first time, aid the working poor. Most states would continue to be involved in making supplementary payments, but they could designate the federal government as their agent in administering their share of the program as well as its own. After lengthy White House discussions including Secretary Finch, Daniel Patrick Moynihan, Richard Nathan, Arthur Burns, and others, the President decided to recommend this startlingly new and liberal piece of social welfare legislation to the Congress. The plan created such strong schisms within the Congress that it became embroiled in endless controversy. (See Chapter V on welfare and rehabilitation.)

Like all Secretaries, Finch had tough decisions to make in the food and drug field. He banned the sale of cyclamates (artificial sweeteners) for use in beverages and food, announced a ban on DDT, with a time delay of two years, for all but essential uses, and made major organizational changes affecting the FDA.

On October 23, three months after the President delivered his "Special Message on Population," HEW established within the Health Services and Mental Health Administration the National Center for Family Planning with a 5-year goal of reaching an estimated 5 million low-income women of child-bearing age who desire family-planning services but cannot afford them. Secretary Finch was a firm supporter of this program, considerably more enthusiastic about it than President Nixon (a circumstance which turned out to be a source of occasional embarrassment).

Legislation continued to roll out of the legislative hoppers, though at a reduced rate compared with the Kennedy-Johnson years. The Older Americans Act of 1969, the Child Protection Act, the Federal Coal Mine Health and Safety Act, increased Social Security benefits, the Migrant Health Amendments, the Community Mental Health Centers Amendments—these and others continued to extend the scope of HEW responsibilities. Two actions, however, removed functions from HEW.

On March 10, 1969, the President approved a law removing the Bureau of Federal Credit Unions from HEW and transferring all its functions to a newly created National Credit Union Administration, an independent agency. On June 24, 1970, President Nixon moved to create the Environmental Protection Agency (EPA), a new federal agency reporting directly to the President and dealing with the problems of environmental pollution. The agency brought together all federal programs for controlling air and water pollution, solid wastes, pesticides, and radiation. All HEW functions related to the agency's purposes were transferred to the new EPA.

Finch found HEW a most difficult and disconcerting Department to administer. He could well understand why its manageability was widely questioned. The press, however, which had started out with an unusually favorable attitude, had little understanding of, or sympathy for, his difficulties and within a year began to show its disappointment. To compound Finch's problems, HEW seemed to be a haven for activist employees who were constantly protesting, demanding, and demonstrating. He had the misfortune to be Secretary during the period when organized dissatisfaction with the Establishment was at its height. He was without experience in handling internal backfires. When employee turmoil erupted, accompanied by press coverage, President Nixon suddenly decided that handling the intricacies and pressures and harassments of HEW were not Finch's "cup of tea." With surprising abruptness in mid-June, 1970, Nixon appointed Finch as counselor to the President and in his place at HEW appointed his under secretary of State, Elliot L. Richardson.

ELLIOT L. RICHARDSON

When, on June 24, 1970, President Nixon swore Elliot L. Richardson in as Secretary of HEW, he had good grounds for believing that he had appointed the best-qualified man in the United States for the job. Trained as a lawyer, Richardson had the unique combination of service in the executive, legislative, and judicial branches of the federal government, and a similar breadth of experience at the state level. After an outstanding record at Harvard Law School, he had served as law clerk to the distinguished jurists Learned Hand and Felix Frankfurter, as administrative assistant to Senator Leverett Saltonstall, and as assistant secretary for Legislation of HEW, positions that were interspersed with the private practice of law. After leaving his key post in HEW, he became U.S. attorney for the Eastern District of Massachusetts, then lieutenant governor, and finally attorney general of Massachusetts, before being appointed under secretary of State by President Nixon. If anyone could master the intricacies of the huge Department, it was Richardson. And if anyone could meet the grueling test of appearing before Congress on a dizzying array of complex issues, it was he.

Almost every Secretary of HEW has entered his office with the feeling that the mission of the Department is poorly understood throughout the nation and that one of his principal roles should be to overcome that deficiency. Elliot Richardson and John Gardner had an especially strong motivation to educate the American public to understand the relationship of health, education, and welfare functions and the advantages of uniting them in a single department. They also shared a strong interest in institutional reform. Richardson finally concluded that his most important single audience for such a message and such a philosophy was the key staff of HEW. He decided to deliver his message in person to several auditoriums full of HEW's staff, particularly its professional and management staff at all levels.

As Richardson laid out what he wanted to say, it seemed to his close advisers that it was too much to put into a single speech. Richardson's response was that he would give it even if it took three or four hours. Though he managed to pare it down to much less than that, it promptly became dubbed, "Richardson's Castro Speech." It was so well received that he decided to publish it in pamphlet form under the title, *Responsibility and Responsiveness.*

Richardson began by emphasizing the dangers of overpromising, of the inadvertent stimulation of cynicism by creating a widening gap between what people expected of government and what it was able to deliver. He wanted to set realistic goals and have them understood and met. But behind the goals, there was a philosophy and a strategy that would guide the selection of objectives. In briefest words, it was "the prevention of dependency and the accomplishment of institutional reform." The concept of preventing dependency was undoubtedly fostered by Richardson's close association with Marion Folsom, under whom he had served as assistant secretary in 1957 and 1958. As earlier mentioned, this was the core of Folsom's social philosophy. But the strong desire for institutional reform came from Richardson's personal experience in his home state of Massachusetts where he was in position to observe at close hand the rigidities and malfunctioning of state and local institutions, and the remoteness and failure of leadership on the part of the federal government to assist in making institutions more responsive to public needs.

His interest in institutional reform led Richardson to give much thought to the question of how the federal government could use its influence and leverage to encourage states to bring together at the community level many different services needed by dependent people to help them overcome their dependency. Although it took nearly two years to hatch, Richardson finally produced on May 18, 1972, a bill called the "Allied Services Act of 1972." The "1972" was obviously its date of conception, since there was no chance of its being acted upon before 1973, at the earliest. If and when it should ever become law, it will owe its institutional life primarily to Richardson.

The purpose of the Allied Services Act is to adjust the services available to people—particularly people who are temporarily or permanently incapacitated—to the reality that although many, if not most, of them have multiple problems that are interrelated, specialized service agencies do not treat them as whole human beings. They must go one place for their physical health problems, another for their psychological mix-ups, still elsewhere for their children's problems, two or three other places for their skill deficiencies and lack of employment, and on and on. Such services are organized for the convenience of the professional specialized providers, not for the puzzled members of society who have, at least temporarily, been defeated by its anomalies and complexities. There is no meshing between the needs of such people and the disparate agencies offering services at the local level. Richardson's program would give special financial incentives for the coordinated delivery of human services.

Richardson's style of administration is described in Chapter XI. He succeeded in mastering the management problems inherent in the complex Department more fully than any of his predecessors. Part of that mastery came from his interest in the subject of management, and part from his extraordinary capacity to read staff memoranda far into the night and return them the next day with comments and decisions. This is undoubtedly one of the reasons Nixon came to regard Richardson as his most talented and flexible administrator, able to serve well in any top post in government.

CASPAR W. WEINBERGER

Three weeks after President Nixon's landslide re-election in November, 1972, he announced that he had requested Elliot Richardson to become his Secretary of Defense in the revamped Cabinet and that he would appoint Caspar W. Weinberger to be the new Secretary of HEW.

Caspar Weinberger, a native Californian, went East just long enough to get his undergraduate and law degrees from Harvard and then returned to his home state to practice law. He became increasingly involved in California politics, serving as a state legislator and as a television public affairs commentator and moderator before being appointed finance director by Governor Ronald Reagan. In the latter post he was known as a tough reviewer of budgets.

Weinberger's Washington career began in 1970 with President Nixon's appointment of him to the chairmanship of the Federal Trade Commission, a position he held for only five months before Nixon made him deputy director of the Office of Management and Budget (OMB) when it was upgraded from its former status and title, Bureau of the Budget. In 1972, Weinberger succeeded George Schultz as director of OMB, the President's right arm in budget and management matters.

Secretary Weinberger has embarked on his new assignment as this book is being completed. His approach and style of administration are rapidly emerging. The President has assigned him the mission of corralling the wild horse labeled "HEW." He is a spokesman and an instrument of Presidential policy aimed at restricting HEW's future pressure on the federal budget. Neither he nor the President think it necessary for him to be a spokesman to the President on behalf of the many groups and interests who look to HEW as the federal government's principal source of concern and money in helping them to solve their manifold social problems. To what degree he will be able to fulfill the President's desire to put a financial lid on HEW will be fascinating to watch.

In organizational terms, Secretary Weinberger took several major steps in rapid succession. He made his new under secretary, Frank Carlucci, the internal manager of the Department with the understanding that he is to accelerate the movement toward regional decentralization of intergovernmental programs begun under Finch and additionally developed by Richardson. He has created a new assistant secretary for Human Development, bringing together the Office of Child Development, the Administration on Aging, and miscellaneous other functions previously scattered. And he has reorganized HEW's health programs, abolishing the unsuccessful Health Services and Mental Health Administration, and putting in its place four health organizations: a Health Services Administration, a Health Resources Administration, a Center for Disease Control, and an Alcohol, Drug Abuse, and Mental Health Administration.

IN SUMMARY

These are but a few sketchy highlights of activities and actions of the first ten Secretaries of HEW. Nothing short of an enormous record could give an adequate sense of the variety of issues coming before each succeeding Secretary and of the competing forces coming to a vortex in that position. Some additional sense of this extraordinarily complex managerial job will become evident in additional chapters. It would be difficult to prove that the unusually short average tenure of HEW Secretaries—2.2 years—is primarily the result of the enormous load placed on them, but that it has been a contributing factor there can be no doubt.

The briefest way to characterize the dynamism of HEW in its first twenty years is to set forth a table showing the growth of its budget. Table 1 shows that growth. And, as we shall see in the chapters to come, the upper limit is not yet in sight.

TABLE 1

DEPARTMENT OF HEALTH, EDUCATION, AND WELFARE
History of Outlays
(In thousands)

	General Tax Funds	Social Security Trust Funds	Total Expenditures
1954	$ 1,971,362	$ 3,404,760	$ 5,376,122
1955	1,992,542	5,585,515	7,578,057
1956	2,066,357	5,551,284	7,617,641
1957	2,285,683	6,726,403	9,012,086
1958	2,614,698	8,332,447	10,947,145
1959	3,041,908	9,828,488	12,870,396
1960	3,344,639	11,742,641	15,087,280
1961	3,684,706	12,595,000	16,279,706
1962	4,132,666	14,358,720	18,491,386
1963	4,927,808	15,788,924	20,716,732
1964	5,321,299	16,625,152	21,946,451
1965	6,029,180	17,357,083	23,386,263
1966	7,450,753	19,857,077	27,307,830
1967	9,944,904	25,323,296	35,268,200
1968	12,147,738	29,019,572	41,167,310
1969	13,095,651	33,901,367	46,997,018
1970	16,472,217	37,423,495	53,895,712
1971	18,731,219	43,122,442	61,853,661
1972 (est)	23,551,774	48,228,358	71,780,132
1973 (est)	25,460,344	58,119,348	83,579,692
1974 (est)	27,494,302	66,327,453	93,821,755
1975 (est)	29,553,000	73,109,000	102,662,000

III

The Structure of HEW and the Office of the Secretary

By 1973, the Department of Health, Education, and Welfare had accumulated no fewer than 200 programs.* This staggering array of programs is administered through 13 operating agencies —three of which are located within the Office of the Secretary— and ten regional offices. The six health agencies are grouped under the Public Health Service and the two education agencies under the Education Division, both of which are legal titles with little meaning. The operating agencies, which might also be labeled program agencies, and the number of personnel employed by each agency at the end of August 1973 are:

Public Health Service
    National Institutes of Health, 12,622
    Food and Drug Administration, 6,503
    Center for Disease Control, 3,238

---

* The index of the HEW part of the *Catalog of Domestic Assistance,* issued annually by the Office of Management and Budget for the use of state, local, and institutional officials appears as Appendix A of this volume. The catalog—for sale by the Government Printing Office— contains such information in respect to each program as: objectives, types of assistance, eligibility requirements, application and award process, formula and matching requirements, and whom to contact for further information. There are also a score or more of direct operating programs not listed in the catalog such as the enforcement functions of the Food and Drug Administration.

Health Resources Administration, 1,214
Health Services Administration, 17,778
Alcohol, Drug Abuse, and Mental Health Administration,†
   6,124
Social Security Administration, 67,660
Social and Rehabilitation Service, 2,376
Office of Human Development (Office of the Secretary)
   Office of Child Development, 481
   Office of Youth Development, 45
   Administration on Aging, 108
Education Division
   Office of Education, 2,971
   National Institute of Education, 378

In addition, the Office of the Secretary employs 5,660 persons, of which 3,195 are located in the Washington area and 2,465 in HEW's ten regions.

THE LEGAL POWERS OF THE SECRETARY

Nearly all the legal powers of HEW except those covering education programs are vested in the Secretary, subject to his delegation. This follows what has been the doctrine of public management for a generation. Congress has resisted, however, efforts to assign legal powers over education to the Secretary, reflecting partly the influence of education lobbies, partly the possessiveness of congressional committees, and partly the continuing hope of both that an organization handling education affairs will some day be elevated to a Cabinet department.

Many observers have erroneously interpreted the failure to vest in the Secretary the legal powers over education programs as seriously circumscribing the Secretary's authority. In practice, this is not true in any important sense. The Secretary continues to control budget decisions and departmental positions on legislation, the two most important policy roles that he needs to exercise. Furthermore, the commissioner of Education and the assistant secretary for Education both serve at the pleasure of the President, and as long as the President has confidence in his Secretary of HEW, the top education officials are usually disposed to follow

† Created September 25, 1973, by reorganization of the National Institute of Mental Health. Employment figure shown is that of NIMH on August 31, 1973.

CHART I.
Organization of the Department of Health, Education, and Welfare

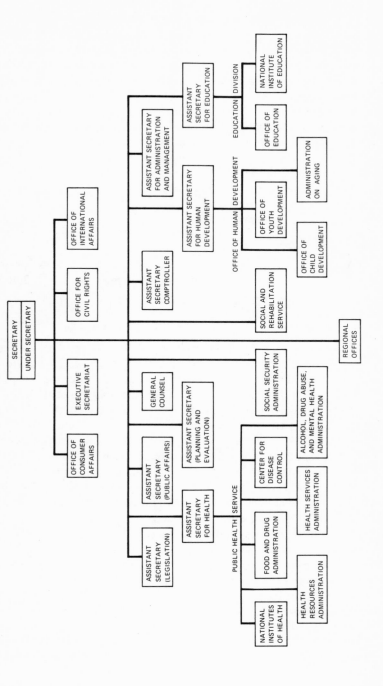

the Secretary's desires in the event of a disagreement. Two commissioners of Education have been fired since the end of World War II, when they attempted to show too great a sense of independence from the policies of their superiors. Vesting legal powers in subordinate officials has less effect than most people think. In actuality, the Secretary of HEW has almost all the legal power he needs or can effectively use over his subordinate agencies.

THE UNDER SECRETARY AND THE REGIONAL DIRECTORS

The HEW under secretary shares the Secretary's responsibilities and duties in whatever way the Secretary may wish. The ideal arrangement is to have an under secretary who is a first-rate internal manager, thus freeing a major part of the Secretary's time for the numerous congressional, White House, and public contacts that place heavy demands on him. Unfortunately, many under secretaries have been chosen for reasons other than their managerial competence, and often with little or no concern for their ability to work in tandem with the Secretary. Some have had very short tenure. Presidents would be wise to allow their Secretaries to select their own under secretaries, as President Richard Nixon did in allowing Robert Finch to choose Jack Veneman. Veneman served four years (1969–73), giving both stature and continuity to the office.

Beginning in 1973, the under secretary was delegated responsibility for the direct supervision of HEW's ten regional directors and their staffs. The new under secretary, Frank Carlucci, recently the deputy director of the Office of Management and Budget, is an apostle of the Nixon doctrine of decentralizing decision-making to "the field," and the first important organizational action of Secretary Caspar Weinberger was to reassign the field establishment to Carlucci so that he might accelerate what had been a significant trend during Nixon's first term—the shift of decision-making from Washington to the ten regional offices. A deputy under secretary for field operations was named to aid the under secretary. The term "decentralization" in the terminology of the Office of Management and Budget (OMB) has not meant transferring authority to state and local officials; it has meant delegating it from Washington federal officials to regional federal officials. Although President Nixon's major interest has been in shifting program decisions to states and communities, the OMB's has been to get federal program decisions made and coordinated at the regional level, believing that regional decision-making will be a step toward more independent and responsive state and local decisions, a premise that deserves much more careful analysis than it has received.

The problem of how best to organize HEW's field operations has been a perennial issue and a classic example of the conflict between those forces that seek to manage by geographic area and those that would prefer to organize by program or functional purpose. The argument has persisted since the early days of the Federal Security Agency and will continue far into the future. The most difficult issue is whether the regional directors will, in effect, be "regional secretaries" or whether they will be regional co-ordinators of the representatives of the several operating agencies of HEW, with limited power to knock heads together when coordination cannot be achieved by leadership and persuasion. The recent trend, with the support of the OMB, has been toward powerful regional directors, possessing substantial grants of author-ity for decision-making. This has been carried out in the Depart-ment of Housing and Urban Development (HUD), but HUD is much more limited in scope than HEW. In its size and complexity it is more like one operating agency of HEW than the whole De-partment. This philosophical and power problem is almost certain to continue as far into the future as it is possible to see. And it seems clear that the more complex a department is, the more difficult it is to vest across-the-board authority in regional directors.

THE OFFICE OF THE GENERAL COUNSEL

One of the earliest functions to be centralized in the Office of the Secretary was legal services. From the initial organization of the Federal Security Agency (FSA), it was recognized that the Administrator needed to have a strong legal office at his immediate beck and call. In consequence, this was the first of the staff func-tions to be centralized. In 1940, the legal services for all of the operating agencies were consolidated under a general counsel, immediately answerable to the Administrator. The purpose was to assure consistent legal advice and to avoid situations in which there would be conflict between the legal opinions of the various echelons of the FSA. So it has remained ever since.

The General Counsel's Office is organized by divisions that serve the operating agencies, and in addition, there are three divisions that serve the entire Department: the Civil Rights Division, the Business and Administrative Law Division, and the Legislation Division. The supervisory staff to oversee the work of all the divisions is tiny, consisting only of the general counsel, an associate general counsel, and, recently, two special assistants. While the staff of the Office of the General Counsel has been out-standing—one of the finest legal staffs ever assembled in any government department or agency—it is inevitable that the division staffs assigned to perform legal services for the operating agencies should acquire, in substantial degree, an operating agency per-spective after working closely with them for five, ten, or fifteen years. It is the role of the general counsel to minimize this tendency, but he has never had sufficient staff to perform this function adequately. Experience with the regulatory functions of the De-partment, especially the Food and Drug Administration, empha-size the need for a larger review staff to assure the Secretary's interests are fully reflected and protected.

The Office of the General Counsel has maintained higher pro-fessional standards, been more continuous in service, and has had a stronger stabilizing influence on the Department than any other component of the Office of the Secretary. Although all of the lawyers are in "Schedule A" positions—meaning that they do not have the same theoretical tenure that other civil servants do—they have been so highly competent that the politically selected general counsel of each Secretary's administration has quickly learned how foolish it would be to seek to shake up the staff with a lot of new blood. Much of the credit for the high quality of the staff belongs to two general counsel who served during the FSA years—the late Jack Tate and Alanson W. Willcox (who also served for the eight years of the Kennedy-Johnson Administra-tions).

How Should Assistant Secretaries Be Used?

For most of the two decades of its existence, HEW has stood out from most other domestic departments in the manner in which it has used its assistant secretaries. The dominant mode in most other domestic departments is to designate assistant secretaries as line officers responsible for overseeing subordinate bureaus. But from the start (see Chapter II), HEW has used its assistant secretaries primarily as staff officers whose role is to try to help the Secretary knit together the related functions in the operating agencies. Their roles—with three recent exceptions—have been Department-wide. Even though they have not had substantial formal decision-making power, they have, nevertheless, had very major influence on decisions.

By 1973, HEW had the following eight assistant secretaries: Legislation, Planning and Evaluation, Human Development, Public Affairs, Administration and Management, Comptroller, Health, and Education. To this list should be added the general counsel, who is of assistant secretary rank and whose role as a cohesive force in the Department is, as mentioned, as great as that of any assistant secretary.

The assistant secretaries for Health, for Education, and for Human Development are the exceptions to the rule; they are line officers, with supervisory responsibility over operating functions in their respective fields. All three are of recent origin—the line duties of the first date from 1968, by decision of the Secretary; those of the second date from 1972, by decision of Congress; and those of the third from 1973, by action of the Secretary.

Many Washington officials measure their own effectiveness and importance by the extent of their explicit decision-making power, and their capacity to use that power to accomplish what they think needs doing. To such officials, the role of being an adviser to the Secretary and his agent in dealing with issues that cut laterally across several components of the Department is difficult to perform—if and when they are given such assignments. They chafe under the advisory role and seek the power to direct particular units of the Department. This sort of frustration caused the assistant secretary for Health and Scientific Affairs to be converted into a line officer in charge of the predominantly health-oriented agencies of HEW. At current writing, there is some talk of converting the present assistant secretary for Health into an administrator for Health, making it very explicit that he is the top health operating official in the Department.

When a staff officer, who is charged with dealing with issues that cut laterally across an organization, is converted into a line officer with an operating agency empire under him, he can no longer serve effectively and objectively as a staff adviser to the Secretary. This has happened in the above-mentioned example of the assistant secretary for Health. He now has an empire to supervise, but he does not have within that empire the components of HEW that spend the most money on health functions. He supervises the National Institutes of Health, the Health Services Administration, the Health Resources Administration, the Center for Disease Control, and the Food and Drug Administration, but he does not have authority over the Medicare program of Social Security or the Medicaid program of the Social Rehabilitation Service. Who, then, can advise the Secretary objectively about the latter programs, about health insurance legislation, and about other key health issues that extend beyond the bounds of the operating portfolio of the assistant secretary for Health? The answer has to be other assistant secretaries and staff officers, serving entirely as staff officers, with no empires to protect.

The Office of Management and Budget would be well advised to conduct both a retrospective and an ongoing study of the contrasting methods and effects of organizing through the use of line, as compared to the use of staff assistant secretaries.

Assistant Secretary for Legislation

The position of assistant secretary for Legislation has been an extremely key post during most of the 20-year life of HEW. Two men who occupied it—Elliot Richardson and Wilbur Cohen—later became Secretary. The dynamics of HEW's legislative concerns are so complex and fast-moving that only an unusual person can keep up with their ramifications. In the early days, the assistant secretary for Legislation operated with only two or three professional assistants, using the general counsel's staff to augment his own, but by 1973, he had more than twenty—still a comparatively modest staff—including four deputy assistant secretaries.

Assistant Secretary for Public Affairs

Large departments need a top-level official to concern himself with relations with the press, the media, and the public. Although he is rarely the HEW spokesman on important issues, he has a myriad of second- and third-level issues and hundreds of organized subdivisions of the general public with which to deal.

Secretary Weinberger decided in the summer of 1973 that the

public affairs and public information area was a good candidate for significant economies. He ordered a 77 per cent reduction in HEW's public affairs staffs (located primarily in the operating agencies), and the elimination of 275 publications. Estimated savings totaled $20 million. Weinberger gave his newly appointed assistant secretary for Public Affairs, Lewis M. Helm, greater and more centralized authority over public affairs and public information matters than had been given to any of his predecessors.

Assistant Secretary for Planning and Evaluation

Three of the five persons who have served as assistant secretary for Planning and Evaluation since it was established in 1965 have been economists skilled in quantitative analysis. Two of them, William Gorham, who served under John Gardner, and Laurence Lynn, who served under Elliot Richardson, cut their analytical eyeteeth in the Office of the Secretary of Defense during the McNamara regime. They brought to HEW the conviction that systematic analysis of problems, establishment of goals that could be defined in quantitative terms, programming and budgeting in terms of these goals, and progress reporting in relation to established objectives should be as applicable to HEW as to the Defense Department. But each of them discovered that there was a wider degree of difference between the two organizations than they had supposed.

The long-range planning role of the assistant secretary for Planning and Evaluation requires sophistication in understanding the competing political forces that act on and through the Congress, as well as in economic analysis. Enormous amounts of energy may be wasted if it is devoted to enterprises that have no realistic chance of acceptance by the Congress. Conversely, analyses of problems from a fresh perspective—analyses of problems that cut across the wide range of departmental functions and that deal with long-range issues in a way that can capture Presidential and congressional understanding and support—provide the Secretary with the most effective instrument he has for giving genuine leadership to the direction of the Department's programs.

The assistant secretary for Planning and Evaluation has a substantial staff, including three deputy assistant secretaries, one for income maintenance, one for health planning and analysis, and one for program systems. When a Secretary shows keen personal interest in the kinds of imaginative analytical work of which this office is capable—as occurred during Richardson's term—its influence can be very large.

Assistant Secretary for Health

The assistant secretary for Health ("Scientific Affairs" was dropped from the title, but not from the duties, in 1972), who has been mentioned earlier in this chapter, is both an administrator and a policy adviser to the Secretary. He supervises the operations of the six agencies under him—the National Institutes of Health, the Health Services Administration, the Health Resources Administration, the Center for Disease Control, the Alcohol, Drug Abuse, and Mental Health Administration, and the Food and Drug Administration—and oversees the work of the ten regional health directors and their staffs. He is *an* adviser, not *the* adviser, to the Secretary on health matters falling outside his six operating agencies and is not in position to be completely objective about such matters, since he has an operating empire to protect.

In the major health reorganization of 1973, creating the new Health Services Administration and the Health Resources Administration, Secretary Caspar Weinberger approved a recommendation of Assistant Secretary for Health Charles Edwards that he be given a much enlarged staff in comparison with earlier assistant secretaries for Health. Most of the new staff was transferred from the Health Services and Mental Health Administration (HSMHA), which was abolished. The 1974 staff of the assistant secretary for Health is budgeted at approximately 700 people, an increase of 500 over the 1972 and early 1973 staff. Such a large staff is tantamount to a restoration of the former Office of Surgeon General of the Public Health Service under a new name and new management. In 1968, the Office of the Surgeon General was thought to be an unnecessary layer of management and was abolished; in 1973, its equivalent was reconstituted to give the Assistant Secretary for Health a full set of the management tools and staff thought to be needed by a top line officer. "The more things change, the more they remain the same."

Assistant Secretary for Education

Under the Education Act Amendments of 1972, a new assistant secretary for Education was created to head a new Education

Division in HEW, consisting of the Office of Education and the new National Institute of Education.

It is too soon to judge what distribution of power will emerge between the assistant secretary and his two subordinates, the commissioner of Education and the director of the National Institute of Education. It will be interesting to watch the struggle of the assistant secretary for staff. Being a legally established line officer, he probably feels that he should have the panoply of staff assistants that is the normal accompaniment of line officer status. But Congress has limited him to a staff of some forty positions, a far cry from the seven hundred positions available to the assistant secretary for Health.

Assistant Secretary for Human Development

Following Secretary Weinberger's decision to put HEW's field establishment under his new under secretary, Frank Carlucci (with the aid of a newly created deputy under secretary for Regional Affairs), Weinberger abolished the position of assistant secretary for Regional and Field Services and in its place established a new assistant secretary for Human Development. (The HEW Secretary has the power to use several of his assistant secretary positions flexibly and can change their titles and duties at will.)

Weinberger announced that his new assistant secretary for Human Development would assume direction of a miscellaneous collection of small agencies and functions drawn from various parts of the Department where they did not fit well. These include: the Administration on Aging, the Office of Child Development, the President's Council on Mental Retardation, the Office of Youth Development, current HEW programs for youth and student affairs, and Office of Economic Opportunity functions concerning Indian Affairs. Several of these are operating programs with combined funds of well over a half billion dollars. The largest of them deserve description and comment here, since they are operating agencies within the Office of the Secretary.

Services for the aging. The late Congressman John Fogarty was the father of the Administration on Aging. Neither the Eisenhower Administration nor the Kennedy Administration wanted it, but John Fogarty did. The Budget Bureau was particularly strongly opposed to it on the dual ground that organizing the government by age-clientele groups was in direct conflict with the preferable policy of organizing by broad objectives and that such an agency would quickly become the mouthpiece inside the government of the external organizations of older citizens. Fogarty admitted the second and said that was one reason why he wanted it. And he won. The Administration on Aging (AoA) was created by the Older Americans Act, which became effective in 1965.

By mid-1970, every state had an organization designated as advocate and developer of services and opportunities for older citizens, a major purpose of the Act. A grant program provided financial aid to such organizations, and they, in turn, sought to stimulate the creation of "senior centers" in communities all across the nation. Thousands of older citizens have been enlisted as volunteers to provide services to their associates. The most recent *Directory of Senior Centers* (1970) lists more than 1,200 such centers.

A Foster Grandparent Program, initiated by the Office of Economic Opportunity, was transferred to the AoA in 1969, providing project grants to organize programs that encourage the use of senior citizens to care for small children while their parents are at work or ill.

A White House Conference on Aging was held in 1971, chaired by former HEW Secretary Arthur S. Flemming, who was subsequently named to head the Administration on Aging. The conference covered health, income, nutrition, housing, transportation, employment and retirement, education, and spiritual well-being. One of the major outcomes of that conference was the recommendation for more emphasis on nutrition programs for older citizens, including "meals on wheels" for shut-ins, conducted for many years in England with much success. A $100 million nutrition program was twice enacted in 1972 and twice caught in President Nixon's double veto of the HEW appropriations bill, but was included in the 1973–74 budget. Home health aids, homemaker service, and transportation assistance are other program emphases of the AoA. The AoA operates entirely through state and community groups, providing no direct services to the aged through federal employees.

Youth development and delinquency prevention. The Office of Youth Development (OYD) deals with a very large set of problems with a small amount of money. It has about $10 million to aid states and communities in strengthening and improving their juvenile justice systems, and to provide preventive diagnostic treatment and rehabilitative services to delinquent youths or those in danger of becoming delinquent. The grants emphasize community planning and training of personnel. The OYD's activities are not confined to the making of grants and the provision of technical assistance, but also include the role of catalytic agent within the government, and particularly within HEW to see that the much larger resources of other organizations are applied with full recognition of what they can do to help reduce juvenile delinquency.

The Office of Child Development (OCD). The Office of Child Development, with a staff of about 400, has one large grant program—Head Start—plus a variety of research, evaluation, planning, and coordinating functions. Its Head Start Program to encourage the provision of educational and other constructive services to children during their preschool years is financed at a level of approximately $400 million per year. In 1974, services will be provided to some 300,000 full-year and summer-enrolled children, and to 20,000 children in experimental programs including "Health Start," "Home Start," and the multiform child development centers. Ten per cent of the Head Start opportunities are required by law to be made available to handicapped children.

The residual functions of the Children's Bureau, which was created in 1912 following the recommendations of the first White House Conference on Children and Youth, are now conducted by the Office of Child Development. These include research and the making of grants to enlarge our understanding of childhood behavior and social problems, as well as the preparation for and follow-up on each succeeding decennial White House Conference on Children and Youth. In 1974, research and demonstration efforts will emphasize child advocacy, day care and early childhood education, adoption and foster care, "social ecology" (a term that means mostly the effect of television on children), child abuse, and education for parenthood.

The OCD has, as yet, no satisfactory measures of achievement from the money they spend, a problem that it shares with many other HEW programs. In his final HEW press conference on January 18, 1973, Secretary Richardson said, in his formal statement:

Sesame Street, the children's educational television program, reaches 7 million pre-schoolers for 1 hour a day at a cost of $1.23 per student per year. By comparison, it is interesting to note that Head Start, a "comprehensive child development service program," costs more than $1,000 per child per year—for results which have not yet been empirically demonstrated to be superior to those achieved through *Sesame Street.*

It seems unlikely that Richardson intended to imply that Head Start had no greater value; rather, the sense was that we are badly in need of careful studies to determine just what the effect of various programs is.

Assistant Secretary for Administration and Management

This post is by law a career post to be filled through the merit system, as recommended by the first Hoover Commission. Through a colossal error, in 1969, James Farmer was offered an assistant secretary position without anyone realizing that the only available assistant secretaryship was the one that was by law a merit position. The Civil Service Commission gulped and turned its eyes in the other direction when it gave approval to the appointment, since Farmer had had no experience that would make him well-qualified to fill that post. Instead of concerning himself with administration, Farmer spent much of his time making speeches and dealing with particular issues in which he was interested. He was succeeded after two years by a young business executive, Rodney H. Brady (1971), who returned to the business world after less than two years. And in 1973, the post was filled by the appointment of Robert H. Marik, another appointee with a business background, but without previous significant experience in governmental administration. It is apparent, therefore, that the Hoover Commission concept of this position as being the apex of career professionalism in governmental administration is no longer being observed.

The assistant secretary for Administration and Management has a large portfolio of responsibilities, each handled by a separate division called an "office" to distinguish it from the divisions of operating agencies. Some concept of the scope of activities can be gained from a simple list of these offices, which employ a total of over 1,400 people:

Office of Personnel and Training

Office of Administration
    Data Management Center
Office of Management Planning and Technology
Office of Equal Employment Opportunity
Office of Investigations and Internal Security
Office of Grants and Procurement Management
Office of Facilities Engineering and Property Management
    Office of Surplus Property Utilization

The functions of most of these are reasonably evident from their names, but the last two units deserve special comment. The Office of Facilities Engineering and Property Management (formerly Facilities Engineering and Construction Agency) provides architectural and engineering guidance and support for all HEW construction and construction grant programs. In 1973, there were some forty construction programs within HEW, expending annually about $1 billion in federal funds and about $4 billion in total funds.

The Office of Surplus Property Utilization distributes property instead of money. The federal establishment, especially the Department of Defense, generates a large amount of surplus "personal property" (it seems odd to call obsolete military equipment, airplanes, machine tools, and the like "personal property" but that is its legal label), which is much too valuable to be junked, and a significant amount of surplus real property. Under the law, the other departments of government are given first opportunity by the General Services Administration to acquire this property for their own needs, and if no agency bids for it, HEW is directed by law to make it available to schools, hospitals, and other public service organizations specified in the law. This activity is handled largely out of HEW's ten regional offices, since the property is usually redistributed within the region where it is declared surplus. Since the end of World War II, the FSA and HEW have transferred personal property with an original price of over $6 billion to these organizations, and real property with an acquisition cost of some $1.3 billion.

Space does not permit a description of the functions of the other units under the assistant secretary for Administration and Management. It is worth noting, however, that HEW has been a government leader in providing organized programs and opportunities for many different disadvantaged groups, including "upward mobility" programs to get people with substantial aptitude out of dead-end jobs, college courses for the disadvantaged on "company time," "new start" jobs and training for former prison inmates, and employment for current mental hospital patients to ease and speed their recovery. Some other department and agency personnel officers are annoyed with HEW for doing so much for the various groups of disadvantaged because it means that they—the personnel officers—are constantly put on the defensive for not doing as much.

Chapter XI provides greater detail on the problems and processes of departmental management.

Assistant Secretary, Comptroller

Even though more than 80 per cent of HEW's $100 billion budget is classified as "uncontrollable" (required by law and not subject to annual budgetary control), its sheer magnitude makes the financial management role of the Department an enormous undertaking. It is also the single top-level position in HEW that has consistently, until 1973, been held by career appointees. This bespeaks both the unusual competence of the two appointees who have held the position—James Kelly and Bruce Cardwell— and the value to the Secretary of having a person who has spent years wrestling with financial issues within the Department and in dealing with the appropriations committees of Congress.

The four divisions of the Comptroller's Office are Office of Budget, Office of Finance, Audit Agency, and Office of Grants Administration Policy. These four divisions employ some 1,100 people, the majority of whom are audit staff.

Though the budget staff is comparatively small, the budget function is large and important. Even with "only" about $15 billion falling under the "controllable" category, the Secretary's determination of relative priorities within that amount, and the role of the assistant secretary, comptroller, and his budget staff, loom very large. Funds are not authorized in huge flexible appropriations to operating agency heads, or to the Secretary, as in the Defense Department, but for specific program purposes. The budget and appropriations process is therefore the principal means of setting program priorities.

More than any other official of the Department, the assistant secretary, comptroller, has found himself in the position of having to earn the respect and confidence of the top political officials of each new administration. Not being a political appointee himself, he has been assumed by White House and Budget Bureau officials, and sometimes by newly appointed Secretaries, to be more interested in defending the interests of the bureaucracy with which he has had long association than in protecting those of the President, which inevitably conflict. Since the Congress has had a continuing struggle with the Presidents of both parties over HEW budgets—with the Congress always wanting to appropriate more money than the President asks for—the comptroller may also be suspected of quietly aiding and abetting congressional efforts to enlarge the Department's appropriations. The circumstances are such as to require the comptroller to demonstrate that his primary loyalty is to each new President and each new Secretary.

One of the most dramatic examples of this occurred in 1969, the first year of President Nixon's Administration, when President Nixon decided to veto the HEW appropriation bill as extravagant and inflationary—his first major veto. Naturally, he was eager to have the veto sustained and put Presidential assistant Bryce Harlow in charge of seeing that the votes were lined up. Harlow succeeded. (As an interesting aside, the White House organized a cocktail party with the President that took place only hours after the congressional action. Every individual who voted to sustain the President's veto was invited so that the President might thank them personally—an unprecedented political gesture—and one which did not become a tradition as other appropriation bills were vetoed.) It then became necessary to get another bill, acceptable to the President, through the Congress. The HEW comptroller, James Kelly, was the lone career man involved in the delicate process of trying to get the new bill. Gradually, the White House faded into the background and gave Kelly the leading role in negotiating a bill that the President could sign. He managed to do so, in large measure, because he was a career man who was extremely knowledgeable and trusted by both sides.

The size of the audit staff—some 700—may seem surprising in relation to other administrative support functions of the Office of the Secretary, but the HEW audit staff performs a function that has utility for the whole government. It audits the books of colleges and universities and of state governments so as to determine not only that federal funds are expended for the purposes for which they were appropriated, but also to determine the applicable "indirect cost rates" for each institution. Grants and contracts allow actual indirect costs (usually within specified limits), but one agency of the federal government must study the books of each institution to determine the allowable rate. HEW is the "cognizant agency."

Even with a staff of 700, many of the HEW programs are not audited with sufficient frequency, or in sufficient depth to give solid assurance of the proper and efficient expenditure of the funds. In 1969, Comptroller Kelly estimated that it would require 3,000 auditors to do a thorough job. Even so, the General Accounting Office, the financial audit agency for the Congress, has sufficient confidence in the HEW audit work that it accepts most of those audits without going over the same ground. And both HEW and the General Accounting Office encourage state audit agencies to develop and achieve quality standards that will enable them both to accept large parts of state audits without duplication.

The Office of the Comptroller, especially since 1969, has had considerable success in harmonizing and simplifying the requirements placed on grantees and contracting institutions in respect to applications, record-keeping, and reporting, thus speeding up the federal review and approval of grant applications.

OFFICE FOR CIVIL RIGHTS

This office, numbering some 700 employees in 1972—most of whom work in HEW's regional offices—was created primarily to carry out the responsibilities given HEW under Title VI of the Civil Rights Act of 1964. Because of its social significance, Chapter X is entirely devoted to this subject.

IV

Social Security

Social Security, as earlier mentioned, was the most important and durable product of the New Deal, which was the first of the five revolutions in the relationship of American citizens to their government. The term "social security" was an American invention, brought into national and then international use by the authors of the Social Security Act. It quickly acquired wide popularity as a phrase meaning, as a minimum, a governmental system for replacing part of each worker's earnings when they were abruptly terminated, or sharply reduced, by old age, death, unemployment, or disability. To most other nations, it includes some form of national health insurance, not just for the elderly but for the entire population.

To many of its pioneers, Social Security has a broader meaning. The late Arthur Altmeyer—who was "Mr. Social Security" during the formative years of the program—believed the term should mean "a specific governmental program designed to promote the economic and social well-being of individual workers and their families through providing protection against specific hazards which would otherwise cause widespread destitution and misery." When used in this way, it is intended to encompass not only the federally administered or sponsored social insurance programs (including certain veterans' benefits and state administered unemployment insurance) and state-sponsored workmen's compensation for industrial injury, but financial assistance programs based on needs tests (public assistance, general assistance, and possibly also food stamp programs).

In this chapter, Social Security will be used in a narrow context. It will mean the social insurance functions of the Social Security Administration (SSA), including its health insurance functions.

Although Abraham Epstein deserves credit as the leader of the organized movement to enact social insurance in the United States, the men who did more to shape Social Security than any others, particularly during its early years, were three men from Wisconsin previously mentioned—Arthur Altmeyer, Edwin Witte, and Wilbur Cohen—plus two men who were later to become regular advisers concerning the modification and evolution of Social Security—J. Douglas Brown, of Princeton University, and Marion B. Folsom, of Eastman Kodak Company. They labored together, and with many other advisers, in the fall of 1934, produced the set of principles and the organizational framework that became what we now know as "Social Security." Since these principles are the key to the acceptance and durability of the social insurance system, it is useful to record and discuss briefly each of the seven concepts that have seemed to stand out in importance above others.

PRINCIPLES OF SOCIAL SECURITY

The basic principles of Social Security are these:

1. *Social Security embodies accepted principles of social insurance.* It is based on a special tax on employee earnings, with the employer and the employee sharing the costs equally. Although it would not be a violation of social insurance principles for the general taxpayer to be a partner to the support of the system, except for very special circumstances, such as military service, no share of the cost of the cash benefits has ever, in the U.S. system, been borne by general taxes. Special trust funds are maintained by the Treasury Department into which all Social Security tax receipts are paid and from which all benefits and administrative costs are met. An actuarial staff computes carefully what rates of taxation will be needed to assure that the income into the trust funds will at all times be sufficient to cover the outgo for the payment of benefits. This schedule of tax rates is written into law, and although changed on many occasions, it has been at all

times set so as not to require supplementation from general revenues.

Social insurance differs from private or mutual insurance systems in a number of respects, foremost of which is that social insurance agencies are not required to have enough assets in their trust funds to pay off their obligations to beneficiaries in the event their income should cease, as private insurance companies are required to do. The premise of Social Security is that the U.S. Government and the Social Security system will operate in perpetuity and that income will always be sufficient to cover outgo. The government always has the power, when it is needed, to raise the tax rate to meet the outgo.

2. *Coverage is compulsory and virtually universal.* The system is intended to assure that all persons in the work force with the exception of certain specifically named groups—principally government workers who are covered by separate retirement, disability, and survivorship programs—are covered by Social Security whether they want to be or not. No one can decide that he prefers to take care of his own economic hazards and opt out of both the taxes and the benefits. There is, of course, no way a person can be forced to accept benefits due him if he does not wish to receive them, but this does not relieve him of the requirement to pay the Social Security taxes.

The social insurance system was designed not only for the protection of the individual against the hazards of an uncertain and complex industrial society; it was also designed to guard society against the hazard of having its members become public charges. To achieve both purposes, there was no alternative but compulsory membership in the Social Security system.

3. *Benefits are wage-related, but with a deliberate bias toward low-wage earners.* Unlike systems providing flat pensions, which had developed in some other countries, and which were becoming a popular idea in the United States in the early 1930's, publicized by the Townsend Movement, the Social Security system was designed to provide retirement and survivorship benefits (and, later, disability benefits) that bore a significant relationship to lost earnings. The designers of the system were acutely aware of one major difference between the United States and the Western European countries, which had pioneered social insurance. The United States had much wider geographic differentials in wages

and cost of living than any other industrial nation. Flat pensions
high enough to be meaningful in large Northern cities with their
high cost of living would be so high in the Southern rural areas
that they would distort the whole economy. Flat pensions also
promised to become extremely expensive, since their floor would
have to be high enough to be meaningful to the majority of
beneficiaries.

The answer to this problem seemed clear to the designers of
the system. They would relate the benefits to the wages previously
received by the wage earner. This would mean, of course, keeping
detailed records on the wages of all persons covered by the program. High-paid workers who contributed substantial amounts
over an extended period in the form of Social Security taxes
should be entitled to receive more when they retired or became
disabled than low-paid workers. And they needed more to avoid
radical downward shift in their standard of living.

On the other hand, if all workers were to receive the same
proportion of their average earnings, the level of benefits for the
low-paid workers would be so low that they could not keep body
and soul together in their old age or cope with the disability or
death of the family's principal wage earner. It was assumed that
the low-paid workers would not be able to make significant savings
during their working years to supplement their Social Security in
old age, while high-paid workers did have this opportunity.

As a result of this line of thought, the benefit formula was
weighted in favor of the low-paid worker. It was reasoned, too,
that the additional payments to the low-paid workers would come
entirely from the contribution of employers, so that all wage groups
in the population would get back all they had put in, plus interest,
and would, in addition, receive a weighted percentage of all
employer contributions. This, it seemed, would help achieve one
of the basic purposes of the program—to protect all members of
the society against the hazard of indigency from lost earning
power. The employer contribution could be used, and should be
used under this theory, to bring the benefits of the low-wage
earner up to a level where he could buy the necessities of life
with his Social Security benefit.

The benefit formula has been changed many times with continued stress on giving the low-paid worker a higher benefit in
proportion to his contributions than higher-paid workers receive.

The formula has now become so complex that it would serve no useful purpose to describe it here in overly condensed form. (The Social Security Administration will furnish information on this subject in any degree of detail desired.)

4. *Benefits are contingent on complete or significant loss of earnings.* This principle has been the hardest for the public to understand and accept. It says that when a person reaches sixty-five (or sixty-two if he wishes to take a reduced monthly benefit), he is not entitled to a retirement benefit unless he retires. On its face, this seems reasonable to many people, but in practice, it seems quite unreasonable to a substantial number of very articulate workers who do not understand the theory and who regard themselves as victims of the principle.

Nobody argues that he should receive a disability benefit if he does not become disabled, or that his family should receive a survivorship benefit if he is still alive and well. But many argue vehemently that they should receive a retirement benefit when they reach some arbitrarily fixed retirement age, even though they are not retired. Many think of "their" Social Security as money which they have paid in over the years and which they should start recovering at age sixty-five (or sixty-two) no matter whether they have any loss of earnings or not. They think of it as a "paid-up annuity" that will fall due at age sixty-five. This is not what it is.

From the point of view of society, what the Social Security system seeks to do is to protect the individual and society against the hazard of indigency caused by the loss of earning power. If there is neither a complete nor a significant loss of earnings, there is no obligation of society or the Social Security system to pay the individual a monthly benefit to supplement his current earnings.

The problem becomes more acute when it is looked at in terms of part-time earnings. If a person retires from a full-time job and takes a half-time job, is he retired? What, in fact, constitutes a reasonable test of retirement? That issue has been plaguing the Social Security Administration since it began paying benefits and is the subject of more bills introduced into Congress, year after year, than any other subject with which the Congress deals.

In 1940, the law read that nobody could earn more than $15 per month and be eligible for a retirement benefit. Since then, the definition of retirement has been liberalized numerous times until today, when the rule is that a person may earn $2,100 per year with no reduction in benefit. If a Social Security beneficiary earns more than the annual exempt amount, his benefit will be reduced by $1 for each $2 he earns. Under this formula, there is never a disincentive to work, and persons classified as poor can continue to work, if they wish, and have little or no reduction in their Social Security payments as a result of their earnings.

Perhaps the easiest way to understand why the designers and custodians of the Social Security system in Congress, in HEW, and elsewhere, have not eliminated the retirement test entirely and made all persons eligible to receive full annuities when they reach sixty-five is to look at the high cost of doing this and the questionable purpose to be served by doing it. Eliminating the retirement test would cost about $3.5 billion annually. The $3.5 billion would be paid to people who need it least—to persons who, for the most part, are employed full time at good wages or salaries and who are at an age when few have the burden of minor dependents. It would be necessary to increase payroll taxes by .7 per cent (theoretically shared equally by employer and employee) to cover the cost. Would the social benefits to people who are better off than the rest of the aged justify such a large added expense? The consistent answer of those who understand the Social Security system best has been no.

5. *Benefits are to be paid as a matter of right, with no means test.* For nearly two decades after the Social Security Act was enacted the idea of paying Social Security benefits to millionaires like the Rockefellers and the Mellons came under varying degrees of attack. The die-hard opponents of the welfare state seized upon this feature of the young Social Security system as one of its most vulnerable aspects. They thought they had an appealing issue when they pointed out that the system would pay benefits to wealthy people who obviously had no need for them. But the argument was a two-edged sword, and the back edge was sharper than the front.

The only alternative to paying annuities to millionaires who had worked most of their lives, paid taxes into the system, and finally retired was to set up a means test and say that nobody who had more than X dollars in assets or who had income exceeding Y dollars from savings and investments would be eligible for benefits. A means test would mean that everybody would be subject to financial investigation, not just millionaires. And it would be a deterrent, it was pointed out, rather than an encouragement, to supplemental saving for the retirement years. Why should people be penalized for being provident? And who would tolerate the indignity of a means test unless he were approaching pauperism?

The last time this issue was raised in any serious way was in 1953 when Arthur Altmeyer was Social Security commissioner. He "laid it on the line" to then Congressman, subsequently Senator, Carl Curtis of Nebraska in very blunt terms. Although his bluntness to Congressman Curtis did not endear him to HEW Secretary Oveta Culp Hobby and President Eisenhower, it seemed to produce an end of serious congressional efforts to modify the concept that Social Security benefits should be paid as a matter of right. Although the issue continues to be raised from time to time, students of the program and advisory councils on Social Security have always concluded that the provision in the law to pay benefits without regard to resources and nonwork income should be retained.

6. *Files and records on individuals are to be kept confidential.* Nothing was said in the original Social Security Act about the confidentiality of records. It was the Social Security Board that made the early and firm decision and publicly pledged that it would protect its records against uses that might impair the confidence of the public in the privacy of the records. It decided against allowing law enforcement agencies, federal, state, and local, to use the records for tracking down persons accused of crime. It decided against the use of the files to help identify persons who were on trial or to provide other possibly incriminating information. And it decided not to allow the use of the records to assist relatives and police to find missing persons. These were extremely important policy decisions. It took stout men to uphold them.

Congress implemented the Social Security Board's pledge in 1939 by enacting a provision prohibiting disclosure of information from Social Security records except in certain tightly circumscribed situations specified in the Act or in regulations. In rare instances (as, for example, in non-Social Security court cases and for the benefit of the worker), the commissioner of Social Security can use his *ad hoc* authority to permit disclosure of specific information. For the most part, the pledge of confidentiality has stood firm, but pressures from Congress and the Justice Department for exceptions have caused several breaches in the dike.

The theory of the board was clear. At the time it made its decision, Social Security was not yet firmly and permanently established as a social insurance system, constructed as an instrument solely to serve the interests of the people. Government was thought of, much more than it is today, as having been established for the purpose of keeping people from doing what they ought not to do, rather than aiding them in doing what they could not do individually. It would have been easy for people to develop an early distrust of Social Security if they had reason to believe that its records were being used against them whenever it suited the purposes of the government. Not only might such mistrust have undermined the future of the system, but it might have discouraged people from providing honest information about themselves, thus making it most difficult to achieve accurate and equitable administration.

The principal exceptions made to the rule of confidentiality are:

- *Immigration and naturalization.* The Justice Department may obtain information, upon formal request, concerning aliens who are suspected of being in the country illegally, and in certain other cases.
- *Inquiries from the FBI and the Secret Service affecting the national security.* SSA may furnish these agencies with information they certify is needed concerning individuals involved in acts or threats of espionage, sabotage, assassination of the President, or other similar acts or threats inimical to the national security.
- *"Runaway pappies."* This is a jocular but common way of referring to a class of cases typified by the need to locate the legally responsible parents of dependent children so that a court may order contributory support from them. Information may only be given to properly authorized public authorities.
- *Identification of otherwise unidentifiable deceased and insane persons, victims of amnesia, etc.*

The problem of preventing the Social Security files from being opened up to broader use is a continuing one. On the whole, the record of SSA and HEW in guarding the files has been good. Much of the pressure to breach the confidentiality rule comes from Congress and from state and local law enforcement agencies, and the greatest pressure came in connection with the problem of fathers of dependent children who had deserted their families. SSA finally justified the use of its files to locate deserting parents on the ground that the public assistance program and the old-age and survivors' insurance system were both integral parts of the Social Security Act, and that it was proper to use Social Security data to avoid unnecessary and improper expenditures under public assistance. It was probably more a rationalization than a reason, since Congress was breathing down the necks of the Social Security Administration at the time and would probably have taken action if SSA had not.

7. *Social Security is to be administered by a single federal agency applying its principles uniformly throughout the nation.* Philosophically, the designers of the Social Security system preferred not to make so large a leap as to bypass state and local governments and establish a single, uniform system, operated by the federal government. If they could have found a way of doing so, they would probably have involved the states, as they did in requiring (not legally, but practically) the establishment of forty-eight state systems of unemployment insurance, operating under minimum standards prescribed by federal law. But the more they examined the matter, the more certain they became that the only durable and equitable way of operating the old-age insurance program was to have it unitary and to have it completely operated by a single federal agency. Thanks to Henry Ford, the United States was already then a nation of mobile citizens and promised to become rapidly more so. If a wage earner had spent his life working in five or six states, how could he deal with five or six different state retirement systems, or they with him, in determining what he should receive as a retirement benefit?

By any test, the decision to have a single, federally operated system was sound. In practice as well as in theory, it has turned out to be far more efficient than any set of state systems could conceivably have been. The quality of its management is unquestionably higher than that found in state unemployment compensation.

Even so, the principle of unitary administration was partially breached in the case of disability insurance. When it was added to the Social Security Act in 1956, the decision was made to have state vocational rehabilitation agencies act as agents of the SSA in determining whether applicants for benefits had any reasonable prospect of being rehabilitated. It was reasoned that it would be in the interest of both the individual applicants and society to spend a good deal of money rehabilitating even the most severely disabled people if long years of disability payments could be avoided and the individuals could become self-sustaining and contributing members of the economy.

Although there are numerous other lesser principles, these constitute the basic structure on which all else is built. All aspects of the benefit formula are written into law, and except for the disability and health insurance sections of the Act, there is comparatively little room for any but technical interpretations. Over the years, however, as more and more groups have been added, hundreds of technical rulings have been necessary. The law and regulations now fill a 450-page handbook, which is the reference book of SSA employees and other persons concerned with the eligibility of Social Security beneficiaries.

THE TAX SCHEDULE AND THE GROWTH OF THE TRUST FUND

The authors of the original Social Security Act envisaged the accumulation of a substantial reserve during the early years when benefit rights would be accruing rapidly, but relatively few benefits would be paid. In 1939, this policy was modified to limit the reserve in the trust fund to approximately three years' outgo. During World War II, however, taxes yielded far more than had been expected and the reserve mounted rapidly. Even though Congress repeatedly postponed scheduled increases in the payroll tax schedule, the reserve grew by 1949 to $12 billion, roughly double the amount projected for that year in the 1939 estimates.

Postwar inflation made the buying power of Social Security benefits drop precipitously. In 1950, Congress increased benefit levels by an average of 77 per cent and extended coverage to a large portion of the workers previously excluded. These and later amendments, together with the steady increase in the number of retirees, brought income and outgo more nearly into balance and led to a tacit "pay-as-you-go" policy, advocated by some from the start. The law, however, continued to provide for a schedule of tax rates in later years which, if allowed to go into effect, would build up large future trust funds. Again and again, Congress postponed the effective date of higher tax rates, establishing levels sufficient only to meet program costs and allow small increases in the trust funds.

The 1971 Advisory Council on Social Security confirmed the "pay-as-you-go" policy with a contingency reserve of one year's outgo. They decried the future tax schedule written into law which, if allowed to go into effect, would produce very large trust fund accumulations—projected to reach a trillion dollars by the year 2025. They did not seem, however, to realize that if the other recommendations they made were adopted—as they were—the revised estimates of *annual outgo* from the trust may well reach a trillion dollars in 2025.

The explicit acceptance of the pay-as-you-go policy, together with a second recommendation of the Advisory Council, became the springboard for an election-year increase of 20 per cent in Social Security benefits. The council recommended that the actuarial cost estimates for the cash benefits program be based on assumptions that earnings levels will rise, that tax and benefit base will be increased as earnings levels rise, and that benefit payments will be increased as prices rise. In other words, Social Security actuaries were asked to be "realistic" by taking account of increases in productivity, wages, and prices. The changed assumptions would permit an immediate, one-time 20 per cent increase in benefit payments with no increase in the long-range tax rates for cash benefits until well into the next century. Needless to say, this aspect of the report was welcomed with particular warmth on Capitol Hill, and enacted into law on July 1, 1972, despite President Nixon's strongly worded preference for a 5 per cent increase.

In addition to the 20 per cent across-the-board increase in benefits effective for September, 1972, the new law says that future benefits will be automatically adjusted to increases in the cost of living, and the tax and benefit base will be automatically adjusted to increases in wages. For years, an automatic adjustment feature was opposed by both Wilbur Mills and Wilbur Cohen, the two most influential experts on Social Security policy in the postwar period. Both felt that repeated congressional reviews and action to raise benefits gave policy-makers the opportunity to make additional marginal improvements in the equities of the system, and, not least in importance, that the President and the congressmen and senators who supported the increases could gain valuable political credit with the voters back home for doing so. Eventually, however, the political push toward automatic increases prevailed. It is an amusing sidelight on the political process that the new law requires that Congress be notified of any prospective automatic increase far enough in advance to permit Congress to take *ad hoc* action to increase benefits and thereby pre-empt and supersede the automatic increase that would otherwise occur.

What did not become apparent to the members of the Advisory Council or the Congress was the magnitude of the increases implied by their new assumptions on constantly expanding economy with accompanying increases in wages. A 6 per cent growth rate per year (somewhat lower than in the recent past) would mean a doubling every twelve years, a quadrupling in twenty-four years, and a sixteenfold increase in forty-eight years. The trillion-dollar trust fund that the Advisory Council thought would be a "very large accumulation" would be a fair estimate of annual expenditures for the year 2025. The average *monthly* benefit for a retired couple, under the new assumptions would by then exceed $2,000. It makes one stop and wonder whether the authors of the recent book *The Limits to Growth* may not be more right than some economists when they caution that past rates of economic growth cannot continue even for two more human lifetimes.

To anyone who feels that 2025 is too far away to worry about, it should be noted that the Social Security benefits of children born in 1960 will fall due beginning in 2025, assuming retirement at 65. More will be said at the end of this chapter about the foreseeable problems of Social Security in the early decades of the twenty-first century.

How Does the System Operate?

The American system of Social Security is the only one in the world built on the foundation of lifetime earnings records for every covered worker. At the time it was designed, it was strongly attacked as being infeasible because it would require such an army of record keepers that a very sizable share of the contributions would be eaten up by the prohibitively high administrative costs. The optimists among those who advocated the system estimated that the cost of administration could be held to 5 per cent of benefit payments, once the system approached maturity. The pessimists who opposed lifetime earnings records predicted the costs would run to 20 per cent or 25 per cent. None could then foresee the electronic revolution. It is fortunate that it occurred when it did, for without computer technology, the burden of paperwork might have broken the back of the system.

With the marvels of electronics, old-age and survivors' insurance operates for only 1.7 cents for each dollar of benefits paid. This fact is not widely appreciated. It is literally astounding that the cost of collecting the taxes, developing and maintaining more than 200 million wage records, operating about 960 local offices for dealing with the public and accepting claims, adjudicating the claims, writing the checks, paying the postage on the checks, and operating an extensive appeals process amounts to only 1.7 cents for each dollar of benefits paid. Other parts of the program are more complex and expensive: 5.3 cents for disability insurance, 2.7 cents for hospital insurance, and 13.1 cents for supplemental medical insurance. The consolidated average administrative cost ratio for the total program is 2.7 cents.

This is one of the great unheralded success stories of governmental management. It is a system that has been examined and admired by experts from large private insurance companies and from foreign social insurance systems. It deserves a closer look as to how it is done.

The central data bank of the Social Security system, on which all else depends, is located in its headquarters building in Baltimore, Maryland. In the Woodlawn complex outside of Baltimore, SSA has the most powerful commercial-type electronic data processing operation in the world. There are: one IBM 370/65, 13 IBM 360/65's, 10 IBM 360/30's, 2 UNIVAC 1108's with 11 satellites, an RCA Spectra, an RCA 301, and other lesser machines. There are 325 tape drives and around 220,000 reels of tape on which is recorded wage and other program-related information concerning the approximately 205 million persons who have acquired Social Security numbers since 1937.

The 90 million wage items from the quarterly reports of employers have to be transferred from those reports to the lifetime earnings records of each wage earner. All are maintained on magnetic tape. Many of the large employers send in their quarterly wage reports on reels of magnetic tape—about 12 million wage items—which can be handled directly by the SSA computers. Other employers usually type or print their quarterly wage reports. More than half of these are put through optical scanning equipment that reads the print (there are hundreds of different type faces and thousands of dirty typewriters) and converts the information reported on the forms to magnetic tape. When the optical scanner cannot understand an item on the wage report, which occurs in about 20 per cent of the cases, it marks it so that human brains will take over and try to figure out what the optical scanner could not. In a very small proportion of such cases, it is necessary to go back to the employer for more precise information. All handwritten reports and all printed or typewritten reports that the optical scanners cannot read—some 50 million wage items each quarter—are handled by manual keying operations.

In order to guard against the possibility of disaster, a duplicate set of records is maintained in a storage vault at some distance from Baltimore. Since the wage records are literally the heart of the system, if any disaster were to destroy the records in Baltimore and there were no duplicates, it would almost certainly be necessary to abolish the Social Security program as we know it and start over again with a new and different system.

When any individual reaches retirement or becomes disabled, or when there is the death of a wage earner, a claim is filed in one of the 960 SSA local offices. (The number of district and branch offices is expected to exceed about 1,150 by mid-1974 to provide more convenient service to the public.) The information contained on each claim is then transferred to teletype, thence to two large government message switching stations at Berwick, Kansas and Romney, West Virginia, where it is put on high-speed electronic tape and relayed over wires to similar high-speed electronic tape on the receiving end in Baltimore.

Each day, on the average, 20,000 retirement, survivorship, and disability claims are received in Baltimore. Each night, the entire wage file is run through the computers, which are directed to produce whatever information they have on the 20,000 claimants. Not only do the computers produce the wage information, but they calculate from the data the amount of benefit to which each is entitled. In cases where all the information seems to be in proper order, with no missing wage reports or inconsistencies, the computer notes that these seem to be routine and properly calculated. Claims reviewers then certify to the correctness of the computer-prepared calculations, giving especially careful review to cases where the computer calculations indicate there may be problems. Some of the cases require considerable work in order to obtain missing data or correct errors of record.

Once the claims are certified, the various forms and control cards are mailed back to the originating district offices. There the claims are given preliminary (and in many instances final) adjudication. The material is then forwarded to one of seven payment centers located in New York, Philadelphia, Birmingham, Chicago, Kansas City, Baltimore, and San Francisco. Each benefit computation is then reviewed again prior to the writing of a continuing monthly check, which, in the simplest cases, will be produced electronically and mechanically from that point forward until some major event such as death intervenes. In the less simple cases, there are likely to be changes of address, changes in earnings that will affect the amount of benefit paid, recalculation of benefit because of changed family situations (for example, when the older child of a widow passes the upper age of eligibility as a dependent), and other factors.

Whenever there are general increases in Social Security benefit levels, as there periodically are, the computers are instructed to change all payment amounts to accord with the revised law. Nothing could better illustrate the simplicity and efficiency of electronic data processing equipment.

The seven payment centers have substantial electronic data processing equipment of their own that prepares the tapes used to write the checks each month to the 30 million Social Security beneficiaries. When the tapes are prepared, they are carried to the nearest Treasury disbursing office (usually in the same city), and there they are fed into high-speed check-writing machines. The checks are mechanically inserted into envelopes, sealed, sorted by zip code, and mailed.

There are hundreds of suboperations in this giant enterprise, but this brief sketch outlines the way in which electronic machines have been put to use to perform a steadily increasing percentage of the work load of the SSA, a work load which would be mountainous if it were not for the machines. The 9,500 employees who work in the Bureau of Data Processing are masters, but also slaves, of those machines. Yet, it is hard to think of anything more deadly than being snowed under the deluge of paper that would be required—there is still too much paper, as it is—if the computers were not available.

EXTENT AND EFFECT OF SOCIAL SECURITY COVERAGE

By 1972, approximately 90 per cent of the jobs in the nation were covered by Social Security. The principal noncovered groups are federal government employees, who have an excellent retirement system of their own, and some groups of state and local government employees whose employers have not exercised the option to obtain coverage under Social Security.

The growth in the number of beneficiaries of Social Security and the cash payments to them can be seen from the following table:

Calendar Year	Number of Beneficiaries (12/31)	Cash Payments from Trust Funds*
1940	222,448	$ 35
1950	3,477,243	961
1960	14,844,589	11,245
1970	26,228,629	31,863
1973 (est.)	29,970,000	51,885

* In millions of dollars.

Disability Insurance

The possibility of including disability insurance in the Social Security program was considered by the original designers of the Social Security Act, but they concluded that it would be the better part of wisdom to defer its incorporation in the Social Security package until the basic system was well established. They undoubtedly thought that would occur well before 1956, some twenty-one years after the Social Security Act was passed. But disability insurance was worrisome to the American Medical Association (AMA) and congressional conservatives. They were concerned that disability insurance might open the door to "cash sickness insurance"—which would partially replace lost earnings due to *temporary* disability or sickness, just as "disability insurance" would do for those who were *permanently* disabled— and the next step after that would be some form of national health insurance. Nothing could be worse from the viewpoint of the AMA.

Eventually, however, the arguments for disability insurance wore down the opposition and Congress passed legislation making disability insurance a part of the SSA's responsibilities. Despite President Eisenhower's coolness toward the legislation, he was persuaded by his Secretary of HEW, Marion B. Folsom, to sign it. Folsom, it will be recalled, was one of the pioneers in the development of social insurance in the United States. (See Chapter II.) If he had had his way, disability insurance would have come much earlier than it did.

As mentioned, the law directed the Social Security Administration to make use of the state vocational rehabilitation agencies in screening applicants for disability insurance to determine whether they might be rehabilitated for some form of gainful employment. Despite the essential soundness of the idea of maximizing rehabilitation efforts, it created a deep-seated conflict in the minds of applicants for disability insurance. A disabled worker who has reached the point of applying for benefits based on his disability is at best dubious about his capacity for rehabilitation and self-support, and at worst firmly convinced that he will never work again. When he submits a claim his mind is set toward proving that he is unable to work and therefore eligible for benefits. It is often difficult to turn his attitude toward the possibility of rehabilitation, especially if he thinks this may delay approval of his disability claim. In 1965, Congress authorized using Social Security trust funds to pay for rehabilitating disabled beneficiaries, thereby removing the apprehension of those who thought that efforts at self-rehabilitation would be considered a sign of ineligibility for disability benefits.

The framers of disability insurance were much concerned about possible abuses of the system. The experience of private insurance companies with disability insurance had not been reassuring. In consequence, the original law was tightly drawn to make sure the malingerers would not be given lifetime annuities. Inevitably, therefore, it also excluded some pathetic cases in which permanent and total disability was hard to prove. Many claimants appealed their cases, first to the Social Security appeals examiners and appeals boards and finally to the courts, with the result that the Bureau of Hearings and Appeals had to undergo a large expansion to handle the load. Whereas in old-age and survivors' insurance, the courts had rarely reversed rulings of the SSA, they reversed numerous decisions concerned with disability. The SSA actuaries began to worry about the solvency of the trust fund if the trend kept up. In 1967, the disability provisions in the law were clarified to the extent that the definition of disability would be applied uniformly and consistently throughout the nation and the definition would no longer be subject to varying and diverse court interpretations.

In the fiscal year ending June 30, 1972, benefits to disabled workers and their families paid from the disability trust fund totaled $4.05 billion. About 3.1 million people—disabled workers and their dependents—were the beneficiaries of these payments. An additional 296,000 persons received benefits as a result of severe disabilities that began before they were eighteen.

Effect of Social Security on Poverty

Social Security was never considered by the American public to be part of President Johnson's War on Poverty. But as that "war" seemed to fizzle out, as the Vietnam war escalated, and as many Community Action Programs discovered that they had neither the money nor the muscle to win even battles against poverty, much less a whole war, Social Security's role in combating poverty was increasingly recognized. It moved large numbers of people above the official poverty line and prevented additional large numbers from ever becoming poor. If it were not for Social Security, there would be at least 11 million more people classified as below the poverty line in the United States—11 million more than the 1971 estimate of 25.6 million. And, as a result of the Social Security Amendments of 1972, an undetermined number of additional persons will be raised above the poverty level.

SUPPLEMENTAL SECURITY INCOME PROGRAM

After President Nixon's welfare reform program (see Chapter V) spent three years (1969–72) in the congressional mill, one part of it finally succeeded of enactment, even though the more prominent and controversial Family Assistance Plan died in battle. The successful part dealt with the needy aged, blind, and disabled, who, beginning in January, 1974, will be covered by a federally financed Supplemental Security Income Program, administered by the Social Security Administration.

Basic assistance payments under this program are established at $130 per month for single individuals and $195 for a person with an eligible spouse. This is higher than the payment levels in many states and lower than the public assistance levels in the predominantly urban, industrial states. The high-cost states will be encouraged, but not required, to supplement the federal payments to avoid any decrease in current payment levels. If states so elect, the SSA will serve as their agent in making the state payments. This will avoid the confusion and added cost of sending out two separate checks to each eligible person.

There are, of course, many rules that define who is needy and who is not, but one provision is especially noteworthy. Recipients of payments under this new program are ineligible for food stamps and surplus commodities.

The Supplemental Security Income Program is a large and very difficult new undertaking for the Social Security Administration. If the SSA handles the transition as smoothly as it did the initiation of Medicare, it will deserve a Presidential award.

BENEFITS FOR BLACK LUNG VICTIMS

Awareness of the ravages of pneumoconiosis, commonly called "black lung," on coal miners became intense in the latter part of the 1960's, and was one of the factors that resulted in the enactment in 1969 of the Federal Coal Mine Health and Safety Act. This law established safety standards and regulations for the coal mining industry and provided cash benefit payments from general tax funds to underground coal miners totally disabled by black lung disease and to widows of miners who died from the disease. SSA was made responsible for administering the program for all persons who filed for benefits by January, 1973 (later changed to June, 1973). The chairman of the powerful Labor, Health, Education, and Welfare Subcommittee of the House Appropriations Committee, Congressman Daniel Flood, from the

Wilkes Barre coal mining area of Pennsylvania, was very instrumental in the enactment of this law.

Lifetime benefits of $161.50 a month (adjustable upward as
GS–2 federal salaries are increased) are paid to disabled miners
or their widows, with additional sums for dependents up to a
maximum of $322.90. The law was amended and liberalized in
May, 1972, to establish a presumption of black lung disease if the
miner had spent fifteen years underground and had any disabling
respiratory disease, regardless of what any X-ray might show.
The cost of this program is estimated at $1.5 billion in 1973,
dropping down to approximately $1 billion in 1974, and very
gradually declining thereafter. After December 31, 1973, compensation for disability is supposed to be taken care of primarily
through state workmen's compensation laws, with the Department
of Labor charged with assuring that adequate protection is
guaranteed.

MEDICARE

To most of the nations of the world, some form of governmental protection against the hazards of illness is one of the most
basic and important forms of social insurance coverage. Alone
among advanced industrial nations, the United States moved into
the last half of the twentieth century with no such component of
its social insurance system. Although national health insurance
received a good deal of newspaper publicity and became a political
issue in the late 1940's, when it was being advocated by President
Truman and Federal Security Administrator Oscar Ewing, it
never really became a "bread and butter issue" for congressional
candidates. But in the 1950's and early 1960's, there developed
a great groundswell for hospital insurance for the aged as part of
the Social Security system. Who the inventor of the word "Medicare" was, we may never know (for every success there are a
thousand parents; for every failure, none is to be found), but the
name caught on quickly and permanently.

The Eighty-ninth Congress, elected in 1964, brought in on the
tidal wave of votes that carried Lyndon Johnson into office and
swamped Barry Goldwater, had numerous members who had
pledged themselves to fight for Medicare and few who had
promised to try to defeat it. The stage was set and Congressman

Wilbur Mills, the powerful chairman of the House Ways and Means Committee, who had a particularly strong interest in Social Security, became the stage manager and director. There was considerable doubt at the beginning of the session as to where Mills stood on the issue, but as the hearings wore on, it gradually became apparent that Medicare was an idea whose time had come. Mills decided to use his leadership powers to see that a good bill was produced.

As the congressional forces began to contend, it quickly became evident that one key issue would be whether the program would be completely administered by the Social Security Administration, with the federal government making direct payments to hospitals and doctors, or whether such intermediaries as Blue Cross/Blue Shield would be put to use, in the name of avoiding the opprobrium of "socialized medicine." The power of the American Medical Association lobby was very considerable (the AMA had one of the largest lobbying organizations in Washington), and they wished, above all, to head off any plan which had the semblance of "government medicine."

From the standpoint of the SSA staff, the concept of making direct payments to the providers of the service without intermediaries seemed more in the public interest and likely to be appreciably more economical in the long run than using Blue Cross/Blue Shield, or other intermediaries. But it had its obvious complications. It would inevitably mean that the federal government would become involved in auditing the books of the hospitals and possibly the doctors, and the Social Security Administration would have to enter into difficult—and parallel—negotiations with the hospitals over the setting of rates, without initially having built up any expertise in this delicate and difficult process. The hazard of running into serious administrative difficulties was no small consideration. In the end, the decision was more of a political one than a rational comparison of administrative alternatives. The die was cast in favor of using the intermediary payment and negotiating agencies.

The Social Security Amendments of 1965, containing Medicare, were enacted on July 30 of that year, less than seven months after the Eighty-ninth Congress convened. For so complex a bill, this was rapid action. In brief, the provisions, as amended up to 1972, authorize:

- *Hospital insurance* covering Social Security beneficiaries sixty-five and over (and most disability retirees) for up to ninety days of hospitalization (plus a lifetime reserve of sixty days), one hundred days of extended care in skilled nursing home facilities, and up to one hundred home health visits from nurses, physical therapists, and so on, in each benefit period. After the first twenty days of hospital care, there is a modest coinsurance requirement that a small portion of the total bill be paid by the patient.
- *Supplementary medical insurance* that helps pay for doctors' services, outpatient hospital services, medical services and supplies, home health services, physical therapy, and other health care services. For each calendar year, there is a $40 deductible, and the patient must pay 20 per cent of costs above that amount.

The hospital insurance program is financed from an earmarked payroll tax, similar to that which finances the old-age and survivors' insurance program. No person who is no longer working pays such a tax. In the case of medical insurance, the beneficiaries are required to pay half of the insurance premium. The full premium during the 12-month period beginning July 1, 1972, was $5.80 per month.

The medical insurance plan was not originally a part of the Medicare program. It was an ironic product of a last ditch opposition stand against Medicare by the American Medical Association. The AMA ran full page ads in the *New York Times* and the *Washington Post* decrying Medicare and proposing in its stead a quickly developed plan of its own, which, it was careful to point out, made provision for some nonhospital benefits not covered under Medicare. It was not, however, to be a program administered through the Social Security Administration, since the AMA was deathly afraid that any program that was financed by Social Security taxes and administered by SSA would lead to socialized medicine. After the ads appeared, Wilbur Mills decided that since the AMA had made such a point of the deficiencies of the Ways and Means Committee bill, he would add medical insurance. He asked HEW's Social Security lawyers to come up with a draft bill, and after an all-night drafting session, they delivered the bill to him the next morning, as he requested. The medical insurance program that emerged was roughly comparable to the Aetna plan available to federal employees at that time. That is the essence of the genesis of the medical insurance component of Medicare.

It has been the administration of Medicare that has provided the Social Security Administration with its greatest headaches. Managing the hospital insurance part has been difficult enough—dealing with many different intermediary insurance companies, each with its own approach, rules, and accounting practices. But the most difficult has been the Supplementary Medical Insurance. Here the problem of medical ethics comes to the fore—a most delicate and awkward problem for the government to deal with, especially since many doctors, themselves, are loath to come to grips with it. For example, there is wide variation in the practice of surgeons in respect to operations to remove cataracts. Since Medicare was enacted, some surgeons have operated on almost every cataract case which came to them, whereas most are highly selective, operating only when they are firmly convinced that it will benefit the patient. Prostatectomies present a similar problem. How should SSA cope with seemingly excessive surgery when it is not dealt with by the medical profession itself? Very rarely do fellow surgeons take disciplinary action against an associate for overzealous surgery. One is reminded of George Bernard Shaw's remarks in his preface to *The Doctor's Dilemma:*

> That any sane nation, having observed that you could provide for the supply of bread by giving bakers a pecuniary interest in baking for you, should go on to give a surgeon a pecuniary interest in cutting off your leg, is enough to make one despair of political humanity.

Recognizing that doctors are human rather than superhuman, and subject to the same temptations and frailties as those in other occupations, Congress took steps in the extensive Social Security Act Amendments of 1972 to bring the practice of medicine under more systematic peer review, at least in respect to the treatment of Medicare and Medicaid patients when it necessitates their hospitalization. The Act provides for the establishment of Professional Standards Review Organizations (PSRO's) consisting of substantial numbers of practicing physicians (usually 300 or more) in local areas throughout the country to review services provided under the programs authorized by the Social Security

Three of HEW's massive office complexes: (*Above*) HEW's main headquarters building at 330 Independence Avenue, S.W., Washington, D.C.

Above: The Social Security Administration's headquarters, located near the Baltimore Beltway. *Below:* The Clinical Center of the National Institutes of Health, the largest biomedical clinical research facility in the world.

(All photos on this and the following pages are from the Department of Health, Education, and Welfare unless otherwise indicated.)

Many Department agencies fight disease. *Above:* National Institutes of Health scientists Harry M. Meyer, Jr., and Paul D. Parkman, who developed a vaccine against rubella (German measles). *Right:* Nationwide immunization programs are part of the business of the Center for Disease Control at Atlanta.

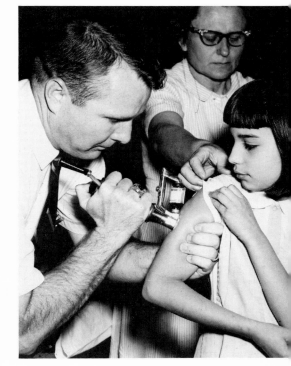

This is one of the nineteen FDA regional laboratories. The agency keeps constant check on food and drugs moving in interstate commerce. (*FDA Photo*)

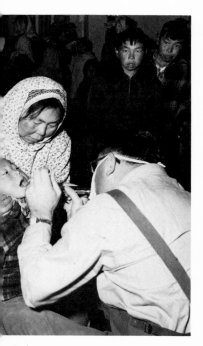

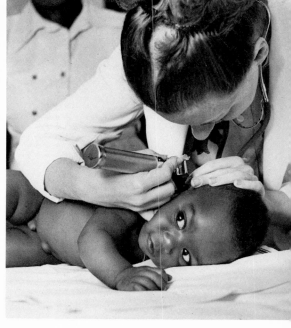

Left: A Public Health Service dentist examines native Alaskans. *Right:* An infant is examined under the Maternal and Child Health program.

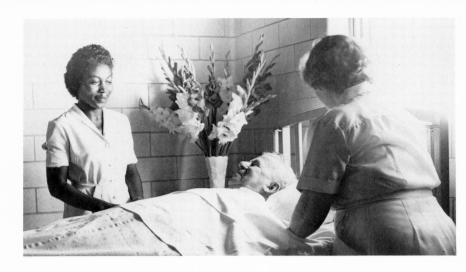

HEW supports vocational training through various programs. *Above:* Practical nurse trainees learn bedside care under WIN (the Work Incentives Program) and Medicaid. *Left:* A blind rehabilitation counselor is instructed in the operation of a lathe. Vocational rehabilitation has been an especially successful HEW program. *Below:* HEW support for vocational training in skills such as mechanics is one of the oldest forms of federal aid to public schools.

Under the Older Americans' Act, senior citizens' centers sponsored by the Department, such as the one in the rest home shown above, are encouraged. *Below:* A Social Security interviewer discusses prospective benefits with a retirement-age couple.

Without help from HEW's programs of Aid to Families with Dependent Children, Social Security, and Supplemental Security Income, the family of this child would be desperate.

HEW educational programs can supplement and expand regular school activities. *Above:* Educational television, aided by HEW funds, adds a new dimension to the classroom for both students and teachers. *Below:* The Teacher Corps supplements normal teaching resources, reaching children from poverty backgrounds.

THE TEN HEW SECRETARIES

Oveta Culp Hobby
1953–55

Marion B. Folsom
1955–58

Arthur S. Flemming
1958–61

Abraham Ribicoff
1961–62

Anthony J. Celebrezze
1962–65

John W. Gardner
1965–68

Wilbur J. Cohen
1968–69

Robert H. Finch
1969–70

Elliot L. Richardson
1970–73

Caspar W. Weinberger
1973–

Act. The purpose of PSRO's is to assure that services are, first, medically necessary and, second, are provided in accordance with professional standards. In a variety of other ways, too, the Act seeks to limit the escalation of costs and provide incentives toward the economical provision of medical services. These amendments may have wide effect on the practice of medicine, not just for Medicare and Medicaid patients, but for the general public.

ORGANIZATION OF THE SOCIAL SECURITY ADMINISTRATION

The organization of SSA seems very simple and functional. It has one bureau for each of three types of insurance: retirement and survivors', disability, and health. It has four other bureaus: a Bureau of Data Processing to handle the consolidated electronic data processing and related activities, a Bureau of District Office Operations, a Bureau of Hearings and Appeals, and a new Bureau of Supplemental Security Income.

A commissioner oversees the work of ten regional commissioners located in the ten HEW regional offices. It is interesting to note that the role of the regional commissioners is modeled on that of the ten HEW regional directors. They are not line operators. They are coordinators, liaison officers, problem solvers, public affairs representatives, and the eyes and ears of the commissioner in the field, but they do not direct the work of the bureau representatives who serve with them. In 1970, the Office of the Secretary of HEW sought to persuade the commissioner of SSA to convert the regional commissioners into line officers, but the Secretary's office was eventually persuaded by SSA that with a few adjustments to upgrade the role of the regional commissioners, the organizational relationships should be left as they were. This is another example of the never-ending philosophical and practical struggle to determine which of four major organizing principles— purpose, place (geographic area), process, and clientele group— is most suitable to a given function or set of functions. In the case of the Social Security Administration, no compelling reason existed to make important delegations of decision-making power to the regions, as was true of other operating agencies of HEW. Other agencies were dealing with numerous project applications and individual grants that required coordination with one another and adaptation to the particular needs of numerous different communities. SSA was dealing with a system that was intended to be uniformly administered all over the United States, so that any person who sought service in any county or city in the country would get the same answers to the same questions and receive the same treatment as any other person in the country. Under such circumstances, major delegation of independent decision-making to the field would vitiate, rather than promote, the national purpose.

THE CAREER TRADITION OF SSA

From its beginning, Social Security has been administered by dedicated career people. It was launched in 1935 when there were thousands of idealistic young college graduates who were eager to participate in the conversion of their government from a stern and aloof set of institutions to an instrument of the people to be used on their own behalf. Also, they believed they could equal or surpass the private insurance industry in the efficiency of management. One of the early directors of the Bureau of Old Age and Survivors Insurance, John Corson, installed a basic work measurement system which, with improvements, has survived for more than three decades. Standards of performance are set for a very substantial proportion of the positions in SSA. Employees are initially aided to learn to achieve those standards, but if they are unable to do so, they are not retained as permanent employees.

The commissioner of Social Security from 1962–73, Robert M. Ball, is a conspicuous example of the group of able members of the Depression generation who have devoted their lives to the objective of making Social Security the most efficiently and warmly administered major enterprise of the U.S. Government. He was recruited as a claims examiner in Newark, New Jersey, in 1939, and rose rapidly to the ranks of top management. In 1954, he was appointed deputy director of the Bureau of Old Age and Survivors Insurance, and in 1962, commissioner of Social Security.

With the exception of half a dozen people brought in from the insurance industry and elsewhere since the enactment of Medicare, and a few experts in data processing recruited to manage the enormous computer system, a very high proportion of the management structure of SSA is composed of persons who have grown up with the system. It is a career-oriented organization.

While it has had many advantages, the career character of SSA may well present it with more of a problem than its top officials are ready to admit. Much of the top officialdom of SSA is eligible for retirement, and it is not at all unlikely that within a very short span of years there may be an unprecedented turnover in its top staff. Even though a concerted effort has been made to send younger, promising employees to executive development programs, it seems somewhat dubious that SSA can sustain the combination of dedication, talent, and productivity that has been its hallmark for a generation.

Even at present writing, the SSA is facing an uphill struggle in keeping the human touch in its mass operations, both externally and internally. In dealing with its enormous clientele, it tries to make the system seem as simple as possible, but the complexity of its regulations and options now exceeds the capacity of some of its district office staff to understand and explain. Internally, it is faced with the universal problem of big bureaucracies of making mass operations seem interesting and important, and of minimizing the feeling that people are in routine, dead-end jobs. There are no easy answers to the curse of bigness.

THE FUTURE OF SOCIAL SECURITY

Social Security has three big issues looming ahead; universal health insurance, short-term disability (or cash sickness) insurance, and partial support of its basic program, particularly for the poor, from the general funds of the Treasury.

By 1972, the leadership of both parties had reached agreement that the American people should all be covered by either a single national health insurance program or a National Health Insurance Standards Act. The latter, which is President Nixon's answer to the bill of organized labor that was endorsed and introduced by Senator Edward Kennedy and associates, would require employers to provide adequate health insurance for their employees, who would share in paying the costs. It would establish a Family Health Insurance Plan, which would meet the needs of poor families not covered by the National Health Insurance Standards Act because they are headed by unemployed or self-employed persons whose income is below certain levels.

The choice between a single national system, as envisioned by

the Kennedy bill introduced January 25, 1971, and known as
the Health Security Act and the National Health Insurance
Standards Act will be a long and hard-fought battle that will begin
in 1973 and probably build up toward 1976. The professional staff
of the Social Security Administration will, during this period, be
caught in the middle of the cross fire. Theoretically, they are
nonpolicy people, with only the commissioner and his deputy
occupying noncareer positions (although both have been career
men since 1962). But the staff is composed of professional
analysts who have worked with this subject for years, and their
involvement in policy issues is inescapable. (During an earlier
period, one of the key staff men who had done much of the work
on the Wagner-Murray-Dingell bill—Dr. I. S. Falk—had become
so identified with it and with its philosophy that when there was
a change of administration from Truman to Eisenhower in 1953,
Dr. Falk became *persona non grata* to the incoming Administration
and left.) The Office of the Secretary should be properly staffed
to provide the analytical talent needed to support the point of view
of the administration in power, but this has never happened in
respect to Social Security. In consequence, the years of controversy
leading up to final enactment of some form of universal health
insurance—which will probably be the late 1970's—are likely to
be difficult ones for the key staff of SSA, which will be called upon
for analyses by both parties in an acrimonious argument.

The short-term disability issue will probably not be so heated.
For nearly twenty years it has been on the back burner. New
York, Rhode Island, New Jersey, California, and Hawaii have
state laws that provide insurance payments to sustain part of the
income of ill persons after their wages have been interrupted.
Marion Folsom was instrumental in designing and enacting the
New York law, and he hoped that it would become a model for
other states. But in the last decade there has been no progress
toward state adoption of such protection except for the state of
Hawaii, and there seems to be no early prospect of such
action.

When the matter does become more active, simple action could
achieve the necessary purpose. That would be to modify the
existing long-term disability concept to include short-term disability. All that would be required would be reduction of the
present waiting period after the onset of disability from five

months to two months, and elimination of the current requirement of the medical prognosis that disability will last at least twelve months.

In the context of national fiscal policy, Social Security presents one especially difficult issue. The flat-rate tax is regressive, since people with low earnings pay a larger percentage of their income in taxes than do those with high earnings. Even though low wage earners receive benefits that are loaded in their favor, the tax burden on many low earners, especially while they are raising a family, is onerous. What, if anything, can and should be done about this problem?

Many persons who are classified as poor are low wage earners with medium to large families. Of these, many are exempt from either federal or state income taxes. But they must pay Social Security taxes on all of their earnings. And the rate they pay on the totality of their earnings is the same as that paid by the president of General Motors on only a small fraction of his earned income.

If one examines the total income and expense budget of the United States, he notes with considerable concern that receipts from Social Security taxes considerably exceed corporate income taxes and are steadily rising. The 1973 budget shows estimated receipts from Social Security taxes of $53.9 billion, compared to $35.7 billion in corporate income taxes. Ten years earlier, receipts from corporation income taxes exceeded receipts from Social Security taxes by an appreciable margin. The Social Security tax has become the most rapidly growing source of federal revenues.

No administration has sought to change Social Security's basic scheme of financing. At some point, however, this may become an important political issue. One proposal that has had some consideration but has never made any progress is to make the federal government a partner in the enterprise by basing the program on one-third support from the worker, one-third from the employer, and one-third from the federal government (meaning the general taxpayer). Since politicians have been actively working to avoid a tax increase and even to find relief for the average taxpayer, future competition for the general tax dollar will be extraordinarily keen. Therefore, it would be very hard for a President to find the fiscal means and the political support for allocating very large amounts of general revenues to finance the government's share of the Social Security program, even if it were to be accomplished gradually, as it would have to be. As in the case of most important issues, there is no easy solution to this dilemma.

On the horizon, but too far away for most people to worry about now, is another problem. It is the question of what will happen when the offspring from the postwar baby boom reach eligibility for retirement and embark on their "golden years." Between now and the end of the century, a large-size work force will be supporting a moderate-sized group of retirees from Social Security taxes, but beginning shortly after 2010, we will enter upon a period when the number of retirees will boom just as the number of babies did after World War II. Under the concept of "current cost financing," tax rates will have to move up rapidly to provide the needed funds. If, by any chance—and this is a good possibility—the birth rates for the balance of this century should turn out to be lower than the Social Security actuaries have assumed, the situation could become more difficult and serious than they now believe. A new era of generational conflict between the bumper crop of active and politically sophisticated senior citizens and the comparatively smaller group of young wage earners seems predictable.

V

Welfare and Rehabilitation

While everyone expected Social Security to grow steadily for at least a generation after 1935, public assistance, commonly referred to as welfare, was expected to wither away. This may have been one reason the designers of the Social Security Act decided to leave to the states and local communities the basic responsibility for providing welfare assistance to the needy, confining the federal role to providing a specified part of the cost and assuring certain standards of equity. This assumption that welfare would gradually decline contributed to the acute shock suffered by the public when the *federal* costs for public assistance, including medical assistance for the needy and social services, grew from $1 billion in HEW's first year (1953) to over $13 billion in 1972–73. The total cost, including federal, state, and local funds, is estimated at $23 billion in 1972–73.

Americans have always been ambivalent about the poor. They are sharply torn between humanitarianism and the belief that a great many people on welfare rolls—some drawing even more money than people with full-time jobs—could find work if they really wanted to. Elizabethan poor laws asserted a residual community responsibility for the destitute, but in New England, where the poor laws were first introduced into the colonies, the poor were expected to work for their food and lodgings. There was agreement that begging was a degrading business, but the work ethic did not condone government relief with nothing in return, if there were someone in the family who could be working.

Many Americans were also conditioned by the frontier psy-

111

chology, which, for nearly three centuries after the English landings in Jamestown, asserted that this was the land of opportunity in which any able-bodied man and his family could find good land to cultivate and could wrest a fair living from the soil. Even when the era of industrialization arrived, the momentum of 300 years of open frontier and rugged individualism carried over into an urban society. The political rhetoric that bespoke unlimited opportunity lingered on and proclaimed that, except in times of depression and heavy unemployment, there were jobs to be found by all who really wanted to work.

Both the Elizabethan poor law tradition and the frontier psychology held that the threat of privation was the greatest single motive force for getting the poor to work. Work was necessary; work was good; and none should be permitted to escape this basic component of "right living." The work ethic was so strong that it greatly overshadowed the humanitarian element of the Elizabethan poor laws adopted by the colonies and enacted by the states after the Revolution. Not for well over 300 years after the British Parliament assumed responsibility for instructing and requiring communities to care for their poor did the U.S. Congress make a comparable commitment. Not until the enactment of the Social Security Act in 1935 did the federal government assume any systematic and continuing responsibility for the poor in the United States, and even then it was in the form of proffered financial aid to the states with no assurance that the states would provide the basic essentials of life to the destitute.

The history of poor relief and welfare aid, particularly as they developed in urban areas in the nineteenth and early twentieth centuries, has been recounted well in a small government publication by Blanche C. Coll, *Perspectives in Public Welfare,* issued in 1969. It records the evolution in public attitudes toward the poor, with indications of a long-continuing and deep-seated fear that collectively the poor constitute a threat to the underpinnings of the social structure. Yet conflicting public attitudes have prevented any permanent consensus regarding proper remedies to poverty.

SOCIAL SECURITY AND WELFARE

A temporary consensus was reached in 1935 in the public assistance provisions of the Social Security Act. The public assistance titles—those that offered aid to the states to finance programs for the aged, the blind, and dependent children and, later, for the permanently and totally disabled—assumed that "open-ended" federal aid would entice the states to fulfill their responsibilities toward the helpless poor. The federal government agreed to match without limit all state payments to the specified groups of needy made according to certain formulas, provided the states agreed to meet specified standards of administration. No minimum—and no maximum—payment levels were written into law or regulation.

The federal government required each participating state to submit a plan to be approved by the Social Security Board for the administration of each of its public assistance programs. The states were thus put on the defensive. They had to satisfy the Social Security Board that they had a sound and acceptable plan of administration in the first place and, continuously thereafter, had to demonstrate that they were living up to the promises made in their plans. It was a means of applying pressure upon the states, through the device of granting and threatening to withhold large sums of money, to administer their traditional responsibilities in ways that would meet with the approval of the newly created Social Security Board. It is not surprising that many states chafed under this new form of federal pressure.

If any state had wished to do so, it could have operated a program of food handouts and almshouses and contract labor without federal help. It was these practices that liberal reformers had sought to supersede through the Social Security Act. They reasoned that matching grants from the federal government would be sufficient to persuade all states to adopt the practice of making money payments to the poor, allowing them at least the self-respect of spending the cash thus allowed them. In one major respect, the reformers were right. All states did "buy in" to the money payments scheme. But this could not prevent, in many areas and circumstances, the paternalistic (or maternalistic) practice of welfare workers scrutinizing the expenditures of their clients to assure compliance with the agencies' welfare policies. This practice later became one of the principal targets of the "negative income taxers" and latter-day welfare reformers.

A small Bureau of Public Assistance was created within the Social Security Board to administer these welfare programs. It was predominantly staffed from the outset by professional social workers, most of whom brought to their duties the firm conviction that all states should not only establish objective standards of need, but that the helpless poor should be assured that these standards would be met. But that was not the way things turned out.

Public assistance law required that all state plans meet the following stipulations:

1. All persons must be "in need" to be eligible for public assistance. The definition of need was to be left to each state, so long as it was not unreasonable in the eyes of the Social Security Board.

2. In determining need, each state must consider all income and resources of the applicant. (As will be seen, this requirement became a very serious problem, eventually necessitating amendments to the law.)

3. Each state plan must set forth its standards for the determination of eligibility, its personnel standards, it methods of administration, its provisions for audit, reporting, and research.

4. Each plan must be operative in all subdivisions of the state and be administered so as to assure equitable treatment to all persons similarly situated, regardless of where, within the state, they might live.

5. There must be some degree of financial participation by the state; no state may require that its local subdivisions bear the total nonfederal share of the cost required to qualify for federal matching funds.

6. A single state agency must be designated as responsible for the administration of the program within the state, and it must have adequate power to assure that the state plan will be carried out in accordance with the state's contractual agreement with the federal government.

7. The states must develop methods of administration that will assure that the agreement will be carried out; the federal government originally agreed to pay half of the costs of "proper and efficient administration." (This arrangement was amended in 1967 to authorize payment of three-fourths of the cost of constructive welfare services.)

8. States must make provision for maintaining the records of applicants and recipients on a confidential basis.

9. Each state must agree to make a prompt investigation after persons apply for public assistance. The federal government strongly encouraged a maximum period of thirty days for determining eligibility.

10. An appeal process was required, including a fair hearing procedure, but there was no requirement that applicants or beneficiaries had to be informed of their right of appeal.

11. No residence requirement could be imposed that was more restrictive than five years' residence out of the last nine, and one year immediately preceding application. (All duration of residence requirements were summarily terminated by the Supreme Court in 1969.) All citizens were equally eligible regardless of the length of their citizenship. And no person could be required to be older than sixty-five to be eligible for old-age assistance.

The law included what seemed to be a conspicuous anomaly of which little notice has ever been taken. It had a built-in incentive for each state to minimize its payment levels if the state was poor and the welfare recipients unorganized, but it afforded the opportunity in comparatively rich states, and even not-so-rich states, where the poor were either well-organized or well-represented, or both, to establish payment levels several times higher than the poor states. Since the law established neither minimum nor maximum levels of payment to needy persons, the Bureau of Public Assistance found itself in the position of trying to negotiate with states with very low payment levels to bring them up, while it was simultaneously trying to keep other states from converting old-age assistance into something resembling an expensive flat pension scheme for the aging. And in some of the well-to-do states in the postwar period appeared the problem of fatherless families with several children receiving larger public assistance payments than the full-time wages of low-paid workers with similar sized families. The gap between the levels of payments in the rich and poor states became a matter of increasing concern to welfare officials and was regularly reported by the Bureau of Public Assistance. In 1971, the average per capita monthly payment under the program of Aid to Families with Dependent Children was $78 in New York and $11 in Mississippi, a ratio typical of the previous two decades.

THE FARM EXODUS AND PUBLIC ASSISTANCE

The mass migration from farms to cities began its resurgence during World War II (continuing a long-term trend that had been interrupted by the Depression) and was much accelerated by the unusually rapid mechanization of agriculture. As the cotton planting and picking machines, the cultivators, and all the other new machines moved in, the sharecroppers and the plantation hands moved out. Where but to the industrial cities, particularly of the North and West (where many of their friends had gone to help spin the wheels of the war machine), could they go? They went, sometimes as whole families, and sometimes with the father of the family moving first and the mother and children following.

The strains on the families often became overwhelming. To the newcomers, the cities were baffling. Much worse, they had no skills to sell. They were proficient at almost no occupation the city had to offer except common labor, and there were not enough such jobs. The cost of living was two or three times what it had been in the rural South. The fact that most of the newcomers were black meant that they were discriminated against in getting even the low-skilled jobs for which they could immediately qualify. It is no wonder that so many of them eventually had to seek welfare aid; the wonder is that more of them did not. They created an enormous pent-up demand for welfare aid, which exploded in the 1960's.

No Federal Funds to Whole Families

Except in the states that operated general assistance programs for whole families using state and local funds with no federal matching money, when a family with an able-bodied father became destitute, it was not eligible for assistance. The Aid to Families with Dependent Children (AFDC) program had been designed for families without fathers (because of death or desertion). The assumption was that if there were an able-bodied father, he should work, not draw relief while idle. It should be remembered that when the Social Security Act was written in the mid-1930's, the federal government had assumed responsibility for employing the employable who could find no jobs in the private sector. The Works Projects Administration, the Public Works Administration, the Civilian Conservation Corps, and the National Youth Administration were strong evidences of this federal commitment. In any event, there was no political support for a permanent federal law that contemplated the support of whole families, including able-bodied fathers, in a continuing state of idleness, no matter what the state of the economy. The law, therefore, was designed explicitly for the relief of dependent children and their caretaker, normally their mother.

To what extent the design of this law became a major cause of family breakup among the poor will never be known. That it has been a contributing cause can hardly be doubted. The strains on rural families, particularly blacks, moving into unfamiliar and uncongenial urban cultures, was so great that a significant increase in family breakdown would probably have occurred in any event, but the lack of any federal program for the employment of able-bodied family heads who could not find work in the private sector, coupled with their exclusion from public assistance, put heavy additional pressure on destitute families to break apart. Except in the minority of states with general assistance programs, the father had to leave his wife and children so they could be eligible for the minimum essentials of life.

As described in Chapter II, Secretary Abraham Ribicoff and his Assistant Secretary Wilbur Cohen, with the support of President John F. Kennedy, succeeded in partly correcting this major flaw in amendments passed in 1961 and 1962. Unfortunately, however, the amendments made it optional on the part of the state to include unemployed parents in their public assistance programs. In the 10-year period from 1962–72, twenty-three states availed themselves of the federal offer. This left twenty-seven states where the father of a destitute family must still desert to make his wife and children eligible for AFDC assistance, or take his family to strange new surroundings in one of the states that does provide welfare aid to whole families.

Other Serious Shortcomings in Public Assistance Law

While strong pressure toward family dissolution among the poor was probably the most publicized of the design failures of public assistance law, there were others of major consequence.

A second serious shortcoming, to which allusion has already been made, was the lack of assurance of payments to the needy that would meet the barest minimum standards of health and welfare. There was nothing to stop a state from adopting a conscious or unconscious policy of starving out their poor in hopes that they would move elsewhere. This is what some of them seem to have done. Many persons in positions of official responsibility were oblivious of the consequences. In 1968, Senator Ernest F. Hollings of South Carolina, hearing reports of starvation in America and being skeptical of them, decided to tour his home state and see for himself the real condition of the poor. He was shocked and apologized for his ignorance of the status of his own constituency. He found ample evidence of such severe undernourishment that it could only be characterized as genuine hunger.

Despite Senator Hollings's findings—and the unrefuted assumption that there were comparable situations in other states—no minimum floor has yet been put under the public assistance payments to the needy. The Department of Agriculture's programs of food stamps and food supplements and school lunches have been substantially enlarged to partially fill this gaping need, but the nation's program of income maintenance for the poor is sorely deficient and inequitable. The Nixon Administration developed a program, commonly referred to as "Welfare Reform," which sought to put a floor under welfare benefits throughout the country, but this became embroiled in lengthy, acrimonious, and unproductive dispute in the Senate for over two years.

A third fault in the welfare titles of the Social Security Act, which took a long time to rectify (and some would say has not yet been fully corrected), was the failure to include any incentive for part-time work. In an effort to minimize program costs, the lawmakers required that every bit of income had to be taken into account and deducted from a person's or family's computed need in arriving at the amount of the welfare payment. Some also felt that equity dictated such a policy. But the consequences were not acceptable in a work-oriented society. If an aged person were able to earn some money—by baby-sitting for example—he or she would have his welfare payment reduced by the full amount earned. If a young boy were enterprising enough to carry papers, his family's payment would be reduced. It was of no economic advantage for any person on public assistance to earn anything unless he or she could suddenly start earning enough to make such assistance completely unnecessary. Another alternative, of course, was to conceal earnings, a not uncommon practice, but one hardly conducive to either respect for law or respect for one's own integrity.

Secretary Ribicoff began correction of this defect in 1961, and the situation was greatly improved by the Social Security Amendments of 1967. The law now requires all states, in computing welfare budgets, to disregard the first $30 per month of earnings of any eligible recipient, and one-third of any additional earnings, thereby providing a positive incentive for the recipients to earn whatever they can. Economists often refer to this as a 67 per cent tax rate on such earnings and most of those who describe it this way are critical of it as being an excessive and unfair rate. In any event, this original flaw in the Social Security Act has been at least partly corrected.

It is particularly interesting to note that in overcoming this defect in the Act, Congress did not hesitate to *require* states to make this change to qualify for funds under the public assistance titles of the law. They were insistent about this as universal social policy, whereas they had been permissive about the inclusion of unemployed fathers.

A fourth serious inequity in the public assistance titles of the Social Security Act became apparent from the practice of paying more in the form of welfare allowances to the nonworking poor than the full-time working poor received in the form of wages. In states with reasonably adequate welfare standards, the hard-working poor with large families were thus worse off than the broken families where nobody worked. Elsewhere in the industrialized world—in Europe and Canada—this problem was alleviated by providing children's allowances of a fairly modest, but still significant, amount, so that the allowances, when added to the minimum wage, would bring a large family up to the level of decency. But this idea never caught on in the United States. It was argued without empirical evidence that children's allowances would encourage the poor to have more children than they could support. Studies showed that this did not occur in Canada. Children's allowances are not and cannot be made a substitute for welfare; they are a means of keeping the working poor off welfare. If systems of governmental support have any influence on patterns of procreation, the U.S. system seems far more likely to encourage irresponsible parenthood.

In any event, it is evident that the policy of paying idle welfare families, even in cases where there may be good reason for their idleness, more than working families of comparable size contains the seeds of serious social discontent, not to mention the destruction of the vaunted work ethic. President Nixon's program of welfare reform sought to remedy this inequity by authorizing payments to the working poor of such amounts that there would always be an incentive and a premium payment for working.

A fifth problem with the public assistance law—an intentional omission—has been ignored by both Democratic and Republican administrations and by Congress for more than three decades. The federal government will have nothing to do with helping states provide welfare payments to needy single individuals or needy married couples under sixty-five if they do not have children unless disability can be proven. The government does provide, through the Labor Department, funds for various manpower development and training programs, with training allowances that are intended to supply subsistence. But there are not nearly enough such opportunities to meet the needs of urban unemployed youth. In states without general assistance programs, the only way these excluded people can become eligible for assistance is to have a child, in or out of wedlock. It seems especially puzzling that no President and no Secretary of HEW has ever tried to provide the leadership that would be required to deal with this vexing problem.

Social workers and public welfare administrators have been very conscious of most of these defects for a long time but have been singularly unsuccessful in educating the press, the public, and the Congress, not to mention Presidents and Secretaries of HEW. A comprehensive report produced primarily by the public welfare profession (*Report of the Advisory Council on Public Welfare to the HEW Secretary*) on these issues was published in 1966 under the title, *Having the Power, We Have the Duty*. The report sank quickly from sight, with hardly a gurgle. Though the price tag on improvements of the welfare system was not explicitly stated, it seemed higher than the public or the economy could stand. The study recommended setting and meeting an adequate standard of need for every person and family in the country, still using a means test. Meteorologists of political winds said it would not fly.

Who Is Responsible for Correcting Errors in Program Design?

How could major laws that turned out to have serious faults have been allowed to stand for decades without correction? It is not an easy question to answer, but some effort to get at the root of so important a matter seems in order.

First, World War II and the Korean War created such broad-scale demand for labor that most of the five problems described above did not become severe enough to seem to warrant action until well after the end of the Korean War. Second, the federal government—both the legislative and executive branches—continued to regard public assistance policy as basically a state matter, with the federal government assuming more of a revenue-sharing than a strong leadership role. There was a traditional and tacit line that the federal government would not cross in intervening in state policy. This was not a carefully thought out philosophy but rather a kind of intuitive attitude, stemming from the political atmosphere of the times. Third, the Department of Health, Education, and Welfare was not staffed to do adequate research into what was actually happening in the welfare field, and consequently top officials operated without adequate knowledge of the creeping social problems that were being aggravated by the defects in the design of public assistance. And fourth, the Secretary and the other top officials of HEW were so heavily pressed by hundreds of other problems with short deadlines that they could give no time to such profound, long-range problems as these.

The last two reasons deserve additional comment. In retrospect, it seems inexplicably shortsighted for the top leadership of HEW to have failed to conduct a careful appraisal of the effect of the expenditures for public assistance, especially after they reached the billion-dollar level with the trend pointing steadily upward. This failure was due partly to the inflexibility of the appropriations made by Congress (only small amounts available for program evaluation), and partly to the generally negative attitude Congress took toward social research. But most of all, it was a leadership failure. It was the direct result of the principle, "The urgent is the deadly enemy of the important." When there are a large number of important things competing with a massive number of urgent things in a department with the unprecedented growth rate of HEW, Secretaries with an average tenure of 2.2 years can hardly expect, or be expected, to grapple with profound social issues on their own initiative. And the bureaucracies, partly for lack of staff and partly for lack of imagination, were not much help to the successive Secretaries. That some corrective action was taken on secretarial initiative was the fortunate result of the combination of Ribicoff and Cohen, each with special knowledge of the problems.

SKYROCKETING WELFARE ROLLS AND PLANS FOR REFORM

As "Welfare Adviser at Large" Daniel Patrick Moynihan has often pointed out, the welfare boom started slowly in the late 1950's, gathered momentum in the early 1960's, and then "took off," without any correlation with the ups and downs of unemployment. (See Chart II.) The accompanying graph (see Chart III) shows the comparison between the number of recipients of Aid to Families with Dependent Children and other forms of aid. (Both charts referred to here are from *Budget Highlights Fiscal Year 1973: The Changes in the Nation's Priorities in Three Years,* which is a 1972 GPO publication.)

A full explanation of the increase would require more space than is available here, but no small part of it was due to the rapid change in attitude about welfare by the recipients themselves. They had become sufficiently numerous that a whole subculture, with its own internal respectability, emerged. Being on welfare no longer carried the social stigma it once had. The National Welfare Rights Organization (NWRO) sprang into being. Legal aid money available through the poverty program became available for class action suits on behalf of aggrieved recipients of Aid to Families with Dependent Children. And when the bright young legal aid lawyers started winning those suits, it gave even greater visibility and respectability to welfare status. Rather quickly, tens of thousands of people who had earlier been eligible for public assistance, but who either had not known it or had preferred not to apply as a matter of self-respect, made application. State and local departments of public welfare were swamped, especially where the NWRO was active.

The great upsurge in the welfare rolls was the result of two deep-rooted factors that could not be overcome by intensive counseling to teach people how to lift themselves up by their own

CHART II.
Welfare Costs: AFDC Payments

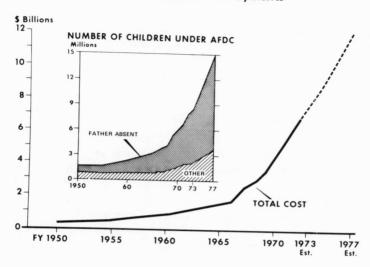

CHART III.
Public Assistance Recipients by Program

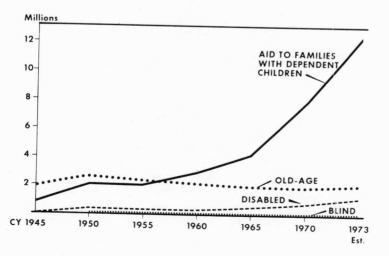

bootstraps. The most profound and inexorable social force was urbanization of great numbers of formerly rural people in a short time, and the consequent misfit between the skill demands of an increasingly technical society and the new urban work force. And the second, which was just mentioned, was the shift in cultural attitudes that caused millions who had been concealing their poverty to shed their shame and ask for what they suddenly became aware was a legal right. Neither factor was or is a reversible condition.

President Nixon's Welfare Reform Plan

When Richard Nixon was elected President in 1968, the "welfare mess" was high on his list of political as well as social problems. It is hardly surprising that one of his earliest postelection decisions was to establish a task force to come up with a fresh approach to its solution. Richard Nathan, later appointed assistant director of the Bureau of the Budget and still later, in 1971, a deputy under secretary of HEW for Welfare Reform, was named chairman of the pre-inauguration task force, which laid out a general plan for overhauling the system. In the spring of 1969, with the aid of Daniel Patrick Moynihan, newly appointed assistant to the President, a second task force, which included HEW Under Secretary Jack Veneman, as well as Nathan and others, produced a welfare reform program that, with some modifications, gained the support of President Nixon. Nixon and his advisers spent a good deal of time arguing the pros and cons of various alternatives before finally deciding on the plan sent to Congress on August 8, 1969.

The essential features of the plan were not complicated. They were:

- A basic minimum cash payment of $1,600 plus food stamps (equivalent to $2,400 without food stamps), to be financed entirely by the federal government.
- A requirement that states should supplement these payments wherever their standards of assistance had been higher than this, but with the federal government aiding the states so that none would have to pay out as much money for public assistance as it had in the immediate past.
- A work incentive that would disregard the first $60 per

month of earnings plus 50 per cent of all remaining earnings.
- Assured eligibility of all families with children (but not single persons or married couples without children), *including the working poor.* Low wage earners with large families would benefit especially from this provision.
- Administration by the federal government, including the extraordinary provision that the states could contract with the federal government to administer the state supplemental benefits at no cost to the states.
- Registration for work and training of all able-bodied parents of children over six years of age, with a stepped-up effort to find suitable work and a requirement that recipients work or have their payments cut off if suitable work were found—a program the President later dubbed "Workfare."
- Social Services to be completely divorced from income maintenance, administered by the states, but continuing to be financed through federal matching grants.
- Federal government assumption (by the Social Security Administration) of responsibility for administration of the aid programs for the aged, blind, and disabled.

President Nixon called the core of the program the Family Assistance Plan (FAP). It was estimated to cost $4 billion more in its first full year of operation than the then existing system and to increase the total number of people receiving income supplements by 11 million, most of the increase coming from among the working poor. It was touted as a not-too-expensive answer to "the welfare mess" with the magic promise of breaking the cycle of poverty and eventually saving billions. FAP's sponsors claimed that it was superior to the "Negative Income Tax," authored originally by economist Milton Friedman and recommended to President Johnson in 1968 by a special task force, principally because of FAP's emphasis on the work requirement—the Workfare part of the program.

The saga of the birth and death of President Nixon's Family Assistance Plan is much too long a story to be fully recorded in these brief pages. It is one of the most fascinating—and depressing —chapters in the annals of recent domestic politics and ended on October 4, 1972, with the defeat of Senator Abraham Ribicoff's lengthy effort to develop a workable compromise between the liberals, who wanted more, and the conservatives, led by Senator Russell Long, who saw welfare reform as disrupting the economy of their regions and inimical to the work ethic. Long's public complaint, "I can't get anybody to iron my shirts," was widely quoted. But Senator John J. Williams dealt the plan its most devastating blow by demonstrating the cumulative value of food stamps, public housing, Medicaid, and other special services to those receiving assistance and showing that many currently on welfare would be worse off under the proposed new Family Assistance Plan.

House Ways and Means Committee Chairman Wilbur Mills, the most powerful man in Congress, had supported FAP, but his support was of no avail, especially in 1972 when the political currents and crosscurrents raged out of control. In the end, Nixon himself became disenchanted with welfare reform and gave no support to HEW Secretary Elliot Richardson in his last-ditch effort to collaborate with Ribicoff on compromise legislation that stuck remarkably close to Nixon's plan. As late as January, 1971, Nixon had listed welfare reform as the first of his six great domestic goals for the American people, but, by the fall of 1972, fighting inflation by holding down governmental spending was far ahead of whatever was second.*

Work Incentives

Despite the failure of Congress to enact President Nixon's "Workfare" program, increasing emphasis has been placed on work incentives for welfare recipients ever since 1962, and especially since 1971. In 1962, when Congress authorized Aid to Families of Dependent Children with Unemployed Parents (AFDCUP), it also encouraged welfare agencies to develop work programs to employ able-bodied but idle parents. In the mid-1960's, the Office of Economic Opportunity and the Labor Department were enlisted in the effort, and in 1968, a new Work Incentives program (WIN) was authorized by the Social Security Act. When the welfare rolls (AFDC) kept going up and up, still more emphasis was

---

* The 3-year drama of the Family Assistance Plan was well observed and succinctly summarized by James Welsh of the *Washington Star-News* in the *New York Times Magazine* of January 7, 1973, and, for those with an appetite for greater detail, was elaborated into a whole book by the more biased participant, Daniel Patrick Moynihan, titled, *The Politics of a Guaranteed Income* (Random House, 1972).

placed on applying both encouragement and pressure to those on the rolls to obtain training to make them employable. Amendments to the Social Security Act in 1971 required that registration for the program be a condition of eligibility for receiving or continuing to receive welfare payments. By 1973, the WIN program was budgeted at $500 million.

The WIN program is a collaborative effort between HEW and the Department of Labor. HEW gets the appropriation from Congress and transfers a large part of it to the Labor Department for testing and counseling welfare workers, and for providing various types of training, public service employment, and job placement. Since nearly half of the WIN participants are mothers who are unable to provide child care for their children while they are undergoing training, it is essential to see that they are provided such services. This part of the program responsibility is retained by HEW.

The average number of work and training participants in 1973 was estimated at 120,000, and the number of children receiving child care at just under 100,000. The number of welfare recipients placed in jobs in 1972 was only 42,100, but the 1973–74 budget predicted with high optimism that 150,000 would be placed in 1973.

The WIN program, which is 90 per cent financed by the federal government and 10 per cent by the states, cannot yet be regarded as a success story. It is particularly in need of the most careful kind of evaluation to determine when and why various approaches are successful or unsuccessful.

AID TO THE AGED, THE BLIND, AND THE DISABLED

While the program of Aid to Families with Dependent Children (AFDC) was growing at an alarming rate, the aid to the aged, blind, and disabled remained within acceptable bounds. As can be seen from Chart III on page 123, the number of people receiving old-age assistance is about the same in 1973 as in 1945—2 million (and about 60 per cent of these payments were to supplement inadequate Social Security benefits). The number of persons receiving aid to the disabled has climbed rather steadily but is still only a little over a million compared with 12 million on AFDC. Blind beneficiaries number hardly 100,000.

Neither the President nor Congress has been happy with the "adult" categories of public assistance, largely because of the wide variation in the levels of aid from state to state. President Nixon's welfare reform had included recommendations for the federalization of the adult categories, and this was the one part of that program that the Congress enacted (in the fall of 1972). As mentioned in the previous chapter, the new law decreed that the Social Security Administration should, on and after January 1, 1974, take over from the Social and Rehabilitation Service, the basic responsibility for all income maintenance for the aged, the blind, and the disabled. States will be permitted to supplement the federal payments if the benefit levels established by the federal government—$130 monthly for an aged person and $195 for an aged couple—are deemed insufficient in their states.

The effect of the federalization of the adult categories (called the Supplemental Security Income Program), and of the assurance of higher levels of payment to these beneficiaries than most states allow for families with dependent children, and of the assignment of the new program to the Social Security Administration, is to leave the Social and Rehabilitation Service even more conspicuously in the role of "manager of the welfare mess." It has an assignment with which it cannot possibly earn a good reputation.

ORGANIZATION AND ADMINISTRATION OF WELFARE

For most of the 35-year history of public assistance, it was administered by a small, clearly understaffed Bureau of Public Assistance, renamed the Bureau of Family Services in 1963. In that year, it had 393 employees divided about evenly between Washington and the ten regional offices. Most of the state plan review and appraisal of state operations was conducted by regional office personnel.

In January, 1963, Secretary Anthony Celebrezze separated the welfare programs from the Social Security Administration, created a new Welfare Administration, and simultaneously upgraded the Office of Vocational Rehabilitation to the new title of Vocational Rehabilitation Administration. The Welfare Administration was composed of the Bureau of Family Services, the Children's Bureau, the Office of Aging, and the Office of Juvenile Delinquency. Four years later, Secretary John Gardner decided that the time had come to see if some of the benefits of the highly successful Vocational Rehabilitation Administration (VRA) could be transferred to the field of welfare by bringing together the VRA and the Welfare Administration and putting the long-time and distinguished commissioner of VRA, Mary Switzer, in charge of the combined operation. The organization that emerged—the Social and Rehabilitation Service (SRS)—continued essentially as it was then created until 1973 when its services for the aging and juvenile delinquency were moved to the office of the Secretary.

In the reorganization, the functions of the Bureau of Family Services were divided among three administrations: the Assistance Payments Administration, the Community Services Administration, and the Medical Services Administration. The most important single reason for this breakup of the Bureau of Family Services was the strong desire to emphasize a new policy that had been decided upon. The Department wanted to make it very clear that the determination of eligibility for public assistance was an entirely separate function from the provision of counseling and other social services. By 1967, when this reorganization occurred, the proponents of the Negative Income Tax had come into prominence and were making much of the demeaning mixture of paternalism and dole that they said characterized the welfare system. Clear separation of the functions of determining eligibility from "constructive social services," supported by the social workers themselves, was intended to enhance the dignity of both the clients and the professional social workers.

The Assistance Payments Administration

To counteract further the arguments of the "negative income taxers" about the demeaning nature of the means test and as a result of pressure from the welfare client groups, the new Assistance Payments Administration launched a campaign to simplify the application process and operate on the assumption that the vast majority of applicants for welfare were honest. They sponsored tests of the "short form," which could be filled out easily and quickly and required no home investigation to determine the eligibility of most applicants. The tests indicated very low levels of dishonesty in filling out the forms. On the basis of this seeming success, Secretary Cohen was so anxious to have the system adopted nationwide that he issued a regulation shortly before he left office that would require all states to test the short form and, if it proved successful, adopt it promptly in their states. By 1972, all states used the method for the adult categories and half used it for AFDC cases.

While the pressure was coming from one side to increase the simplicity and dignity of the means test, pressure on the other was coming to get rid of the cheaters on the fast-growing welfare rolls. Senator Robert Byrd of West Virginia had long been suspicious of laxity in the administration of welfare and was a leader in efforts to minimize illegal and improper payments. He advocated tracking down deserting fathers, identifying the "man-in-the-house," and doing a more thorough job of checking on eligibility and possible cheating (through such actions as nondisclosure of income). The two pressures stemmed from opposite philosophical orientations and have been difficult to accomodate in practice.*

Not too many years ago, HEW used to make a point of its extremely low ratio of administrative costs to total payments to states and individuals. Administrative costs have been about *one-quarter of a cent per dollar* of total payments to states and individuals. Year after year, articles in national magazines have railed against the high administrative costs of federal bureaucracies, skimming off "up to 25 per cent" before the taxpayers' funds were returned to the states. This—the largest federal grant program—has probably skimmed off too little.

The Community Services Administration

Well before social services and eligibility determination were organizationally separated, the Bureau of Family Services was moving toward emphasis on constructive social services. Limited and not too conclusive studies seemed to tell the social work profession what it wanted to hear—that intensive individual casework, involving counseling, testing, and referral to appropriate agencies, could help families become self-reliant and no longer dependent on welfare. The idea combined humanitarianism

---

* Some indication as to which of these pressures was most successful in the preparation of the 1973–74 budget may be judged by HEW's request for the largest one-year staff increase in the history of the administration of public assistance—725 positions—"to provide better management of the public assistance program."

and the prospect of long-range economy and was not too difficult to sell to the Congress. The Social Security Act Amendments of 1965 reflected this concept by offering premium payments to states for constructive social services. Such social services had been matched 50-50 as part of normal administrative costs. The new amendments increased the matching to three federal dollars for every one state or local dollar spent on such social services. It was the beginning of a social service bonanza.

The theory at this stage was that case loads were generally so large that intensive casework was usually impossible. States were told that if they hired enough caseworkers to reduce their loads to fewer than sixty cases per worker, they would qualify for the 75 per cent matching funds. Many more caseworkers were taken on, but a major difficulty was the shortage of well-trained people. How much good the additional personnel were able to do will never be known. No definitive control studies were made.

Then with the 1967 Social Security Amendments came the opening of Pandora's box. Mary Switzer had just been appointed to head the newly formed Social and Rehabilitation Service, and with her long background in vocational rehabilitation, she wanted to draw on some of SRS's successes to improve the welfare program. Rehabilitation agencies operate by having a complete analysis made of the rehabilitation needs of each candidate and then contracting with the various community health and education agencies, first to restore the individual physically as fully as feasible, and then to provide suitable occupational training or retraining. Miss Switzer wanted to adapt the same idea to welfare clients. Up to then, the law had not authorized federal participation in payments from state and local welfare agencies to other community agencies for services purchased for their welfare clients. On the recommendation of Mary Switzer and HEW, the 1967 SSA Amendments contained such an authorization. Unfortunately, it did not have the necessary safeguards, and it opened up what became, after her retirement and death, a multibillion dollar Treasury raid.

Suddenly a few of the sophisticated states discovered the gold mine. There was no upper limit to the federal matching agreement, nor was there anything to prevent the welfare agencies from contracting with other state agencies, not to mention Community Chest agencies, and others to perform services on behalf of welfare clients—and *potential* clients—which they had been performing for years without federal subsidy. And now, for every state or local dollar spent, they would get three federal dollars. California led the way in developing ingenious devices to obtain federal matching funds without actually performing new or added functions. The states could then rebudget the funds they had been using for these purposes. It took a while for all the states to realize that they had struck it rich, but by 1972 there were very few states not reacting to this as a heaven-sent form of revenue-sharing that existed whether or not the Administration's general revenue-sharing bill was enacted. The situation was clearly out of control.

Federal expenditures for social services were approximately $346 million in 1968. They reached $1,598 million in 1972. An informal tally in the summer of 1972 of the potential state claims for federal matching funds for 1972–73 totaled nearly $5 billion. Seeing this, Congress slapped a $2.5 billion limit on federal grants for social services in 1972–73.

In this situation, the Social and Rehabilitation Service and its Community Service Administration as well as HEW officials found themselves ambivalent. On the one hand, they saw great needs for constructive social services that had been underfinanced for years and, on the other, they realized that to an undetermined degree some of the states were "taking Uncle Sam for a ride." Some of the social services involved were: child welfare services, family planning services, group care of children, services to unmarried mothers, adoption services, homemaker services, prevention of serious child abuse, foster family care, services for mentally retarded children, day-care services, research and training in respect to child welfare problems and practices, occupational counseling and referral for public assistance recipients, and services to the aged, handicapped, and disabled. Their keen awareness of the importance and shortage of such services caused some HEW and SRS officials to be more concerned to see that the federal spigot was not abruptly shut off or constricted than to assure that the added federal funds did not simply supplant state, local, and private funds. Even White House officials showed concern when state governors protested any abrupt cut off. Nobody seemed to know for what the funds were being spent; perhaps the auditors would find out later.

This is an excellent example of the extraordinary importance of careful program design and legal drafting of both law and regulations in respect to open-ended grant programs in which the federal government agrees to match all state and local expenditures for specified purposes with no upper limit. Unfortunately, this function has never been performed with the care it deserves, either by HEW or by Congress.

Despite the debacle of 1972, constructive social services represent a vital component of HEW responsibilities to which too little attention has been paid. Those who believe that a good negative income tax would solve most of the poor's problems should spend a bit of time in the company of a social worker dealing with multiproblem families.

The Medical Services Administration and Medicaid

Medical assistance to needy persons, like so many other subjects covered here, deserves a volume to itself. Space permits touching on only a few highlights.

The original 1935 Social Security Act made no special provision for the medical treatment of needy people. States could provide additional cash to needy people to pay their doctor bills, but this did not work well. In 1950, Congress authorized a "vendor payment" plan, with the state public assistance agencies making payments, under agreed fee schedules, to doctors and hospitals for the necessary medical care of public assistance recipients. By 1960, it had become apparent that an enlarged medical assistance program was needed to take care of the numerous aged and disabled people who did not need public assistance for normal maintenance but who had no reserves for expensive illness. The result was the enactment of the Kerr-Mills bill, named after the late Senator Robert Kerr from Oklahoma and Congressman Wilbur Mills, who were the bill's two principal sponsors.

What we now know as Medicaid, administered by the Medical Services Administration, was a natural outgrowth of the Kerr-Mills bill. In 1965, the Social Security Act Amendments authorized a consolidated and expanded medical assistance program now universally called Medicaid, and even authorized the inclusion of fully employed low-income families. The basic coverage required by this legislation now includes in-patient hospital care, out-patient services, laboratory and X-ray services, skilled nursing home services for people over twenty-one, screening and treatment for persons under twenty-one, physicians' services, and home health services. States have the option of including such additional services as prescription drugs, dental services, eyeglasses, hearing aids, and even chiropractors' services. In consequence, no two state plans are alike; they have a wide range.

New York and California led the way in taking advantage of the liberal provisions of the Medicaid law, covering not only those eligible for public assistance, but near-poor, full-time workers and their families as well. What the legislators and executive policy-makers had not counted in their calculations was the elasticity of the demand for medical services, and the readiness of the medical profession to respond to the pent-up demand of those who had relied on Mother Nature and home remedies for much of their lives. The following brief table shows what happened after Medicaid became effective in 1966:

PUBLIC EXPENDITURES FOR MEDICAL ASSISTANCE

Fiscal Year	New York Expenditures*	California Expenditures*	Total National Expenditures*
1965	$ 202,692	$ 186,335	$1,255,652
1966	230,414	294,974	1,591,620
1967	495,832	549,157	2,270,996
1968	1,006,475	616,465	3,451,376
1969	1,235,403	759,330	4,273,439
1970	1,195,404	974,202	4,807,535
1971	1,477,086	1,019,770	5,939,236
1972	1,999,039	988,700	7,374,872

* Includes federal, state, and local monies.

For all practical purposes, the era of charity medicine ended with the start of the Medicaid program. By 1974, it was estimated that 27 million people would be receiving benefits under the Medicaid law. Doctors collected their bills from governmental agencies and agents, a few drawing as much as $200,000 a year from their Medicaid payments alone. The drain on state treasuries became so heavy that several states, with New York again in the forefront, tightened their eligibility regulations and their systems of administration. New York required the medically needy to pay 20 per cent of their bills for services other than for patient care in a medical institution.

The authors of Medicaid could not have realized the extent to which the law would contribute to the "blue collar blues." Few low- and moderate-income workers have health insurance with as broad coverage and protection against prolonged illness as that provided by many Medicaid plans. Catastrophic illness could throw them into bankruptcy. From a medical standpoint, they are now the forgotten people. The piecemeal approach to social ills often exacerbates problems lying just at the fringes of the difficulties it tries to solve.

Rehabilitation of the Disabled

While the program of Aid to Families with Dependent Children became a steadily larger drain on the federal Treasury with each passing year, and more unpopular with the voters of all political persuasions, a companion program was growing larger and simultaneously more popular. This was the program of rehabilitating the disabled, primarily the physically handicapped—and enabling them to acquire new vocations and become self-supporting. The contrast between the evolution of the two programs is interesting and, to some degree, instructive.

The federal government first became involved in rehabilitation of the handicapped in 1920, when it enacted Public Law 236 (Sixty-sixth Congress) "for the rehabilitation of persons disabled in industry or otherwise." The "otherwise" did not refer to veterans disabled during World War I; these were taken care of through separate legislation. Public Law 236 authorized 50–50 matching of state and local expenditures up to a total of $1 million in federal expenditures. The program was administered by a newly created Federal Board for Vocational Education, located in the Department of the Interior alongside the Office of Education.

With the increase in the industrialization of the nation, spurred by the automobile boom of the 1920's, and with very little safety regulation of working conditions to protect workers from the increasing number of hazardous machines, it is not surprising that both industrial accidents and automobile accidents increased dramatically. Disabilities from poliomyelitis and other crippling diseases and numerous congenital handicaps also afflicted hundreds of thousands of persons, most of whom simply bore them stoically.

After the United States's entry into World War II, there was a sudden turnabout in the labor market, with the nation needing to put all its available manpower into the feverish war effort. The reservoir of disabled and handicapped people who might perform useful service, if rehabilitated, became conspicuous. Lengthy hearings were held in the House Committee on Education and Labor, resulting in the enactment of the Barden-LaFollette Act, the first comprehensive vocational rehabilitation program authorized by the federal government.

The Barden-LaFollette Act of 1943 established a new Office of Vocational Rehabilitation in the Federal Security Agency and directed that it conduct a program of federal grants to assure that each state could provide the following range of services:

- Early location of persons in need of rehabilitation to prevent the disintegrating effects of idleness and hopelessness.
- Medical diagnosis and prognosis as the basis for a plan of rehabilitation.
- Vocational counseling.
- Medical and surgical treatment to overcome static handicapping conditions.
- Physical and occupational therapy, when needed.
- Vocational training to develop new skills.
- Financial assistance to needy persons for maintenance and transportation.
- Placement services to help rehabilitated persons find jobs.
- Follow-up services to avoid retrogression during the initial difficult period.

Public support was substantial for the development of greatly enlarged programs using the new matching formula that made it easier for the poor states to emphasize vocational rehabilitation. Vocational rehabilitation began a significant upward climb after the enactment of the new law, and within a few years all forty-eight states had enacted legislation to take advantage of the federal grant program. In 1950, Mary E. Switzer was appointed director of the Office of Vocational Rehabilitation, and she became a talented promoter of the interests of the handicapped. She was a career civil servant who had entered the Treasury Department in 1922 as a junior economist, fresh out of Radcliffe, and had worked her way up to adviser to the Secretary of the Treasury on matters concerned with public health (until the Public Health Service was moved to the new Federal Security Agency in 1939), and then adviser to the Federal Security Administrator on health matters. She became a legend in her time, one of the most successful program advocates in Washington. The HEW South Building became, in January, 1973, the Mary E. Switzer Memorial Building.

Miss Switzer was aided in her enthusiastic promotion of vocational rehabilitation by the results of a study made in the late 1940's that showed that the costs of rehabilitating each person, on the average, would eventually be returned ten times over to the federal Treasury. This did not mean that every case would render such profit, of course, but it did assert that the taxes that would be paid by the average rehabilitated worker, assuming he worked for the rest of a normal working lifetime at the wage rates being paid him a year after his rehabilitation, would be ten times as large as the average federal outlay for his rehabilitation.

This was one of the earliest examples of cost-benefit analysis of social programs within the U.S. Government. Its technical quality left something to be desired, but its impact on policy-makers did not. Vocational rehabilitation became, and remained, the one program of all federal social programs to which government policy-makers turned when asked, "Do these programs ever pay for themselves?" It became a showpiece.

During the eighteen years of Miss Switzer's leadership, the number of persons rehabilitated annually increased from 66,000 (1951) to 241,000 (1969). Although the cost per average rehabilitation rose substantially during this period, so, too, did wages so that there was still a high ratio of benefits to costs, but with far more rehabilitants. "Taxpayers, not tax-eaters," became the slogan of the Vocational Rehabilitation Program.

The contrast between the success of the Vocational Rehabilitation Program and the failure of the "welfare program" (meaning Aid to Families with Dependent Children) to get people into gainful employment and self-reliant status could hardly have been greater. The AFDC program was not designed, of course, as a rehabilitation program, but as an income maintenance program; nevertheless, the public seemed to expect those responsible for administering AFDC to do something that would stem the alarming growth in the number of beneficiaries. That expectation was eventually reflected in the action of Secretary John Gardner in establishing the Social and Rehabilitation Service, bringing together welfare and rehabilitation, and putting Mary Switzer, then aged sixty-eight, in charge of the combined enterprise. It was too late. If it ever did have a reasonable chance of success, the idea of applying vocational rehabilitation approaches and techniques to welfare mothers in sufficient numbers to make a major difference in the size of the welfare rolls would have had a far greater chance if started a decade or more earlier. Conceptually, it had merit, but practically, it has not been very successful.

It would be easy to exaggerate the design failures of AFDC as a cause of our current large welfare load and overemphasize the merits of the vocational rehabilitation law and its administration. But there is a far more subtle reason for the contrast. A large proportion of the clients of the Vocational Rehabilitation Program are, as its name implies, being *re*habilitated. Many are the victims of auto accidents, home accidents, work-connected accidents, and illnesses that prevent them from continuing in a previously chosen occupation. The vast majority of these people have acquired the discipline of work and the confidence that they can succeed at something. Others may have had a handicap since birth or early childhood but have spent much of their young lives learning that they can rise above a handicap that fate has dealt them. Both of these groups are motivated to prove to themselves and their associates that they can do more than society might reasonably expect of them. Nothing is more important to the success of any human being than attitude.

Many of those who have sought help from the welfare program, on the other hand, have been psychologically defeated people. If they ever had any self-confidence, it has been ground down before they ever show up at the welfare agency. For them, the psychological situation is exactly the reverse of the handicapped rehabilitant. Society expects more of them than they can produce at the same time that it denies them work opportunities at which they might have some chance of gaining at least modest self-confidence. Society has treated them cruelly, they feel, and they can expect little from either society or themselves. They lapse into a defensive and often apathetic attitude. This is not intended to be a characterization of the whole of the AFDC case load, but it is true of a sufficiently large proportion to warrant a different public expectation than that which usually prevails.

VI

Education

After the New Deal successfully launched the social welfare revolution in this country, by initiating Social Security and accepting major responsibility for welfare, education became a second lever in changing the relationship between Americans and their government. Even though historians emphasize that federal aid for education began with the Land Ordinance of 1785, sustained federal aid did not come until there was a basic change in American society, brought about by the Great Depression, World War II, technology, urbanization, and the postwar baby boom.

THE LONG ROAD TO FEDERAL ADMISSION OF RESPONSIBILITY

The Founding Fathers were undeniably prescient and wise in respect to education. The Land Ordinance of 1785 provided that the public domain, extending from Canada to Mexico, and from the Appalachians to the Mississippi, was to be sold, and that one thirty-sixth of the land was to be dedicated for schools. One square mile section ("Lot #16") in every township of thirty-six square miles was to be set aside for educational purposes. Two years later, the Northwest Ordinance said: "Religion, morality, and knowledge, being necessary to good government and the happiness of mankind, schools and the means of education shall forever be encouraged." For more than a century thereafter, land grants were the principal tangible evidence of that encouragement, so far as the federal government was concerned.

139

The practice of dedicating public land, or the proceeds from its sale, to education was a brilliant conception of the founders of the Republic, and one that was continued as the lands west of the Mississippi were opened for settlement. The importance of this practice to the development of public education has been too little recognized. The total of federal land grants for educational purposes came to more than 175 million acres. Without such a foundation, the evolution of public schools would probably have proceeded at a much slower pace and compulsory education might have been delayed for decades.

This farsighted action by the Congress was, however, not so much the beginning of a tradition of federal aid and support of public education as the affirmation of responsibility by the state governments for public education. In 1803, the year of the Louisiana Purchase, Congress vested in the state legislatures the control of the land it had dedicated for educational purposes. In a sense, Congress did its noble deed—which cost it nothing—and then washed its hands of further significant responsibility for supporting education for well over half a century.

When it revived its interest in the late 1860's, Congress focused on the need for education and research in the practical arts. Church-sponsored colleges were springing up all over the Midwest, but none of these placed particular emphasis on the needs of farmers for better understanding of agricultural sciences. The Land Grant College Act of 1862 (Morrill Act) was explicitly directed toward the development of institutions for the encouragement of the agricultural and mechanic arts. This was the foundation stone for the great state university systems of the nation. Again, Congress did its good deed and with one exception retreated into its shell for another three decades, coming out just long enough to pass the Second Morrill Act making modest annual cash grants to state universities.

The exception occurred in 1867 when Congress thought it desirable to show its continuing interest in education by creating a small, non-Cabinet Department of Education, renamed the Bureau of Education in 1870 and located in the Department of the Interior. In 1934, it became the Office of Education. Its mission was "to collect such statistics and facts as should show the condition and progress of education, to diffuse such information as shall aid the people of the United States in the establishment and maintenance of efficient school systems, and otherwise to promote the cause of education." From its creation until World War II, some seventy years later, the Office of Education remained largely a token of federal concern for education, never having funds for the support of elementary and secondary education, and only having responsibility for a routine distribution of a small set sum to land-grant colleges. Even during World War I, when the federal government decided to underwrite vocational education through the enactment of the Smith-Hughes Act, responsibility for its administration was not put in the Office of Education but in a separate Board for Vocational Education.

The Office of Education was not without men of vision during these seven decades. Philander P. Claxton, for example, appointed by President William H. Taft and serving through all of Woodrow Wilson's two terms, had high hopes for the federal role in education. He was imaginative in his concepts and a national missionary for the extension of educational opportunity to all citizens of the nation but he had minuscule financial resources. He and John W. Studebaker (1934–48) did more with less money than any other commissioners in the century-long history of the Office of Education.

In the light of Claxton's outstanding reputation, and especially in view of subsequent history, President Warren G. Harding's removal of Claxton from office in the spring of 1921 is of special interest. Following his inauguration, Harding asked Claxton to prepare a bill establishing a separate Cabinet-level Department of Education and Welfare, with the implicit understanding that Claxton would be made its Secretary. Claxton complied with the request but sent word to the President that he did not approve of the bill. Claxton felt strongly that there should be a nonpartisan National Board of Education, which would meet quarterly and would select an executive officer of the highest ability and stature. This was in the reformist tradition of the late nineteenth and early twentieth centuries when it was thought that the only way to improve and purify the administration of public functions was to remove them as far as possible from the immediate influence of politically elected officials. Harding's plan went to Congress where it was buried, and Claxton's resignation by request became the unfortunate result of the disagreement. Harding is not frequently remembered as the first President to try to establish a Cabinet-level department dealing with education and welfare.

Dynamics of the Demand for Federal Aid

Not until another quarter century elapsed did the profound change begin in the federal role in education. When the Office of Education was transferred to the Federal Security Agency in 1939 it had about 219 permanent employees and a budget of $28 million, compared with about 160 employees and about $11 million for comparable functions in 1930. In the aftermath of World War II, education turned out to be the fastest growing public industry in the country and continued so for over two decades, multiplying federal expenditures through the Office of Education more than a hundredfold. The interrelated factors that caused this explosive increase and radically changed the federal role are not well understood. There were seven of them:

1. The postwar baby boom. Demographers had predicted a short-lived baby boom after World War II, as had occurred after World War I, but American parents crossed them up. The number of babies born each year kept on going up for more than a decade after the war, and even when the crest of the boom was reached in 1957, the baby crop continued very large well into the 1960's. The result was a completely unforeseen and unprecedented demand for new schools, for more teachers, and for all the educational paraphernalia that went with them. The cost was extremely high, so high as to overburden most local school districts that were primarily dependent on real property taxes for both operating and capital expenditures. The baby boom was probably the single greatest factor in the ultimately successful demand for federal aid to education.

2. Enlarged educational aspirations. Upward mobility has been the hallmark of American society. Better than riches, to many American parents, was the thought that their children might become doctors, lawyers, architects, teachers—the respected professions of the Old World. The Depression had put a damper on these aspirations, but World War II and its aftermath revived them. Congress nourished these dreams by enacting the "GI Bill of Rights," providing education and training allowances to all who had served in the armed forces. The colleges and universities thus felt the boom in the educational industry more quickly than any other sector. But eventually the postwar babies grew into teen-agers, eager to leave home and find out what college life was like. And when that eventually happened, the GI bulge in college en-rollment in the late 1940's seemed small and easy to absorb by comparison. College enrollment was to skyrocket from just over 2 million students in 1946 to over 8 million in 1972–73 when the college boom came to at least a temporary end. Over half of all Americans between eighteen and twenty attended school or college in 1972–73, by far the largest percentage of any country in the world. Especially during the 1960's and early 1970's, the college boom has been close to the center of American social change.

3. *Urbanization and specialization.* Not only high aspirations, but urbanization, technology, and specialization put pressure on students to increase their education. Urbanization and technology took an unprecedented forward leap during and after World War II, and with it came the necessity to get a lengthy education to get a good job.

4. *Federally generated burdens on local school districts.* The sudden build-up of industrial and military installations during World War II and the Korean war became a justification for tem-porary and then continuing federal aid on a completely unfore-seen scale—up to $612 million in 1972. The war installations had to have workers, and the workers' children had to have schools. Three laws—the Lanham Act during World War II and Public Laws 815 and 874 (Eighty-first Congress)—authorized payments for the construction and operation of schools in areas overburdened by nontaxable federal installations. Once on the books, these last two laws were treated by Congress as a peace-time substitute for some form of payment-in-lieu-of-taxes by the federal government to more than three thousand school districts for the education of children of federal workers who either lived or worked on federal property, or both.

5. *Equal educational opportunity.* The Civil Rights Act of 1964 thrust upon HEW, with the aid of the Justice Department, the task of offering money both as carrot and stick to bring about the desegregation of schools. Title VI of that Act directed the withholding of federal funds from noncomplying school districts, and Title IV authorized the granting of funds to school districts

that needed financial help to desegregate. This led the way to substantial federal payments.

6. *Sputnik and its aftermath.* The very idea that the Soviets could shame American technologists by their Sputnik in 1957 was enough to generate support in Congress for whatever it might take to overcome the scientific, or at least the technological, lead that this event had dramatized. The Space Age was upon us and so were the educational demands that went with it.

7. *A rapidly growing GNP.* Until the Vietnam war strained the nation and drained its pocketbook, the GNP was sufficient to provide not only for a rising material livelihood for the great majority of the American people, but to provide a surplus out of which a growing allocation could be made to education without great difficulty. In fact, heavy investments in education were generally expected to result in more than corresponding increases in the GNP—after a time lag, of course. Accelerating expenditures for education and a rapidly growing GNP were, until Vietnam took precedence, mutually reinforcing trends.

These seven changes that occurred in the wake of World War II piled a second large set of responsibilities on HEW. Federal aid for education was certainly stimulated by Franklin Roosevelt's reorientation of the American mind toward government financing of any important and universal function that overburdened local and state governments. In the two decades following World War II, nothing seemed more important to the American public than educating its children. Federal aid to education in multiple billions became the inexorable result.

The Act That Broke the Ice

In the late 1940's, President Harry Truman sought to get Congress to approve general aid for elementary and secondary education, but he failed. The influential Republican Senator Robert Taft also had a bill for "general aid" that might easily have been reconciled with Truman's, but it was to no avail. The Congress still felt that education belongs to the states and should remain that way. After Dwight Eisenhower became President in 1953, and after the ending of the Korean war eased the condition of the federal budget, pressures from hard-pressed school districts began to build up the demand for federal financial assistance.

Eisenhower resisted those pressures as long as he could until Secretary Marion B. Folsom persuaded him he could no longer hold back. (See Chapter II.) That was 1956. But still the Congress balked, for reasons that Stephen K. Bailey has characterized as "Red, Religion, and Race." The "Red" referred to the apprehension that federal aid to education meant federal control of what was to be taught, one of the surest evidences in the minds of many that it would lead to socialism and communism.

Russia's Sputnik changed the picture. Right after the Sputnik spectacular, Secretary Folsom appointed his assistant secretary, Elliot Richardson, to head a task force to develop a bill that would capitalize on the nation's desire to catch up with the Russians. Folsom, Richardson, and the officials of the Office of Education agreed that the bill should not be so narrowly drawn as to become merely a crash program to overcome the Russians' lead in space. The elements of the bill—which was carefully and strategically titled the National Defense Education Act (NDEA)—can be seen as a blend of efforts to build up the nation's scientific and technical competence, and to provide a vehicle for channeling funds to substandard schools for designated purposes that had some relation to building up the scientific and technological capacity of the nation or had some other supportive relation to the national defense. These were its main features:

- Support for guidance, counseling, and testing to assure that those with latent talent, especially scientific talent, were identified and properly encouraged to develop their skills.
- Aid for expanding and improving the teaching of science, mathematics, and foreign languages.
- Vocational training on an areawide basis.
- Support for training more college teachers and specialists in the language and culture of areas about which Americans were comparatively ignorant.
- Research in the use of television and other modern media.
- Loans to qualified and needy college students.

The NDEA appropriations were small in relation to the need, beginning with less than $50 million, and gradually moving up to more than $200 million, but the law stood as evidence that it was possible to get the nation's lawmakers to use federal tax resources to expand federal aid to education if only the right formula could be found.

The Kennedy Prelude to the Final Break-through

Increasingly, the central legislative hang-up seemed to be the religious issue, and on that score the election of John F. Kennedy was advantageous for the public school forces. Being a Catholic who carried the necessary credentials with the rank and file laity of the Church but who paid little heed to the political views of its leaders, he could take positions that would have been called anti-Catholic if they had come from others. Yet his election was so narrow that he decided to begin by seeking federal aid in an area where the church issue was of minor consequence: higher education. The College Facilities and Scholarship Act of 1961 was promptly introduced and eventually passed both houses in different form but died when the House refused to pass the conference committee's report. Meanwhile, Sterling McMurrin, Kennedy's first comissioner of Education, was trying continuously, along with Abraham Ribicoff and Wilbur Cohen, to find some way out of the maze of conflicting views on the kind of bill the Administration should sponsor to aid elementary and secondary schools, a struggle that waxed and waned for two years.

McMurrin passed the baton to his successor, Francis Keppel, in December, 1962, and within a month the Administration had put the finishing touches on its new federal aid bill, introduced by Congressman Adam Clayton Powell on January 29, 1963, as H.R. 3000. It was an omnibus bill that had something for everybody, including the higher educators, the vocational educators, and the advocates of general aid for elementary and secondary schools. But its beneficiaries were more competitors than co-operators, and it did not take long for the omnibus bill to be split up into separate bills. In November, 1963, the wrangling on two of the bills was brought to an abrupt end by the assassination of President Kennedy, and both became law the following month. They were called the Higher Education Facilities Act of 1963 and the Vocational Education Act of 1963. Both were important pieces of legislation, but in the Kennedy Administration's Thousand Days, the President had been unable to achieve what he had especially wanted—a general aid law for elementary and secondary schools. It was to be another year and a half before it finally happened.

The Johnson Congress and Fast Enactment of ESEA

Even after Kennedy's death, the warring factions could not agree during Lyndon Johnson's first year as President on an aid-to-education bill that could make it through Congress. Commissioner Keppel spent most of his time on this, treating it as his main mission. Although some progress was made, it was not until Johnson's sweeping victory of 1964 that there suddenly appeared a bright future for federal aid. White House and HEW strategists decided to come forward with a new bill, one destined to have a happier fate than earlier efforts.

The Eighty-ninth Congress, which came into office in January, 1965, was undoubtedly the most liberal Congress on domestic issues in the history of the country. Some might rephrase it to say that after the Johnson landslide in which many new congressmen slid into office, there was a very strong predisposition to follow the powerful President's lead in respect to almost any domestic legislation he asked for. Johnson's reputation for "jaw-boning and arm-twisting" had an indirect but potent effect on many congressmen who had never experienced "the treatment" directly. The conditions were perfect for the eager beavers in the White House and in the departments and agencies to help their expansive and enthusiastic leader launch his Great Society programs.

Douglas Cater, as White House negotiator, Francis Keppel, the commissioner of Education, and Wilbur Cohen, HEW assistant secretary for Legislation, agreed that an entirely new bill should be drawn up. With the active participation of key staff of the Office of Education and the Bureau of the Budget, they developed one in a hurry—probably too much of a hurry, as it turned out. The bill went to Congress on January 12, 1965, even before inauguration day. The rapidity with which it was enacted surprised even its authors. It took less than three months to run the legislative gauntlet, and it might have taken even less if Adam Clayton Powell had not taken advantage of his strategic position as chairman of the House Committee on Education and Labor to insist on certain appointments in the Office of Education. The most influential members of Powell's committee—Carl Perkins of Kentucky, Edith Green of Oregon, John Brademas of Indiana, and Frank Thompson of New Jersey—gave strong support to the bill, and the changes were minimal. In a sentimental ceremony at Stonewall, Texas, in the one-room schoolhouse where his schooling began, Lyndon Johnson signed the bill on April 11, 1965, in the presence of the teacher who had taught him there.

The Elementary and Secondary Education Act of 1965 (ESEA) authorized the appropriation of $1.3 billion in 1966, and larger amounts in subsequent years for the following purposes:

- $1 billion to local school districts to aid "educationally deprived children," meaning children from low-income families.
- A 2-year extension of aid to school districts overburdened with tax-free federal installations.
- Supplementary educational centers and services to provide counseling, remedial instruction, vocational guidance, new teaching methods, creative uses of mass media and other services available to parochial as well as public school students and teachers.
- Support for educational television and radio and mobile educational services.
- Aid to states for school library resources, textbooks and other instructional materials for children and teachers in public and private elementary and secondary schools (a major concession to the parochial school lobby).
- Educational research, operated largely on a project grant basis, and funds for the operation of regional research laboratories.
- Funds for strengthening state departments of education.

The ESEA was baptized with high hopes that it would begin, in Johnson's words, "a new day of greatness in American society." Its birth came four months before American bombs started raining down on North Vietnam. Both Presidential and public attention were soon diverted from the wars on poverty and illiteracy to a strange and sad test of American military might halfway around the world. Johnson had undoubtedly expected the funding of federal aid to elementary and secondary education to move up rapidly from its initial billion-dollar level, but the money he had hoped to use for a purpose so close to his heart bought bombs instead of books. During the remainder of his Presidency, Johnson's budget for ESEA never got above $1.5 billion.

Unfortunately, too, the delay that occurred in providing funds for the ESEA, coupled with the failure to provide adequate lead time in the law, started it off under a cloud. Congress did not finish its action on the appropriation bill until fall—a chronic failing of the Congress with more serious consequences than is generally realized—and many school districts did not get their 1965–66 grant funds until the spring of 1966, when the only thing they could do with them was to splurge on new equipment. Equipment manufacturers with the slickest gadgetry and the fastest talking salesmen had a field day. It was a bad start from which ESEA never fully recovered. More than most programs enacted during the legislative outpouring of the Great Society, this one needed the most careful kind of planning and administration. Unlike most other grant laws, it had no requirement for state or local financial matching—a common practice to increase local responsibility for the prudent expenditure of funds—and, therefore, was in extreme need of first-rate management oversight with ample lead time. It got neither. Administrators are still trying to make up for the handicap of that bad start.

LEGISLATING FOR VOCATIONAL, TECHNICAL, AND ADULT EDUCATION

The blockage of general aid for education in the years 1961 to 1965 may have been advantageous for the less controversial grant programs in the field of vocational education. The pressure was on Congress for some form of action in respect to educational aid, and vocational education was the first beneficiary. It was a long-accepted form of aid, having been in existence since 1917. The Budget Bureau hoped it would be phased out when some form of general aid was finally enacted, but, as we shall see, the political judgment of the Budget Bureau left a good deal to be desired.

Earmarked grants for specific forms of vocational education, authorized in 1917, were the earliest form of continuing federal aid for public schools. After the Smith-Lever Act of 1914, creating the Agricultural Extension Service, had pioneered conditional federal grants to states, vocational education was not far behind. Shortly after the United States entry into World War

I, the Smith-Hughes Act of 1917 provided grants to states with the stipulation that the money be used for four types of vocational training, intended initially to aid the war effort, and subsequently to help the nation's economy: trades, industrial skills, agricultural methods and practice, and home economics. Administered by an independent Board for Vocational Education until its functions were transferred to the Office of Education in 1933, this grant program developed a nationwide group of vocational teachers whose salaries came, in part, from clearly identifiable federal grants. It is hardly surprising that they founded in 1929 the American Vocational Association (AVA) and that the AVA subsequently developed an extremely effective lobby on behalf of vocational programs.

Distributive education—training in the retail trades—was added in 1936. During World War II, short, intensive occupational training took a big jump, and after the war vocational education got an additional boost from the enactment of the George-Barden Act of 1946 which enlarged the programs considerably. So it continued for nearly a decade until the Bureau of the Budget decided in 1955 that parts of the program had served their purpose and ought to be phased out. A cut of a mere $1 million in the vocational education appropriation seemed to the Bureau of the Budget to be modest and reasonable but that was enough to galvanize the AVA into a frenzy of defensive lobbying. Once it had marshalled its troops, it decided to take the offensive and seek what it thought was an overdue increase in the level of federal funding. It had no difficulty in persuading Congress to add $5 million instead of cutting $1 million, bringing the annual appropriation up to $23.7 million. Having succeeded once, why not try again? The following year, the AVA got Congress to add another $3 million to the President's budget and then another $5 million the year after that. The vocational education lobby had graduated into the big leagues and had become alert to its opportunities and sophisticated about exploiting them.

After the election of President Kennedy, the Office of Education, with the support of the AVA, recommended that the President appoint a committee to study the whole field of vocational education in relation to the skill needs of the economy and the aptitudes of the numerous high school students who were becoming disenchanted with the traditional curriculum and were dropping out of school. The result of the study was a recommendation for a substantially enlarged program of federal aid for vocational training, which culminated in the Vocational Education Act of 1963, increasing and extending the existing programs, adding authorizations for teacher training and curriculum development, and providing greater flexibility in programming.

In the decade from 1963 to 1973, federal appropriations for basic vocational educational programs grew from $60 million to $384 million and the scope of the vocational enterprise was greatly enlarged. States have been encouraged to restructure the curriculums to emphasize career planning and development. Special programs for the disadvantaged to help combat problems of youth unemployment and delinquency, cooperative education programs that combine work experience with schooling, work-study programs that provide financial assistance to disadvantaged students to help them stay in school, and consumer and home-maker education all have received specially earmarked funds. In addition, funds have continued to go to the basic vocational pro-grams. Still more millions have become available for research and demonstration projects.

Closely related in various ways to vocational education is adult education. Adult basic education—principally literacy training—was covered under the Economic Opportunity Act of 1964 and, two years later, following enactment of the Adult Education Act of 1966, became a function of the Office of Education, together with a variety of other activities authorized by that Act. The 1966 Act stressed types of training that would aid adults to prepare themselves for better jobs.

All told, appropriations for occupational, vocational, and adult education reached the half-billion dollar level in 1972 and 1973. Under the Nixon budget for 1974, however, all operational aid would be folded into the special revenue-sharing package for edu-cation, leaving only $45 million earmarked for vocational re-search. To nobody's surprise, the AVA strongly opposed this recommendation.

AID TO HIGHER EDUCATION

The postwar baby boom gave eighteen years notice—to those who comprehended the birth statistics—that an unprecedented wave of college students was on the way. California and New York laid plans to cope with the deluge of degree seekers by establishing new campuses of their university systems, but most states were much slower to accept their expensive duty. It was clear that a disproportionate burden would fall on the public institutions, since private colleges and universities had much more limited resources in prospect.

By the time the "big bulge" approached junior high school age, university administrators and HEW officials began to get very concerned. In 1958, they persuaded President Eisenhower to appoint a Committee on Education Beyond the High School with instructions to make a thorough study of the problems of financing higher education and postsecondary technical education and report within a year. It showed clearly the urgent need for added facilities and student aid. Eisenhower bequeathed the very useful report to his successor, John F. Kennedy.

The colleges' most urgent need was financial aid for building classrooms. The Office of Education and Assistant Secretary Cohen collaborated with congressional leaders in producing a bill that managed to escape being sidetracked by the church-school controversy. Labeled the Higher Education Facilities Act of 1963, it authorized federal grants and loans to assist eligible colleges and universities finance construction and rehabilitation of buildings. The law also authorized aid to build, expand, or improve graduate schools and cooperative graduate centers. This was to be the beginning of a series of bills to aid higher education as the burden from increased enrollments got heavier and heavier.

With the opening of the "do-everything" Eighty-ninth Congress in 1965, the Johnson Administration was almost as ready with its new higher education legislation as it had been with its elementary and secondary bill. But it took longer to get it through. The Higher Education Act of 1965 approved November 8, 1965, authorized:

- Grants to help colleges and universities become service-oriented toward their communities' needs and problems—a sort of urban version of the Agricultural Extension Service, but without a similar scientific base.
- Aid to college and university libraries.
- Grants to upgrade academic standards of developing colleges and to provide a National Teaching Fellowship program.

- Student scholarships, low-interest insured loans, and an expanded work-study program.
- A National Teacher Corps, graduate fellowships for teachers, and grants to improve college and graduate teacher training.
- Funds for teaching equipment, including closed-circuit television.
- A doubling of funds authorized for construction grants in 1963.

This was a legislative milestone almost as important to higher education as the Elementary and Secondary Education Act had been for its beneficiaries, for it established the expectation by many that the federal government would aid colleges, universities, and students for an indefinite period in the future.

The representatives of higher education were slower to comprehend the benefits to be gained from organized lobbying than their pedagogical brethren at lower levels of education, perhaps because they were more self-consciously individualistic, but by the late 1960's they had gotten the message. Although it would be impossible to demonstrate a connection, it is interesting to note that the higher education fraternity completed a new National Center for Higher Education on Dupont Circle in Washington in 1970, and two years later Congress passed, and the President signed, a very far-reaching bill to aid higher education—more generous in many respects than any that had been enacted for elementary and secondary schools. These are some of the inhabitants of the new center:

American Association for Higher Education
American Association of Colleges
American Association of Colleges for Teacher Education
American Association of Community and Junior Colleges
American Association of State Colleges and Universities
American Association of University Professors
American Council on Education
Association of American Medical Colleges
Association of American Universities
National Association of State Universities and Land Grant Colleges
National Council of Independent Colleges and Universities

Organizations that live together lobby together—at least better than when they live separately.

THE EDUCATION AMENDMENTS OF 1972

When Congress passed the Education Amendments of 1972, HEW Secretary Elliot Richardson hailed them as the most far-reaching education bill ever enacted, but by the time he left office a few months later the Nixon Administration had concluded that they were too far-reaching. Most of the Act, which was 146 pages long, dealt with higher education, but Congress decided to include provisions about such unrelated topics as busing, judicial review, sex discrimination, and summer camp safety. The law turned out to be so comprehensive and complex that it is not feasible even to provide a summary of it here, but a few highlights will give a glimmer of its scope:

- Many of the money authorizations contained in the Higher Education Act of 1965 were considerably increased and new ones were added.
- Basic Opportunity Grants were authorized to assure every person the opportunity of pursuing some form of post-secondary education regardless of his financial need. A grant of $1,400 was available to each student less whatever amount he and his family "may reasonably be expected to contribute."
- A Student Loan Marketing Association was created to serve as a secondary market and warehousing facility for insured student loans.
- The administration of the talent search, of Upward Bound, and of special services programs for disadvantaged college students was consolidated and their scope broadened.
- A National Institute of Education was created.
- An Indian Education Act (Title IV) authorized financial assistance to elementary and secondary schools to meet the special educational needs of American Indians.

This was also the law that sought to circumscribe the power of federal courts to order school desegregation plans that had the ostensible purpose of achieving racial balance through busing, and to defer the effective date of court orders until all appeals had been exhausted. The law also prohibited the use of federal funds for the busing of students to overcome racial imbalance. These provisions made a big splash at the time but have had little effect in practice.

When college and university administrators looked at President Nixon's first budget following the enactment of the Education Amendments of 1972—the 1974 budget—it seemed to them as if the President had "item vetoed" a substantial part of that bill. No funds were included for the support of graduate programs; none for the construction of academic facilities; none for community service and continuing education programs; and none for several other programs authorized by the new Act. The President, the Secretary, and the assistant secretary for Education justified their budget on the ground that avoidance of inflation and increased taxes was of highest priority and that the programs that had been "zeroed out" of the budget were of low priority or should now be picked up by states, communities, and institutions if they regarded them as truly important. As much as any area of the budget, aid for education may become a major sector of the "no-man's land" in the fiscal battles of 1974.

EMERGENCY SCHOOL ASSISTANCE

The 1964 Civil Rights Act sought to soften the difficulties of desegregation by offering financial aid to school districts that voluntarily desegregated or complied with desegregation orders, if it was clear that the process placed a significant additional financial burden on the school district. There is little doubt that this aid did ease the transition measurably. In 1972, Congress went a step further and enacted (as Title VII of the Education Amendments of 1972) the Emergency School Aid Act to provide aid to meet the special needs incident to the elimination of minority group segregation with authorizations of up to $1 billion annually in 1973 and 1974 for this purpose. Special attention was given to problems such as bilingual education in Spanish-speaking areas as well as to the traditional and more prevalent educational needs stemming from minority group disadvantages and isolation. Earmarked funds for educational television and various special programs were also authorized. Funding in 1973 and in the 1974 budget is only at a quarter of the authorized billion-dollar level.

EDUCATIONAL DEVELOPMENT

"Educational Development" has now officially replaced the term "Educational Renewal," and both are euphemisms for educational reform. Educational Renewal was a kind of potpourri of educational aids intended to stimulate educational change and improvement, particularly in areas that had been shortchanged or neglected. Some of the programs that came under this rubric in 1972 and 1973 were: the Teacher Corps, aids for the development of elementary and secondary school teachers, demonstrations of educational technology, drug abuse education, the Right to Read program for adults with English language deficiencies, environmental education, dropout prevention, data systems improvement, a national achievement study, bilingual education, Follow Through (a program for the early primary grades, especially designed to follow Head Start).

In shifting to the new title, Educational Development, in its 1974 budget, the Administration has dropped half of these programs and transferred funds and authority for them to the proposed special revenue-sharing package for education, allowing the states to decide where and how much they wish to spend on each of these. Support will be continued for such popular programs as "Sesame Street" and "The Electric Company" (both of which are partially supported from foundation and other funds) but will be reduced for National Educational Television.

EDUCATION FOR THE HANDICAPPED

Under the Education of the Handicapped Act, enacted in 1970, both grants to states and a variety of special aids on a project basis were authorized. Under the President's 1974 budget, the state grant program, operated at the level of $37.5 million for 1972 and 1973 would be thrown into the special revenue-sharing package in 1974. The special project funds, however, would be retained. These cover deaf-blind centers, early childhood projects, special learning disabilities projects, regional resource centers, media services and captioned films, and special education and manpower development programs. These special target programs and manpower development have been financed at just under the $100 million level.

AID TO LIBRARIES

Perhaps the most surprising of the budgetary turnabouts in the field of education that occurred in President Nixon's 1974 budget was the sudden elimination of all funds for aid to libraries without so much as saying—as the budget does in several other instances —that funds for this purpose are included in the proposal for special revenue-sharing. The budget merely says: "In 1974, Federal support will be discontinued."

Until this sudden switch, the library program had fared well under both Democratic and Republican administrations. Grants have been of three basic kinds: for public libraries, for college libraries, and in 1972–73 for public school libraries. The omission without warning of some $137 million from the budget for this form of educational support will certainly make orderly replacement of the funds from other sources difficult. The timing of such changes in financial responsibility is often as important as the fact of change.

POLITICS VS. RATIONALITY:
SCHOOL ASSISTANCE IN FEDERALLY AFFECTED AREAS

As mentioned earlier, communities that had been overburdened by military installations and war industry had persuaded the federal government during World War II and the Korean War to help bear their unusually heavy educational costs. One of the two laws passed in September, 1950 (Public Law 81-874), authorized payments to school districts based on formulas written into the law defining what constituted a sufficient burden to qualify for aid; the companion law (Public Law 81-815) authorized aid for construction of schools. The federal government agreed to pay what amounted to the full educational cost for children whose parents lived on and worked on federal property—a kind of payment-in-lieu-of-taxes—and about half the cost for students whose parents worked on federal property but who lived on taxable property. The latter turned out to be a bonanza for the wealthy suburban counties near Washington, D.C., and many other suburban counties.

Year by year, this program grew as the number of federal employees grew and as the cost of education moved rapidly upward. From a modest outlay of $123 million in the school year 1951–52, the federal costs reached $612 million in 1971–72. Each successive President, from Eisenhower to Nixon, has sought to get Congress to amend the two laws to cut back on the payments to school districts where there are substantial numbers of parents living in their own homes, or on other taxable property, but working in federal buildings. But these efforts have been to no avail. Payments have been made annually under Public Law 874 to more than 3,000 school districts located in the congressional districts of almost every congressman. On one occasion when Eisenhower sought to gain amendments to the law, his congressional assistant could find no congressman willing to sponsor the amendments. An extension of the two laws was passed *on the consent calendar,* meaning that not a single congressman objected to their enactment.

In his 1974 budget, President Nixon recommended complete elimination of payments to school districts for children whose parents live on taxable property and work on federal property. Although the elimination of such funds may well be the most fully justified of all the cuts in the federal budget, cuts made on short notice that have an abrupt and traumatic effect are both hard to absorb in practice and to achieve politically. The outcome of the political contest will be interesting to observe.

A NEW DAY FOR EDUCATIONAL RESEARCH: THE NATIONAL INSTITUTE OF EDUCATION

Ever since the discovery of miracle drugs and polio vaccine, Congress and the public have had great faith in biomedical research and have supported it handsomely, but they have never had much confidence in social science. In 1972, appropriations for educational research to the Office of Education were less than $100 million, compared to more than a dozen times that amount to the National Institutes of Health for research in the health sciences. Social scientists working in the field of education do not yet have, as a matter of fact, much proof to demonstrate that heavy investments in this field will result in high pay-offs.

Finally, in the Education Amendments of 1972, the proponents of more and better research gained approval of a new National Institute of Education (NIE), hoping that some of NIH's magical power to attract large appropriations and first-rate scientists might be acquired by a bright new national institute in the field of education. The central core of the Office of Education's research functions was vested in the new institute. Its 1973–74 budget as proposed by the President was $162 million, with about 450 positions. By law, the NIE must expend at least 90 per cent of its appropriated funds through grants and contracts for basic and applied research surveys, evaluations, experiments, and demonstrations.

President Nixon's 1974 budget indicated the hope that the new enterprise would contribute more to progress than grants for the support of operating programs. He asked for a $19 million increase in funds, including money to recruit a group of scientists as federal employees to conduct "in-house" research. Part of the enlarged research program would be directed toward areas that have heretofore been neglected by the social science community—such as the relationship between various types of learning and work capabilities. If they can make significant progress in this field alone, they will have earned their salt.

ORGANIZATION OF HEW's EDUCATION FUNCTIONS

Organizations undergoing explosive growth usually have severe pains of adjustment. The Office of Education has had more than its share of such pains. In 1960, Commissioner Lawrence Derthick tried to cope with organizational problems by appointing a study group, headed by Assistant Commissioner Homer Babbidge, to recommend changes. The reorganization plan it produced de-emphasized its traditional clientele groups and emphasized the processes of administration (for example, it grouped grants to all levels of education in one division). The plan turned out to be short-lived. When the Elementary and Secondary Education Act of 1965 was enacted, the White House, the Bureau of the Budget, and Commissioner Keppel agreed that the Office of Education needed a quick organization study. They selected Dwight Ink—then assistant general manager of the Atomic Energy Commission—to head a 3-man task force to make the study. The report, submitted within sixty days, called for a 4-bureau structure —Elementary and Secondary Education; Adult and Vocational Education; Higher Education; and Research—plus centralization of financial and personnel management. In one of the most sudden and traumatic reshuffles in modern bureaucratic history, the reorganization, which necessitated massive assignment changes and physical moves, was attempted over a Fourth of July weekend only days after the submission of the report. It took months to recover from the ensuing chaos.

In concept, today's organization of the education functions of HEW follows the basic lines of the Ink Committee report of 1965 except that the top executive responsibility has now been shifted (by the Education Amendments of 1972) to the assistant secretary for Education and the Bureau of Educational Research has now been upgraded to the National Institute of Education. When John Ottina became commissioner of Education, the position was occupied in 1973 for the first time by a man with higher credentials as an administrator than as a professional educator—a long-felt need of the Office of Education. This position has essentially become that of a multiple program manager.

All other HEW assistant secretaries are in the same building and on the same floor with the Secretary, but the assistant secretary for Education and his small staff are located in a separate building, surrounded by the Office of Education. The physical arrangements are symbolic of a scarcely suppressed hope that the education agency may some day be elevated to full Cabinet status.

The Office of Education bureaucracy, which administers some one hundred programs, dispensing over $5 billion annually, and offering technical assistance in a variety of areas, is very small, as bureaucracies go—about 2,800 positions. Excessive size has never been a major problem of the office; its central problem has been that of continuous upheaval. For most of HEW's twenty-year span, it has been in a state of administrative flux. There have been eight commissioners during this period with wide variations in administrative philosophy and management style. With or without the drastic reorganization of 1965, the Office of Education was not well prepared for the burden of administering the mass of new program responsibilities thrust upon it by the Johnson Administration and the Eighty-ninth Congress. If it could have started from scratch with adequate lead time and continuous leadership by a brilliant and orderly administrator like Arthur Altmeyer ("Mr. Social Security"), it might have had a reasonable chance to develop traditions and methods of administration that could carry it through all kinds of external buffeting, but it had no such good fortune.

Even the most competent educational administrator in the nation, however, would have been faced with a more difficult set of problems than Arthur Altmeyer ever had to cope with. The commissioner of Education, and now the assistant secretary for Education, are caught in the middle of contending forces, pulling and pushing in opposite directions. Power to determine educational policy is more jealously guarded by its keepers at the local and state levels than any other function. And that, according to President Nixon, is as it should be. But HEW and its high education officials are under great pressure—often by the President's own subordinates—to bring about educational innovation and reform so as to assure that appropriated funds are effectively spent. How can they do this without running headlong into the counterthrust of decentralizing federal power to decide how money is to be allocated and spent and of giving state and local officials more decision-making power over the expenditure of federal grant funds? More will be said in the pages that follow and in Chapter XI about this problem, for it is a dilemma that runs through other HEW programs, but nowhere is it so acute as in education.

As currently organized, the Office of Education has five deputy commissioners, one for each of the following: planning, evaluation, and management; school systems; development; higher education; and external relations. In addition, it has special organizational units to operate the Teacher Corps, the "Right To Read Program," and the "Office of Special Concerns."

Special Institutions

The Secretary of HEW gives general oversight to several independent educational institutions, which receive annual appropriations from the federal government. These are:

- The American Printing House for the Blind, in Louisville, Kentucky, which produces Braille books and a variety of other educational materials for blind students.
- Gallaudet College in the District of Columbia, the only 4-year college in the nation specifically for deaf students; it also has a graduate school program concerning deafness.

- Kendall School, an elementary school for deaf students, operated by Gallaudet College.
- Model Secondary School for the Deaf, associated with Gallaudet College.
- National Technical School for the Deaf, in Rochester, New York, authorized in 1965, which has a new building due for completion in 1973.
- Howard University, in Washington, D.C., founded in 1867 to educate liberated slaves, which is now a university of international importance. More than half of its 10,500 enrollment is in its professional and graduate schools. Fourteen per cent of its student body comes from seventy-eight foreign countries. The Howard University Medical School has supplied a significant share of black physicians in the United States.

These institutions are in no sense federally controlled—each has its own board of trustees that sets the policies of the institution —but none, except perhaps for the American Printing House for the Blind, could exist without the federal aid they receive. Each is a unique institution and national resource.

Education Functions Outside of HEW

There are, of course, numerous education programs conducted by the federal government outside of HEW, especially in the Veterans Administration, the National Science Foundation, the Bureau of Indian Affairs (in the Department of Interior), the Department of Labor, and the Department of Defense. Some proponents of a separate Department of Education would like to see a number of these functions brought together with the education components of HEW and elevated to Cabinet status. In the light of President Nixon's efforts to enlarge HEW by converting it into a Department of Human Resources, the likelihood of a separate Department of Education before the late 1970's looks remote.

WHO MAKES EDUCATION POLICY?

Conventional wisdom used to assert that the Office of Education was the mistress of the powerful education lobbies, particularly those at the elementary and secondary level. These are:

American Association of School Administrators
American Federation of Teachers
American Vocational Association
Council of Chief State School Officers
National Association of State Boards of Education
National Congress of Parents and Teachers
National Education Association
National School Boards Association

There was at least a half-truth in the implication of a very cozy relationship between the Office of Education and the national education organizations, a half-truth whose validity has been considerably diminished in recent years.

In the years prior to 1958, the Office of Education had comparatively little money to dispense on a discretionary basis and consequently not much influence over educational programs and policies. The office's principal stock in trade was statistical and other information and technical assistance to state and local school officials and teachers. The money that the Office of Education did have—for vocational education and for aid to federally affected areas—was distributed according to legal formulas, leaving the office hardly any discretionary control. Under these circumstances, it was natural and understandable that the office should seek to achieve some leavening of public school performance through close cooperation with major organizations of teachers and school officials. The staff of the office was so small that it could not hope to reach directly the numerous local school systems. Conversely, the public education organizations developed a special interest in the Office of Education, believing it to be their spokesman within the government on behalf of educational needs.

The extent to which career personnel and commissioners of Education became influenced by, and spokesmen for, the views of the various educational organizations varied considerably, depending on the personalities and characters of the persons occupying key positions, the strength of their own independent views, and the degree to which they received conflicting signals from the President and the Secretary who served as their superiors. There is no doubt that when the educational organizations demonstrated their political power by persuading Congress to add even modest sums of money not requested in the President's budget or restore cuts proposed by him, this influence did not go unnoticed in the Office of Education.

In the 1960's, however, the psychological relationship changed noticeably. As the size of the office's budget reached the multi-billion-dollar level, and thus became a matter of major budgetary concern to Presidents and Secretaries, dissatisfaction with the conservatism of the major educational establishment of the country became more and more in evidence at the top levels of government and was likewise shared by the Congress. Both Democratic and Republican Presidents—Kennedy, Johnson, and Nixon—seemed to feel that it was more important than previously to appoint commissioners of Education who would be both innovative and capable of independence from the public educational organizations. More than this, however, they wanted them to see that the multiple billions that were by then being spent for education were effectively spent, meaning that the Office of Education was not to be a mere transmission belt for federal funds but was expected to use the big appropriations as leverage to change the school systems, with particular emphasis on finding better ways of educating disadvantaged children.

This also fitted in with the mood of Congress, which was developing the distinct impression that most of the public educational organizations were only interested in more money to do the same things they had always done—which did not seem to be working very well. Without fully realizing what was happening, therefore, both the Congress and the executive branch fell into the trap of earmarking specific funds for a hundred different purposes. Some of the money was to be divided up among the states on a formula basis, and most of the rest was to go to institutions on a project basis. All purposes were undoubtedly meritorious, but the net effect of trying to decide educational policy in this manner was demoralizing to state and local school administrators. Conditions vary widely and school administrators need flexibility. There developed scores of vested interests in these earmarked funds, all with the realization that to keep the money flowing, they had to develop their lines of communication to influential congressmen in Washington. This was the legacy of the Kennedy-Johnson legislative boom in education.

The excessive earmarking of funds for specific program purposes that became rampant in the mid-1960's—a policy that originated in the executive branch and was sponsored by the Congress—finally had its inevitable reaction after the change of administration in 1969. In his State of the Union message in January, 1970, President Nixon stressed the difficulties of running the nation from Washington and the need to revitalize state and local institutions to make their own policy decisions effectively. In his message, he recommended not only "general revenue-sharing," which was finally approved by Congress just before its adjournment in 1972, but several forms of "special revenue-sharing," including an important bill to consolidate many grant programs in the field of education. The effect of this bill would be to give states and local communities much greater flexibility in the use of funds to fit their own needs and purposes than they have had under the numerous categorical grants. The effect would be to transfer much policy-making in the field of education back to states and local communities where it used to be. But in the three years 1970–73, Congress has ignored it. The explanation for this is worth discussion.

Essentially, the reason Congress has paid no attention to the President's special revenue-sharing bill for education is that the national educational organizations are more concerned that their members might lose money under the plan than they are interested that they might gain decision-making power and flexibility. Even though President Nixon's plan tried to assure the school organizations and state and local school officials that they did not mean to use the special revenue-sharing program as a device for cutting back on appropriations for education, it seemed impossible to persuade the beneficiaries of the categorical grants that they would be as well off under the consolidated grants as under the earmarked categorical grants. They felt, and feel, that they can trust the Congress to look out for their interests more fully than they can trust their own state legislatures and school boards. And the Congress enjoys, both politically and emotionally, the feeling of being relied upon to look out for these special interests.

Nixon's commissioner of Education, Sidney Marland (later appointed assistant secretary for Education), managed to get himself in difficulty with the Congress over a closely related issue. Marland, with the active support of HEW Secretary Richardson, sought to make maximum use of the latitude permitted under existing law to achieve some of the flexibility that would be encouraged and allowed under the special revenue-sharing bill. This was a central feature of his plan for "Educational Renewal"—a systematic encouragement to states and school districts to develop the most effective means they could devise to meet their own special educational problems and needs, with the Office of Education helping them to use the existing categorical grant structure to put the money where they felt it was needed. Key members of the Congress were very much put out that the commissioner seemed to be exceeding his legal authority. He did not exceed his legal authority, according to HEW's general counsel, but he may well have exceeded what some powerful members of the Congress had in mind when they enacted the laws and approved the appropriations under them.

It is evident that it is not easy to answer the question as to who makes education policy. In any list of prime examples of pluralistic decision-making in a pluralistic society, education policy must surely be close to the top. All kinds of special educational interests are at work, often in active competition and at cross-purposes. We see the ironic pattern of a President wanting to give the states and local school officials more power of self-determination, only to find that the dominant theme of their concerns seems to be simply more money, not more power to use available funds more flexibly and imaginatively. Some educational leaders have concluded that their long-range interest lies in regaining opportunity and power to manage their own households, even at the risk that such a course may not yield the maximum number of federal dollars. But many educational specialists seem unlikely to be persuaded that states and school districts can be depended upon to look out for their interests as well as can the U.S. Congress.

FUTURE FINANCING OF EDUCATION

Unless and until it is overtaken by health, education is and will continue to be the largest and most expensive public industry in the nation, by a wide margin. Yet despite the rapid build-up in federal appropriations for the support of education, federal aid is still not as large a proportion of the revenues and expenditures of state and local school systems as is generally supposed. Of the $51.8 billion of estimated revenues of public elementary and secondary schools in 1972–73, federal funds constitute only about $4 billion, or roughly 8 per cent of the total. State funds contribute about $21 billion, while local and other funds make up the balance.

Two factors will greatly influence the future form and magnitude of federal aid for elementary and secondary education. The first is the outcome of the struggle between the President and Congress over congressional power to determine how much shall be spent for what—the power to set national budgetary priorities. Judging from its past actions, Congress places a higher priority on expenditures for educational aid than does President Nixon, but whether Congress will be able to enforce its will remains to be seen.

The second factor involves a policy struggle previously discussed, namely Nixon's reiterated proposal for special revenue-sharing (education), grouping some thirty categorical programs into a single grant to each state with greater latitude for state and local decision-making concerning the allocation of the funds. Governors and mayors and county commissioners seem increasingly concerned that "power to the people"—the slogan in support of revenue-sharing, general and special—may mean the power to spend less money to provide for increasingly expensive public services. If the choice is seen as one between more adequate money and more flexible authority, money is likely to win.

Higher education, too, is nervous about its uncertain financial future. President Nixon's 1973–74 budget stressed the use of the "market mechanism" under which the federal government would undertake to see that qualified students were granted or loaned sufficient funds to assure them the opportunity to attend college and graduate school, and leaving to them the choice as to what institution they wished to attend. This plan also involved a significant reduction in the funds paid directly to colleges and universities. Thus, students are expected to shop around and get the best educational bargain they can. Understandably, this increases the nervousness of some of the high-cost institutions. The problem becomes particularly acute in respect to graduate and professional schools where the educational costs per student are very much higher than tuition costs. Sharp cutbacks in fellowships, proposed in the 1974 budget, were alarming to graduate and professional schools.

VII

Health Research

The third revolution—federal acceptance of responsibility for the people's health—seems approximately halfway toward its denouement. It began after World War II, with the sudden, euphoric prospect that medical research might be the golden key to ending many of mankind's oldest scourges. In the United States, research led the profound change, but could not, by itself, fulfill the people's aspirations for greatly improved health. Before this third revolution ends, it seems highly probable that there will be a nationwide, government-sponsored system for assuring equitable access to good medical care, regardless of a person's income or economic status. In only a quarter century, the distinction between public health and private health has been blurred almost to the point of obliteration.

The Rise of Medical Research and NIH

As mentioned earlier, health insurance was promoted soon after World War II by President Harry Truman, Oscar Ewing, and various senators and congressmen. In retrospect, it is clear that it was simply not an idea whose time had come. The health insurance concept was so badly mauled by Congress that many of its supporters decided that the wisest strategy was to begin capitalizing on the almost universal faith in the efficacy of research and wait until the public realized how indispensable some form of health insurance really was. There was an enormous amount of work needed in biomedical research, in professional training, and in communications before a groundswell was likely to emerge for a national guarantee of basic health services to all people.

In 1939, at the time when HEW's forerunner—the Federal Security Agency (FSA)—was created, the U.S. Government had only minor concern with medical research and almost none for the training of doctors, dentists, nurses, or the scientists needed for biomedical research. The Public Health Service had a modest laboratory called the National Institute of Health (NIH) overlooking the ground on which the John F. Kennedy Center for the Performing Arts now stands, and Congress had just authorized the creation of a National Cancer Institute, also of modest size, to be built in Bethesda, Maryland. These, together with several small field laboratories, made up the biomedical research component of the Public Health Service, with a budget of scarcely a million dollars.

During World War II, little new manpower was allocated to civilian medical research, but as soon as the war ended, plans on a grand scale were presented to the Bureau of the Budget by the director of the National Institute of Health, Rolla Dyer, with the active support of the surgeon general, Thomas Parran. They had a design for the greatest medical research center in the world, to be located adjacent to the National Cancer Institute in suburban Washington. The time was ripe and the postwar budget could stand the cost.

Penicillin and other miracle drugs that came into sudden and widespread use during and after World War II, followed by radar, the atomic bomb, and other dramatic outcomes of wartime research and development, led the nonscientifically trained public to hope for, and even expect, easy and rapid discoveries of ways to cure all manner of illness. Both the public and Congress jumped to the understandable conclusion that research was the potential answer to the diseases that had been killing off too many of their families and friends, and might shorten their own lives. Most of the communicable diseases had been conquered, but the chronic diseases—particularly cancer and various diseases of the heart, the arteries, and the lungs—were becoming more lethal as each year passed. Members of the House and Senate saw their own ranks weakened as some of their outstanding members died of such diseases, sometimes in the prime of their careers. Senator Robert Taft, a revered man among his colleagues, succumbed to cancer not long after his unsuccessful effort to become the Republican Presidential nominee in 1952.

This climate of opinion stimulated burgeoning medical research, using the federal taxing and spending power to finance it. Fortunately, the key committee chairmen in both the House and the Senate had a deep interest in medical and health matters, and particularly in research. The chairman of the Senate Committee on Labor and Public Welfare, which handled the legislative authorizations affecting medical research, during most of the 1950's and 1960's was Lister Hill of Alabama. He was also chairman of the subcommittee that handled the Appropriations Committee's funds for medical research. The son of a surgeon, with five cousins and two brothers-in-law who were doctors (and himself named after the father of aseptic surgery, Joseph Lister), how could he fail to be sympathetic to a great leap forward in the field of medical research?

In the House of Representatives, the Labor and Welfare Subcommittee of the Appropriations Committee was chaired for sixteen years during the same period by Congressman John Fogarty of Rhode Island. He was a self-made man, starting as a bricklayer, becoming a union official, and then, at the age of twenty-eight, successfully seeking a seat in the U.S. House of Representatives. After his election in 1941, he quickly learned all the tricks of the congressional trade and simultaneously acquired a profound interest in exercising congressional leadership to help improve the health of the American people. Within a decade, he controlled the House Appropriations subcommittee that dealt with health, education, welfare, and labor functions.

With public opinion strongly favorable, and with the controls of the key congressional committees in the hands of Hill and Fogarty, the medical research activities of HEW, particularly those of NIH, entered upon an extraordinary postwar boom that extended to the late 1960's before coming to an abrupt, but temporary, halt.

A National Heart Institute and a National Institute of Dental Research were created in 1948, and the former National Institute of Health was renamed the National Institutes of Health. Two more institutes were authorized later in the same year: the

National Microbiological Institute and the Experimental Biology and Medicine Institute. In the following year, 1949, the National Institute of Mental Health was created, and in 1950 the Omnibus Medical Research Act authorized the National Institute of Neurological Diseases and Blindness and the National Institute of Arthritis and Metabolic Diseases (which absorbed the Experimental Biology and Medicine Institute).

Fortunately, when the rush of new institutes reached this point, there was a lull to enable NIH to build new facilities and complete those that had been authorized. In July, 1953, NIH opened its new Clinical Center—the finest clinical research facilities its sponsors could design. A 500-bed hospital was surrounded by laboratory facilities with the most advanced equipment to enable research scientists to touch elbows and compare observations with clinicians caring for patients. Patients were selected on the basis of the relationship of their illnesses to the research program of the Clinical Center and the institutes that shared research space in the center. The decision was made not to charge patients for any of their hospital expenses, but they had to agree to cooperate with the center in its research effort.

Meanwhile, as each year passed, the appropriations for NIH went up at an unprecedented rate. They jumped from less than $3 million in 1945 to more than $50 million in 1950 and, after a lull during the Korean War, resumed their upward climb. Important as the new Clinical Center was, it was always intended to be a minor part of the total federal biomedical research effort. The main thrust was to support research through grants to universities and other nonprofit research centers. This worked well during the late 1940's and early 1950's, but then the universities began running out of space and facilities within which their scientists could work. One of the early strategies of the NIH had been to invest a significant part of its grant funds in fellowships and traineeships, and these were producing research scientists who were eager to work but who had neither adequate facilities nor equipment. To help overcome this lack, the Health Research Facilities Act was passed in 1956, authorizing matching grants to universities and other nonprofit research centers. And, in the same year, the Armed Forces Medical Library was transferred to HEW, placed under the Public Health Service, and renamed the National Library of Medicine. It was later to become a component of NIH

(1968), and the government's principal arm for the preservation and dissemination of biomedical scientific information.

Lobbies for "senior citizens" and for children stimulated the creation of research programs in 1958 and 1961. First was the Center for Aging Research, as would be expected, followed by the Center for Research in Child Health, in whose founding and development the Kennedy family took a special interest in order to increase research on mental retardation. These did not remain centers long; they were upgraded at the suggestion of NIH Director James Shannon to the National Institute of Child Health and Human Development in 1963. In the following year, Congress authorized the construction of a National Environmental Health Sciences Center—not as a part of NIH—and located it in the Research Triangle Park of North Carolina. This was raised to the status of an institute in 1967 and transferred to NIH.

Until 1967, one function after another was being added to NIH and nothing was being taken away. But at the beginning of 1967, it was decided to remove the National Institute of Mental Health from NIH and make it a separate bureau. The dual reasons for this were that the supporters of mental health thought their program would thrive better if elevated in status and that the mental health program, unlike those of the other institutes of NIH, had developed into as much or more of a service program than a research program.

In 1968, a relatively new bureau of the Public Health Service— the Bureau of Health Manpower Education—was transferred to the jurisidiction of NIH, even though the scope of its functions greatly exceeded research manpower. The new bureau had been created outside NIH because it was becoming increasingly difficult to separate the training of health personnel according to whether the personnel would ultimately wind up as research scientists and technicians or as clinicians and other professionals and paraprofessionals engaged in service activities. But after brief experience with an independent bureau, it was decided that NIH had so many contacts with the training institutions that it could best perform the leadership role in the development of adequate professional manpower.

In briefest summary, this is the sequence in which the organization of NIH developed. As of current writing, NIH has nine categorical or disease-oriented institutes: cancer; heart and lung; eye, allergy, and infectious diseases; arthritis, metabolism, and digestive diseases; child health and human development; dental research, environmental health sciences; and neurological diseases and stroke; plus the National Library of Medicine and several supporting divisions and centers.

By the fiscal year 1972–73, NIH had reached an appropriation level of $2.4 billion and was supporting approximately half of all the biomedical research being conducted in the United States, as well as some being done abroad.

As is apparent from the evolution of the institutes, most of them were organized around particular disease categories, stimulated by persons who were either afflicted with such diseases or who had loved ones who suffered from them. When the National Microbiological Institute was converted to the National Institute of Allergy and Infectious Diseases, it was reported that the change was precipitated by the assertion of an influential congressman that the first title had no "sex appeal." "Nobody ever heard of a person dying from microbiology," he was reported to have said.

Organizing the NIH by disease categories is not the pattern that the top officials of the agency would have adopted if the same amount of money had been appropriated in lump sum to them each year, with full latitude to the director to organize as he thought best. In that event, there would have been far more emphasis on putting the related scientific disciplines together than on grouping staff on the basis of disease categories. But the disease approach appealed strongly to the public and to Congress, and it produced larger appropriations than would have been made if NIH had followed its own organizational inclinations. Furthermore, it focused research on the purposes for which the public funds were being spent, so its top officials decided to relax and make the best of their affluence.

THE POLITICAL FORCES BEHIND NIH

Except for the Army Corps of Engineers, there is probably no better example in the U.S. Government of the power of a triangular political force than that exhibited by NIH, with the support of Congress and outside pressure groups. This symbiotic relationship has long been the object of study and comment by political scientists, particularly by the late Wallace Sayre.

A federal agency develops simultaneous support from key members of Congress and from outside pressure groups that have an interest in the products and services of the agency. The key congressmen and senators find it highly advantageous, in terms of their own political fortunes, to support the programs of the agency and the interests of the pressure groups, especially when these seem to coincide with what they regard as the public interest. The delight of the pressure groups in obtaining the support of both the key members of Congress and the program agency that dispenses money hardly requires comment.

It is surely not surprising that the NIH has developed a very supportive following. A few of the numerous organizations that have a deep interest in the success of NIH programs and appropriations are:

American Cancer Society
American Heart Association
American Nurses' Association
Association of American Medical Colleges
American Association of Dental Schools
American Public Health Association
American Association of Colleges of Pharmacy
American Speech and Hearing Association
Association of Schools of Allied Health Professions
Planned Parenthood-World Population

Since 1970, more than a score of these and other organizations interested in federal support for health programs have associated themselves in the Coalition for Health Funding, but this is a recent development, the product of unhappy experience in the late 1960's.

For most of the 1950's and 1960's, there was no umbrella organization comparable to the Rivers and Harbors Congress, which knitted these and other organizations together in a concerted effort to achieve common ends. But in place of the Rivers and Harbors Congress, there was the most remarkable one-person lobby in the United States. She was—and is—Mary Lasker. She has been applying her extraordinary political talents to the shaping of NIH (and other health programs as well) ever since the late 1940's.

Mary Lasker, philanthropist and widow of Albert Lasker, millionaire advertising entrepreneur, has had a consuming interest in finding ways to improve the health of the American people for most of her adult life. In the early 1940's, she and her husband founded the Albert and Mary Lasker Foundation and became particularly interested in biomedical research as an avenue to the increase in man's life span and the reduction of disease and suffering. She acquainted herself with the research that was going on in the country and gradually realized that the only way to get money on a grand scale for this vital purpose was to figure out how to extract it from the federal Treasury. In 1949, she tried to persuade the Bureau of the Budget to add substantial sums to the President's budget. She soon discovered, however, that the Budget Bureau was a place that reduced budgets; they almost never increased them no matter how worthy the purpose. Congress, she decided, was the place to focus her effort.

In John Fogarty and Lister Hill, Mary Lasker found two men who reveled in the opportunity to make their reputations as champions of medical research. With the help of an old friend, Florence Mahoney, and an ex-newspaperman turned promoter of the cause of mental health, Mike Gorman, she developed a technique that was successfully used year after year to get Congress to overbid the President's budget request for NIH, usually by scores of millions of dollars. The system involved the full participation of Fogarty and Hill and assistance from the officials of NIH. During most of the 1950's and 1960's, NIH was headed by a respected scientist, James Shannon, who combined an intuitive political skill with his medical research background. The repetitive pattern of appropriations that developed sent Budget Bureau officials, White House staff, and even Presidents into a frenzy of annoyed frustration, and precipitated unprintable comments.

Each year, the various institute directors would develop a budget based on how much money they thought they could effectively use, assuming there were no over-all fiscal restraints on the budget as a whole. These were reviewed by the NIH director, and after he modified or approved them, they were sent to the Office of the Surgeon General of the Public Health Service, which normally treated them like hot potatoes and passed them on to the Office of the Secretary as quickly as possible. The Office of the Secretary would usually cut them back appreciably, following fiscal constraint guidelines set by the Bureau of the Budget, and then pass them on to the Bureau. The competition for funds in the final budget of the President would always necessitate cutting the NIH budget further. So there was at least a double cut by the time the NIH budget reached the Congress, but the amount requested was always enough to carry forward the big boost from the previous year, plus a little more.

When the NIH budget reached Congressman Fogarty's Appropriations subcommittee, he would make it appear that the budget had been butchered. He would ask each institute director how much his original request had been and then proceed to put the Secretary, as the Administration's spokesman, on the defensive for having slashed those budget requests. At the end of the departmental hearings, Fogarty would then invite testimony from public witnesses. The Lasker lobby was ready with its stable of nationally known doctors to present their "Citizens' Budget."

The witnesses were some of the most distinguished names in American medicine, all of whom were carefully selected, well-prepared, and well-rehearsed. Dr. Sidney Farber of Harvard and Dr. Michael DeBakey of Baylor were two of the most regular and influential of the scientific witnesses. The Citizens' Budget oftentimes bore a significant resemblance to the funds requests of the institute directors but in some respects was almost always higher. At the end of each budget review, Congressman Fogarty never tried to get the rest of his committee to go along with any such increases as the Citizens' Budget called for, but he was always able to persuade them to make significant increases above the President's budget.

The same procedure was always repeated in the Senate where Senator Hill was usually successful in adding more, and usually larger, increases. A well-mannered Southern gentleman, Senator Hill was reluctant to use the needling tactics of John Fogarty, but the results he got spoke for themselves. The growth in the NIH appropriations, as shown in the table at the end of this chapter, shows clearly the success of the collaborative effort during the golden Fogarty-Hill-Lasker-Shannon era of NIH.

Mary Lasker's largesse to key politicians and friendship with Presidents of both parties, coupled with the advantageous location of sympathetic and powerful men in the Congress and the executive branch, created a kind of political dynasty that seems to have been without precedent and that may never be matched again. It lasted until Fogarty had a massive heart attack and died in his office in January, 1967, and Lister Hill retired from the Senate at the end of 1968, and James Shannon retired as director of NIH in 1968. These events coincided with, or touched off, a retributory assault on the NIH budget, led by the White House and the Bureau of the Budget. The medical research institutions that depended on NIH grants found themselves for the first time in their memories faced with a cutback in federal funds. Mary Lasker and her lobby had to pick up the pieces of their broken dynasty and begin again to build a new health coalition on the ruins of the old. They had to pursuade Congressman Daniel Flood of Pennsylvania—Fogarty's successor—and Senator Warren Magnuson of Washington—Hill's successor—to become congressional champions of medical research and other health programs. In their efforts, they found bipartisan cooperation from Senator Norris Cotton of New Hampshire and Congressman Robert Michel of Illinois. All of these men had been quiet supporters of HEW health programs. As we shall later see, Mary Lasker's indefatigability still pays off.

THE RESEARCH GRANT SYSTEM

Well before HEW came into being as a department, two critical policy decisions had been made by the Public Health Service in respect to the support of biomedical research, and they were never basically changed thereafter. It was decided, first of all, that biomedical research could thrive best where the most talented research people were then located and wanted to remain—primarily on university campuses, in teaching hospitals, and in nonprofit research institutes. The expansion of such research, it was reasoned, could be achieved best and made most effective by making grants to the institutions in which these people were located to enable them to carry on projects that the institutions could not otherwise afford to finance. Second, it was decided that the determination as to which projects were of genuine scientific merit should not be made by a government bureaucracy but by highly respected representatives of the scientific community serving in an advisory capacity to government.

This combination of decisions resulted in a national research program dominated by thousands of small projects that were generated by the scientists themselves wherever they were institutionally based. While most of the individual scientists who have been recipients of grants under this system do like it, it has been the subject of controversy—especially as the years have gone by, and some of the killer diseases still seem very far from being conquered. Impatient research watchers have counseled strong leadership in research planning, applying large sums to "targets of opportunity," and giving greater emphasis to large-scale screening of drugs and other applied research. These have been tried, but not in sufficient degree to satisfy the proponents of all-out efforts to find cures for killer diseases.

The Division of Research Grants acts as a central control and reference point for all research grant applications, referring them to the appropriate study sections. The study sections are composed of recognized scientists from all over the country, mostly from the very institutions from which the grant applications emanate. This system is called "peer group review."

Some concept of the scope of biomedical research supported by NIH can be gained from the list of review groups:

Allergy and Immunology
Applied Physiology
Bacteriology and Mycology
Biochemistry
Biomedical Communications
Biophysics and Biophysical
    Chemistry
Cardiovascular
Cell Biology
Communicative Sciences
Computer Research
Dental
Development Behavioral Sciences
Endocrinology
Epidemiology and Disease
    Control
Experimental Psychology
General Medicine
Genetics
Hematology
History of the Life Sciences
Human Embryology and
    Development
Immunobiology
Medicinal Chemistry
Metabolism
Microbial Chemistry
Molecular Biology
Neurology
Nutrition
Pathology
Pharmacology
Physiological Chemistry
Physiology
Radiation
Reproductive Biology
Surgery
Toxicology
Tropical Medicine and
    Parasitology
Virology
Visual Sciences

Despite the fact that individual members of these review groups are required to absent themselves whenever a grant application from their own institution is under consideration, there is unavoidably some conflict of interest built into this system. No man can be completely objective about a grant application from an esteemed colleague who has just stepped out of the room, or even from one of the colleague's close associates.

Organizational expert Harold Seidman has characterized scientific research as "the only pork barrel for which the pigs determine who gets the pork." Surprisingly, statistical analyses have shown no substantial difference between the approval rates of grant applications of institutions when they are represented on the review groups and when they are not. In any event, it is a risk that NIH and HEW have elected to take because they believe it to be preferable to the alternative of doing all the review work with full-time government employees. First-rate scientists could certainly not be enlisted to spend their careers as project reviewers.

Projects that pass the scientific screening of the study sections are referred to the appropriate institutes and to the statutory advisory councils of those institutes. Purists in public administration have long looked with exceeding disapproval on the unusual legal power of these advisory councils. They are composed of an approximately equal number of scientists and lay citizens, appointed by the Secretary, and they have, for all practical purposes, the final legal approval power over all projects. Theoretically, the director of NIH may veto projects approved by the councils, although he never has, and he does not have the power to approve any project that has been disapproved by any one of the councils. The councils are not, therefore, *advisory* councils, in a true sense, but legally constituted bodies that have basic decision-making power.

But the appearance of power vested in the councils is much greater than the actuality. The preliminary screening done by staff personnel in the Division of Research grants and particularly the reviews conducted by the scientific study sections (whose members are appointed by the director of NIH) are largely determinative in establishing the order of scientific merit. Each grant application is assigned a rating, and the hundreds of applications are transmitted to the councils in priority order. The councils make no attempt to go over each application, although they occasionally discuss specific projects in which individual council members have a special interest. Rather, they are inclined to discuss the desirability of giving special emphasis to particular types of grants. When they are agreed on this course of action, a whole group of grants (for example, those which seem likely to lead to improved contraceptive techniques) may be elevated in relative ranking. Thus, the councils' role tends to be primarily policy-oriented.

CONTRACT RESEARCH

Separate from the project review and grant mechanism is the system of contract research. The most notable example has been the cancer chemotherapy program, developed to screen thousands of drug compounds to see whether any of them had unsuspected power to inhibit the growth of cancerous tissue. Under this program, the large drug manufacturing companies were drawn into the research effort by contractual arrangements under which they not only tested the properties of the numerous available compounds but also developed thousands of new drug formulas for the screening program. This program has proceeded since the late 1950's, with only limited success. The $250 million that has been spent on the program has yielded a number of useful drugs, but they have not been spectacular in "curing" cancer. Nevertheless, the program has been an essential part of the continuing search for all useful means of inhibiting the devastating growth of cancer cells.

A somewhat different use of contract research resulted from President Richard Nixon's announcement in 1970 of the ending of all bacteriological warfare activities by the Department of Defense. This rendered surplus the excellent set of laboratories developed by the army at Fort Detrick, Maryland, just outside Frederick. After extensive bureaucratic jockeying, this facility was turned over to NIH for biomedical research. NIH, in turn, decided that it could best be operated by a nongovernment contractor, Litton Bionetics, a subsidiary of Litton Industries.

Most contract research is applied research that requires testing on a larger scale than is normally feasible in the small projects for which grants are made. Decisions on contract research are made by the officials of the various institutes of NIH and are not required to be reviewed by the study sections and councils. As time has gone on, a gradually larger proportion of all research funds have been spent on contract research, reaching 17 per cent in 1972 ($205 million—most of it on cancer, heart, and lung research). To what extent this increase reflects a desire on the part of the officials of these institutes to gain control over the programming of research and to what extent it reflects the inadequacy of coverage of all good research leads by the system of project applications and grants, it is impossible to determine. Both factors are clearly present.

Supporting Scientific and Professional Manpower Development

The system of depending on the pluralistic scientific community to come forward with imaginative research projects relies heavily on a continuing and growing flow of first-rate scientific manpower into the biomedical research field and the availability of suitable laboratories and instruments. It was found quite early in the explosive growth of NIH that scientific manpower was not in large supply and that the only way to expand it at a reasonably fast pace was for NIH to foot the bills. A fellowship program was initiated by the National Cancer Institute in 1941, and in the years that followed World War II, a steady stream of new fellowship and traineeship programs was created to meet the manpower needs of each succeeding research institute. The rapid growth of research would not have been possible without this extensive encouragement toward doctoral and postdoctoral work in the biomedical sciences.

Later, in the 1950's and 1960's, the federal government became increasingly concerned with the need to enlarge the supply of professional personnel available to provide health services for the rapidly growing population. When this occurred, it led to the creation of a Bureau of Health Manpower Education (1967), originally an independent bureau of the Public Health Service, which was subsequently transferred to the National Institutes of Health where it remained for the 5-year period, 1968–73. Secretary Weinberger's health reorganization moved it to the newly created Health Resources Administration in the summer of 1973 (see Chapter VIII).

ORGANIZING TO CONQUER CANCER:
SHOULD THE NASA MODEL BE FOLLOWED?

The void left by the death of John Fogarty in 1967 and the retirement from the Senate of Lister Hill at the end of 1968, and the consequent abrupt ending of the escalation of appropriations to NIH, made it inevitable that the backers of biomedical research would fall back, regroup, and find a new strategy for a fresh effort to extract more money from the Congress. It came in the form of a renewed dramatization of the horrors of cancer and the urgent need for a kind of "moonshot" for the conquest of this most dreaded of all diseases.

On April 27, 1970, the Senate passed a joint resolution authorizing the Senate Committee on Labor and Public Welfare, with the assistance of an advisory committee, to report to the Senate on the current status of scientific knowledge about cancer, the prospect of finding its causes and cures, and measures necessary to facilitate success at the earliest possible time. Subsequently, the House and Senate passed a concurrent resolution expressing the unanimous sense of the Congress that "the conquest of cancer is a national crusade" and that "the Congress should appropriate the necessary funds so that the citizens of this land and all other lands may be delivered from the greatest medical scourge in history." The rhetoric left little doubt that the medical syndicate of Mary Lasker, Mike Gorman, and Florence Mahoney was back in high gear.

On November 25, Benno C. Schmidt, a New York business executive who served as chairman of the Committee of Consultants on Cancer—and who was also a good friend of President Nixon—submitted the committee's report to Senator Ralph W. Yarborough of Texas, who, as a last act of his senatorial career, gave it maximum publicity. It asserted that cancer was the number one health concern of the American people; that the amount spent on cancer research was grossly inadequate; that cancer was increasing, even though the cure rate was gradually improving; that there have been major advances in fundamental knowledge of cancer in the last decade; that a national program for the conquest of cancer was essential; and that an independent National Cancer Authority, analogous to the National Aeronautics and Space Administration (NASA) and directly answerable to the President, should be created with the explicit mission of conquering cancer at the earliest possible time.

It took hardly any time at all for the report to be converted into a bill that was introduced by Senators Edward Kennedy and Jacob Javits and fifty co-sponsors on January 25, 1971. It generated more than a dozen identical bills in the House, likewise with bi-partisan support. Needless to say, it created consternation at NIH, partly out of bureaucratic possessiveness, but even more out of deep concern over the profound and little understood ramifications of the proposal. The NIH was convinced, with good cause, that the only reason the categorical disease institutes work as well as they do was that they are all organized under the umbrella of the NIH, which is responsible for basic biomedical research and for relating this research to the more directly disease-oriented studies of the various institutes. To make an excision of the cancer program, followed probably by the heart and lung program, and then by others, from the body of basic biomedical research, would be like dismembering an organic whole and expecting its member parts to thrive better by themselves.

While not unaware of this analogy, the proponents of the "cancer crusade" proposal preferred a different one. They felt that the mission-oriented technological feats produced by the Manhattan Project of A-bomb fame and the Apollo Program of NASA were clear demonstrations that the combination of indepen-dence, strong leadership, and lots of money had worked miracles and should be able to do so again. They felt that the NIH and its subordinate institute, the National Cancer Institute, had not demonstrated that they were imbued with the same intense dedi-cation to their mission and sense of urgency that characterized the men of Los Alamos and the Apollo team. And, at least as im-portant, they felt that an independent organization with a clear-cut mission, answerable directly to the President, would be likely to be financed much more generously than the National Cancer Institute had been.

The battle was thus joined in the spring of 1971 between the cancer crusaders on the one side and the NIH and supporters of integrated medical research, on the other. The NIH director, Dr. Robert Marston, and his associates perceived it almost as a life and death struggle, since the loss of the cancer program would seem to presage the beginning of a series of such efforts, and the end of an integrated medical research organization. The cries of anguish were so loud that they were heard and heeded by both Secretary Elliot Richardson and President Nixon. Simultaneously, Mr. Nixon was getting pressure from the opposite direction. One of Mr. Nixon's close personal friends, Elmer Bobst, was a member of the Committee of Consultants, which recommended the independent agency. Nixon's political friends, too, were telling him that a NASA-like agency had great political sex appeal.

As is frequently the case, there was still one further complicating factor. The President had based an important part of his 1971 State of the Union message on what he described as one of the most important changes in governmental structure since the writing of the Constitution. He recommended consolidating most of the domestic functions of the federal government into four departments: Human Resources, Natural Resources, Community Development, and Economic Affairs. Seven existing departments would be abolished. The President's very wide span of control would thus be narrowed, and most domestic activities would be logically arranged by purpose in these four departments, thus seeking improved governmental management. Creating an independent national cancer authority would run directly counter to the President's expressed organizational philosophy.

After months of behind-the-scenes maneuvering, a compromise was reached: a compromise that violated all the principles of good administration and simultaneously fulfilled the purposes of politics. It placated everybody and satisfied nobody. Under the law, approved December 23, 1971, the National Cancer Institute was retained as a component of NIH. Its director was ostensibly to be a subordinate of the director of NIH, but both officials were converted to Presidential appointments, and the director of the National Cancer Institute was given powers that made him one of the most ambiguous subordinates in the federal government. Among other things, the new Act directed the director of the NCI to:

> Prepare and submit, directly to the President for review and transmittal to Congress, an annual budget estimate for the National Cancer Program after reasonable opportunity for comment (but without change) by the Secretary, the Director of the National Institutes of Health, and the National Cancer Advisory Board; and receive from the President and the Office of Management and Budget directly all funds appropriated by Congress for obligation and expenditure by the National Cancer Institute.

The first part of this citation establishes a budgetary channel running direct to the President from an organizational unit four levels down in the hierarchy, and the final clause removed from the President a piece of his cherished authority to withhold appropriated funds from any program if he thought it desirable on fiscal or other grounds. Any management or public administration expert would have advised the President to veto the bill, but the issue was obviously not decided on those grounds.

A 3-man President's Cancer Panel was created by the Act to monitor the progress of the program. It was directed to bring immediately to the President's attention any delays or blockages in the program (implying that the director of the NCI is to have his way within NIH and HEW), and to make periodic reports directly to the President about the progress of the cancer research program. Nothing was said about consulting with, or making their reports available to, the Secretary of HEW, the assistant secretary for Health, or the director of NIH.

Perhaps the crowning administrative indignity was the creation of a National Cancer Advisory Board, within the National Cancer Institute, composed of twenty-three members, eighteen of whom are to be appointed by the President, and five of whom are to be ex-officio members: the Secretary of HEW, the director of the Office of Science and Technology (in the White House), the director of NIH, and representatives of the Veterans Administration and the Department of Defense. The Secretary of HEW and the director of NIH are thus directed to participate as two of twenty-three in *advising* the director of the National Cancer Institute, but he need not heed their advice if he chooses not to. His outside support may be far more important than his inside support, and his outside supporters and critics mean to have him understand this well. It would be interesting and useful for a panel of the National Academy of Public Administration to monitor this operation and report their observations and evaluation to the public.

THE NIH CLINICAL CENTER: LARGEST IN THE WORLD

When Dr. Rolla Dyer presented his ideas for the world's largest and finest clinical center to the Bureau of the Budget in 1946, he exuded confidence that a new era in rapid medical discovery would grow from the collegial relationship that he proposed to establish between the research-oriented clinicians, working directly with their patients, and the research scientists working in supermodern laboratories. Up to that time, few research laboratories of consequence had been built adjacent to the hospital rooms of patients being studied. Dyer reasoned that there needed to be a continuing dialogue between the microbiologists and the pathologists, between the surgeons, the oncologists (specialists in cancer), the biochemists, and the epidemiologists—and on and on. The insights of each should provide additional understanding to all his associates, and the result, in medical terminology, should be synergistic—the total effect should exceed the sum of the individual outputs if the scientists were to operate separately. This is the philosophy that underlies the architecture, the organizational arrangements, and the procedures of the NIH Clinical Center, which was dedicated on July 2, 1953. The actual planning of the Clinical Center was done under the supervision of Dr. Jack Masur, who also served as its distinguished director from 1956 until his death in 1969.

Six of the ten National Institutes of Health and the National Institute of Mental Health are allotted bed space within the Clinical Center. The institutes select patients—referred to NIH by physicians throughout the United States and other countries—for current clinical studies of specific diseases and disorders. About 15 per cent of the patients have been "normal volunteers"—healthy persons who provide scientists with an index of normal body functions against which to measure the abnormal. Although there has been a steady diminution in the number of these "normal volunteers" admitted in recent years, NIH says this is because of the accumulation of an adequate supply of information about them, rather than a steady diminution of normal people in the population.

The Clinical Center attempts to assure medical care of the highest quality to its patients. Research and experimentation is conducted under the strictest standards to assure patients that their well-being comes ahead of the desire for clinical study and scientific knowledge. Although not a "teaching hospital," the Clinical Center does perform various educational functions, including two residency programs.

Some 67,000 patients—about 4,000 per year in recent years—have been admitted to the Clinical Center for study. Eleven hundred laboratories envelop the 516 beds of the center. An extremely modern and expensive surgical wing was completed in 1963, which, by rights, should be named the "Herman Downey Surgical Theater." Downey was Senator Hill's powerful Appropriations subcommittee clerk, a gruff Tennesseean who hugely enjoyed being at the elbow of power. He probably put more of his own initiative and talent for kibitzing into the construction of the surgical wing than into any other aspect of NIH.

It is difficult to measure the extent to which the Clinical Center has fulfilled Rolla Dyer's dream. As a concept, it was impossible to fault, but the hopes and expectations of some were more than it was realistic to ask. In two decades of operation, it has not produced the cures for chronic killer diseases, as its ardent supporters had hoped, but it has made progress in improving forms of treatment. The linkage of clinical and laboratory sciences has certainly been worthwhile, and the pattern has been followed in numerous smaller clinical centers, both here and abroad. It has been the crucible within which a number of useful scientific advances have been made, and many fine scientists, including Nobel laureates, have achieved distinction.

THE NATIONAL LIBRARY OF MEDICINE

The storage, retrieval, and communication of biomedical knowledge have suddenly become a large, complex, and very important business. Although all components of NIH are engaged in this business, the organization with the most central responsibility for it is the National Library of Medicine (NLM).

The roots of the library extend back to 1836 when the surgeon general of the Army established a library. It was given a great boost in 1865 by the appointment of John Shaw Billings to head it up. He built it into a national resource of biomedical literature. In 1880, it began issuing a bibliography of medical literature, *Index Catalogue* (later renamed *Index Medicus*), which became pre-eminent among biomedical bibliographies of the world. By the beginning of the post-World War II era, it was rapidly becoming apparent that the Armed Forces Medical Library, as it was then called, was a national library resource that would be more appropriately administered by the United States Public Health

Service. By act of Congress it was renamed the National Library of Medicine and transferred to the Public Health Service on October 1, 1956.

With the electronic age at hand, the NLM embarked on the development of the most modern conceivable application of electronic data storage and retrieval systems to biomedical literature. Under contract with the NLM, the General Electric Corporation developed new equipment to meet the special needs of the NLM. The new system took several years to complete and became operational in January, 1964, with the name Medical Literature Analysis and Retrieval System (MEDLARS). Among other things, it involves the cross-referencing of abstracts that range across the whole field of medical literature, using key words, somewhat like the concordance of the Bible on a grand scale, as only computers could do.

In October, 1965, the Medical Library Assistance Act was passed, authorizing grants to help the nation's medical libraries expand their services to the health community. Grants were authorized to public and private nonprofit institutions for training, research, publication, and the development of regional medical libraries. Traineeships and fellowships were also authorized. And in 1967, the NLM acquired the National Medical Audiovisual Center. In 1968, as Lister Hill's illustrious career in the Senate was drawing to a close, Congress decided to name a planned new facility to house the developing biomedical communications network the Lister Hill National Center for Biomedical Communications. It was a warm tribute to the Senator, but nothing could adequately reflect the indebtedness of the NIH to Senator Hill.

THE JOHN E. FOGARTY CENTER

Only days after John Fogarty's death from a heart attack in January, 1967, Congressman Melvin Laird, then the ranking Republican member of Fogarty's Labor and Welfare Subcommittee of the House Appropriations Committee, proposed to Congress the creation of an International Research and Study Center at NIH as an appropriate memorial to Fogarty. Shortly thereafter, President Lyndon Johnson announced that he would seek funds for the creation of the John E. Fogarty International Center for Study in the Health Sciences. The center became operational on July 1,

1968, and all functions of the NIH Office of International Research were transferred to the new center.

The International Post-Doctoral Fellowship Program within the center provides training opportunities in the United States for young foreign scientists from forty-two countries. Institutes may invite foreign research scientists to work in NIH laboratories as part of the center program. Resident scholars from the United States are also supported in the performance of advanced study in the health sciences. International conferences and seminar programs are regularly sponsored by the center.

The center's name, like the Lister Hill Center, seems like a small tribute to one of NIH's two greatest benefactors.

NIH APPROPRIATIONS

No sketch of the development of NIH, however brief and limited, should end without providing a table of the growth of its appropriations. (See Table 2.) It speaks for itself—almost. What the figures do not show is that most of the increases made between the end of the Korean War in 1953 and the death of John Fogarty in 1967 were made at the initiative not of the President, but of Congress, and specifically Congressman Fogarty and Senator Hill. The immediate aftermath of Fogarty's death and Hill's retirement from the Senate is evident in the figures.

TABLE 2

NIH APPROPRIATIONS, FISCAL YEARS 1938–73

1938	$ 464,000
1939	464,000
1940	707,000
1941	711,000
1942	700,000
1943	1,278,270
1944	2,555,020
1945	2,835,000
1946	3,020,000
1947	7,952,000
1948	26,573,000
1949	45,668,000
1950	52,146,000
1951	60,059,750

TABLE 2 (*Continued*)

1952	57,675,291
1953	59,030,750
1954	71,153,000
1955	81,268,000
1956	98,458,000
1957	213,007,000
1958	241,183,000
1959	324,383,000
1960	430,000,000
1961	577,161,000
1962	736,585,000
1963	930,800,000
1964	974,454,000
1965	1,058,992,000
1966	1,244,406,000
1967	1,412,983,000*
1968	1,178,924,000
1969	1,394,052,500
1970	1,525,239,974
1971	1,688,799,000
1972	1,751,921,000
1973	2,015,196,000

* More than half of the decrease in amount from 1967 to 1968 occurred because Health Manpower Education was removed from NIH in that year, but even so the year 1968 was conspicuously the end of the Hill-Fogarty-Shannon-Lasker boom era in medical research.

VIII

Health Services and Resources

Not all of HEW is still expanding. For eighteen years, Presidents have been seeking to divest the Public Health Service (PHS) of its marine hospitals, and HEW of St. Elizabeths Hospital, the huge mental hospital in the District of Columbia. In his 1973–74 budget, President Nixon not only reiterated this position but also recommended terminating the Hill-Burton hospital construction program and the regional medical programs created in 1965 to improve the treatment of victims of cancer, heart disease, and stroke, and stated the intent to end federal support for community mental health centers. All told, Nixon asked Congress to cut the staff of the Health Services and Mental Health Administration— the agency that administered these programs until it was replaced by three agencies in mid-1973—by more than a third in a single year. The Public Health Service was directed by President Nixon to reverse its propellers. However, Congress did not agree to so drastic a change in direction.

THE RISE AND ECLIPSE OF THE PUBLIC HEALTH SERVICE

From 1912 until 1968, the U.S. Public Health Service was a growing organization, proud of its traditions, directed by a surgeon general, and staffed in its professional positions primarily by officers of its commissioned corps. Many of its highest officers had spent their entire careers in the Public Health Service, starting as interns in PHS hospitals immediately after graduation from medical school. That it was not able to continue as a cohesive organization after 1968 became a deep wound to many PHS officers.

Hospitals and health services for merchant seamen are the historical roots of the U.S. Public Health Service. In 1798, President John Adams signed the Act creating the Marine Hospital Service to care for sick and disabled American seamen. The struggling young American merchant fleet was operating at a severe disadvantage compared with those of other maritime nations of Western Europe, and it was imperative to maintain healthy crews for the new merchant ships. For a century, the Marine Hospital Service was the backbone of what was, in 1912, to become the U.S. Public Health Service.

Other responsibilities were assigned to the Marine Hospital Service during the latter part of the nineteenth century. The waves of immigrants who crossed the Atlantic after the nation began its recovery from the deep wounds of the Civil War brought increasingly severe public health problems. The immigrants brought with them a variety of contagious diseases and transmitted them to thousands of city dwellers with whom they came in close contact. Something had to be done. Congress decided this was a national, not a local or state, problem and passed the first Foreign Quarantine Act in 1878, giving the Marine Hospital Service the difficult task of keeping communicable diseases from being brought in from outside the country. Thus began the performance of a function that has continued to the present, though it has greatly changed in character since most travel is now by air instead of by sea.

To perform its role effectively, the Marine Hospital Service concluded as early as 1889 that it needed a mobile corps, subject to assignment anywhere, anytime. It also needed to pay more than the tiny salaries that were then being paid to civilian doctors. It concluded that the best device was to adopt the military personnel system, pay scale, uniforms, and perquisites. It designated its chief medical officer as "surgeon general of the Marine Hospital Service" (after 1912, surgeon general of the Public Health Service) and sought to follow—usually successfully—the War Department in the rank it accorded its surgeon general. The Commissioned Corps, as it was called, used the titles of medical director, senior surgeon, and surgeon to correspond with captain, commander, and lieutenant commander in the navy. Their uniforms followed the navy color tradition—dark blues and whites.

The commissioned officers of the Public Health Service became a proud group of career professionals. And, like all commissioned corps that require their top officers to have spent most of the professional lives in the service, the PHS inevitably became somewhat ingrown. Its leaders in one generation came from those who had made their career decisions a generation earlier. When times changed rapidly and the demands upon the Public Health Service ballooned far beyond anything that was earlier imaginable, the officer corps was caught without many of the talents it needed, but it was reluctant to assign high positions to persons outside the corps.

The quarantine functions of the PHS—which were extended in 1890 to curb interstate transmission of communicable diseases— led also to the beginnings of its medical research responsibilities. The Hygienic Laboratory, which later evolved into the National Institute of Health (NIH), was created in 1887 for research on cholera and other infectious diseases. (As noted in Chapter VII, NIH remained a modest undertaking until after World War II.)

The Great Depression of the 1930's became not only a spur to the development of a new social insurance system, accompanied by various welfare programs, but to the beginning of federal leadership in the improvement of state and local health departments. And it was the Social Security Act that became the vehicle for the new era of public health.

As governor of New York, Franklin Roosevelt had had the sense or good fortune to name an unusually competent and dynamic physician, Thomas G. Parran, as his state health director. So close became their relationship that Dr. Parran was Roosevelt's inevitable choice as surgeon general of the Public Health Service when the position became vacant in 1936. But before he was named surgeon general, Dr. Parran was instrumental in persuading those who developed the bill that became the Social Security Act— including, of course, President Roosevelt—that provision should be included in the already large bill to build up state and local health departments. Title VI of the Act, which became effective in 1936, authorized the Public Health Service to make general support grants to states to vitalize their generally weak public health organizations.

A companion part of the Act, Title V, authorized the Children's Bureau to make grants to state and local health departments for maternal and child health services. These two provisions, with their matching requirements to elicit the appropriations of more state and local funds, produced a substantial improvement in the performance of public health work.

Even with the addition of its new grant program to state health departments, the Public Health Service was small by present-day standards when it was transferred to the new Federal Security Agency from the Treasury Department in 1939. It had a dozen marine hospitals, strategically located at the major seaports and on the Great Lakes and the Mississippi; an interstate and foreign quarantine program; a leprosarium at Carville, Louisiana; two narcotics hospitals at Lexington, Kentucky, and Ft. Worth, Texas; a small National Institute of Health and a newly authorized National Cancer Institute; a communicable disease prevention program, with special funds for venereal disease work; and a few other and smaller functions. Its total employment was 6,200, and its budget was a little less than $30 million. This was the size and shape of the Public Health Service at the dawn of the era of public interest in public and private health.

Thomas Parran was an appropriate surgeon general to usher in that new era. He thought of himself and behaved as a genuine national promoter of public health. No previous surgeon general had ever behaved so. Venereal disease had been an unmentionable subject in polite company and in the public prints until Dr. Parran turned the spotlight on it. He did this even before the miracle drugs, such as penicillin, were found to be effective cures. He undertook to educate the American public about gonorrhea and syphilis, their method of transmission, their serious potential effects, and their treatment. As a crusader, he was unusually influential.

After the discovery of penicillin and the realization of its extraordinary utility in the cure of venereal disease, an enlarged program was authorized during World War II to bring the spread of the diseases under control. The program turned out to be so effective that a similar program was developed at the end of the war to combat tuberculosis—with appropriately different case-finding methods, medication, and other treatment. The so-called miracle drugs and antibiotics raised such high hopes that Congress seemed ready to vote additional funds for anything the Public Health Service asked, and for some things they did not ask.

In 1946, Congress passed the Hospital Survey and Construction Act, better known as the Hill-Burton Act, to provide hospital facilities in areas where they were nonexistent or sparse. Although Senator Lister Hill was the most important single driving force behind the bill, Senator Robert Taft made a singular contribution. As the Senate was considering the formula by which the funds should be allocated among the states, Senator Taft noted how intense the need was for hospital construction in the poorest states, which also were predominantly rural. He said that if the funds were allocated among the states on the basis of population, the funds would not go where the need was most acute. The formula that he was instrumental in devising made state allotments on the basis of the *inverse ratio of per capita income squared*. And after the funds were alloted, there was a variable matching formula that required the communities in the richest states to put up two dollars for each federal dollar of contribution, while the ratio in the poorest states was one state or local dollar for each two federal dollars. This was the strongest dose of financial equalization between rich and poor states ever to be enacted by Congress. It is especially noteworthy that its author was the highly respected and popular leader of the conservative wing of the Republican party. If a liberal Democrat had sponsored the idea, it would never have been enacted.

Other new responsibilities followed in steady succession:

- Transfer of the National Office of Vital Statistics from the Bureau of the Census (Commerce) to the PHS (1946).
- Creation of a Communicable Disease Center in Atlanta, Georgia (1946), an outgrowth of the malaria control programs of World War II.
- Establishment of the National Institute of Mental Health (1949).
- Broadening of the Hill-Burton program to include chronic disease hospitals, nursing homes, rehabilitation centers, and modernization of existing hospitals (1954).
- Transfer of the Indian Health Program from the Bureau of Indian Affairs (Interior) to the PHS (1954).

- Legislation of water pollution control measures giving the Public Health Service increasing responsibility, power, and money, but finally removing it from PHS (1965) because of increased expression of concern about the low organizational levels of water pollution control functions. (President Nixon and Congress eventually solved this by creating, in 1970, an Environmental Quality Council and an Environmental Protection Agency to which water and air pollution functions were transferred, but not until after water pollution control had been promoted to agency status in HEW and shortly thereafter transferred to Interior, then headed by the ardent conservationist, Stuart Udall.)
- Legislation for mental retardation and mental health centers (1963 and 1965).
- Amendments on drug abuse control (1965).
- Amendments to establish regional medical programs for heart disease, cancer, and stroke (1965), to make available to patients everywhere the latest advances in medical science and technology.
- Legislation for comprehensive health planning and the Partnership for Health program (1966) designed to give states greater flexibility in the administration of health programs and encourage them to take a more active role in coordinated planning.

Except for a lengthy struggle between the Bureau of the Budget and its successor, the Office of Management and Budget (OMB), on the one side, and HEW and Congress, on the other, over the proposed abolition of the PHS marine hospital system, this is a list of some of the major developments among the scores of legislative and other program changes that shaped the Public Health Service up to 1968. As described in Chapter II, in that year Secretary Wilbur Cohen reorganized the health functions of HEW, taking most of the power away from the surgeon general and altering entirely the meaning of the institution called the Public Health Service. The struggle over the PHS hospital system is so significant that it deserves to be recounted as one of the factors leading to the eclipse of the Public Health Service as a cohesive organization managed by officers of its Commissioned Corps.

THE CRUSADE TO ABOLISH THE MARINE HOSPITALS

Through its Federal Health Programs Service, the PHS provides direct medical care to merchant seamen, Coast Guard personnel, PHS commissioned officers, federal prisoners, and federal employees injured in line of duty. The largest and most controversial of its functions has been the operation of its marine hospitals—now called Public Health Service hospitals—of which there are now eight remaining. For a century and a half, these formed the backbone of the Public Health Service. The eight general hospitals are located at Boston, New York (Staten Island), Baltimore, Norfolk, New Orleans, Galveston, San Francisco, and Seattle, and there is a leprosy hospital at Carville, Louisiana.

For most of the last two decades, the PHS hospital system has been the subject of a deep-seated and running controversy between the Budget Bureau-OMB, HEW, and Congress. It all started in 1955, with a recommendation of the second Hoover Commission that the system was no longer needed. The report said that the service could be provided by community hospitals at the port cities and elsewhere and that the efforts and manpower of the PHS could be better used on other programs.

In its follow-up on all Hoover Commission recommendations, the White House, acting through the Budget Bureau, asked for HEW's reaction to these recommendations. HEW responded by saying that the Labor Department and the Commerce Department should also be consulted because the provision of adequate and free health services to merchant seamen might become an important issue between the maritime unions, the industry, and the government. As to the question of whether the hospital system was an undue burden on the officers and other personnel of the Public Health Service, HEW pointed out that it had been the training ground for most of the top PHS officers, and in consequence was rated as more of an asset than a burden. If equivalent service were to be performed in community hospitals and paid for by the government, the cost would substantially increase, according to HEW. The cost per patient day at that time was appreciably below that of good general hospitals in the port cities. And, as a final note, they pointed out that in some of the port cities, the community hospitals were overloaded.

The Budget Bureau was far from satisfied. The bureau, like the Hoover Commission, was convinced that in the long run equal or better medical care could be provided to merchant seamen through community hospitals, and that such services should not be performed by the federal government if there were an acceptable alternative. The bureau embarked on a crusade to rid the Public Health Service of its hospital system whether or not it would save the taxpayer any money. The crusade has lasted, at current writing, for some seventeen years, and has involved four Presidents and ten Secretaries of HEW.

The kernel of the Budget Bureau-OMB case was and is that these hospitals were created in a day when circumstances were utterly different, and now that times have greatly changed, appropriate adjustments should be made. It became a *cause célèbre* to demonstrate that federal functions can be terminated when they are outmoded, that bureaucracies are not automatically self-perpetuating. The idea of reducing the federal payroll by three or four thousand employees, even when the same service actually costs as much or more when performed under contract, has been almost irresistible to most Presidents and Budget Bureau directors, and therefore has been very hard for Secretaries to oppose when they had—as they always do—far more important matters to fight for in their budgets and their personnel ceilings. In consequence, most Secretaries have agreed to the recommendation of the Budget Bureau-OMB (some might have agreed anyway, but none would have regarded it as a matter of high priority) and have sought congressional approval for elimination of the PHS hospital system, if not at one swoop, then one by one until the hospitals are all gone. But Congress has not, up to present writing, agreed to more than a reduction of the system from twelve to eight hospitals.

The saga of the attempt by various Presidents and Secretaries, goaded always by the Budget Bureau-OMB, to get Congress to end the PHS hospital system is much too long to cover properly here. It deserves a case study by public administration scholars. To the author, who participated in and observed this lengthy struggle, year after year, one observation stands out above all others. If the same amount of effort—a massive amount over the seventeen years, including a special study by Ramsey Clark when he was a White House assistant to President Johnson in 1964—had gone into the improvement of other HEW programs that were in need of revision, including some that might have achieved substantial savings, it would have been enormously more productive for the American public. Each Secretary has a certain amount of good will in his congressional bank account, and if he is wise, he will spend it with care. If he spends a lot of it on a matter of third or fourth order consequence about which the Congress feels strongly, he has far less to spend on truly important matters. If this issue had involved substantial savings, it might have been worth it, but it was one of substituting contract services for direct federal services. It has been not an economic but an ideological issue, and an issue about which the general American public had neither knowledge nor interest.

It now appears that the matter may resolve itself—as it might have without the 17-year fight—because of the difficulty of staffing the PHS hospitals when the doctor draft is ended. The quasi-military status of the Public Health Service has been a godsend in staffing PHS hospitals. Without it or its equivalent, the PHS hospital system's days are numbered. But the long and acrimonious disagreement has been both debilitating and demoralizing to the leadership of the Public Health Service.

THE UNCLEAR ROLE OF THE SURGEON GENERAL

By the 1960's, national health policy had become a very important matter to Presidents, Congress, and the body politic. Clemenceau's dictum that war was too important to be left to the generals became applicable to surgeons general. Health policy moved to the highest echelons of political leadership. This left the surgeon general in a state of confusion as to what his proper role should be. He had become accustomed to thinking of himself as the top professional administrator within the government concerned with public health and, as such, thinking himself entitled to a key role in the discussion and development of health policy. But the formulation of health policy was outgrowing him and his staff, and he realized it.

To compound the problem, ideological and partisan views increasingly influenced health policy discussions. Democrats led the fight and eventually gained enactment of Medicare and Medicaid, and the more liberal among them wanted to go on from there to an expensive form of national health insurance managed by the federal government. The American Medical Association (AMA) and most Republicans in Congress took a very dim view of national health insurance and of each step that they thought might make its ultimate adoption more likely. Surgeons general, appointed for a 4-year term, were supposed to be chosen for their professional competence, not their ideological views. Inescapably, the policy issues made it awkward for a surgeon general to occupy so powerful a position unless he was able to make a postitive contribution to the development of health policies that coincided with the basic philosophy of the administration in power. Inevitably, health policy moved into the hands of the Secretary of HEW and his politically appointed subordinates.

Thus it was that Secretary Wilbur Cohen, in April, 1968, took both administrative and policy leadership functions away from the surgeon general and gave them to the assistant secretary for Health and Scientific Affairs, later renamed the assistant secretary for Health. Thus it was that the surgeon general was downgraded to a staff advisory role. When the term of its last occupant—Dr. Jesse Steinfeld—ended in early 1973, the position was not even filled. At present writing, there seems to be no intention of filling it. It is a casualty of the health revolution in mid-course, the victim of policy issues too big for the office.

THE REORGANIZATION OF 1973

From 1968 to 1973, Cohen's administrative concoction—the Health Services and Mental Health Administration—carried on almost all of the traditional functions of the Public Health Service except for the research, communications, and manpower responsibilities vested in NIH. With the coming of Secretary Weinberger came a new era and a new organizational arrangement. Both the 1974 budget and the new organization were intended to reflect clearly the nonexpansive philosophy of the administration in the field of health. Under this philosophy, the federal role in health was defined as:

- Financing of health services to reduce financial barriers affecting access to health care.

- Health and medical research activities that have broad national benefits but require high investment costs that cannot be adequately provided from other than federal sources.
- Preventive health and consumer protection activities that can be achieved best through collective action.
- Limited support to influence structural changes in the health system through technical assistance and special start-up funding for demonstrations.
- Limited health manpower activities that are essential to meet especially difficult problems that cannot be addressed through the basic student assistance programs of the Office of Education.
- Direct provision of medical care, only as a last resort, to segments of the population whose right to such care is recognized in law or whose need is especially acute because of the failure of more traditional means of providing health services.

Emphasis is clearly upon *limited* support and on direct medical care *only as a last resort.* This means major cutbacks in programs that have been regarded by many as foundation blocks of the federal health structure. But President Nixon and Secretary Weinberger share the firm conviction that unless constraints are applied, following the philosophy set forth above, the demands for federal health subsidies can overwhelm the federal budget.

The Weinberger reorganization of 1973 strengthened the hand of the assistant secretary for Health and made him the administrator of all health programs except for the health insurance functions of the Social Security Administration and the medical assistance programs (Medicaid) of the Social and Rehabilitation Service. In place of the Health Services and Mental Health Administration, Weinberger created four new units: the Health Resources Administration, the Health Services Administration, the Alcohol, Drug Abuse, and Mental Health Administration, and the Center for Disease Control. All are answerable directly to the assistant secretary for Health, as are the Food and Drug Administration and the National Institutes of Health.

The most traumatic effect of the new philosophy, budget, and organizational shake-up was felt by the National Institute of Mental Health (NIMH). Under the new policy, federal support for the community mental health center program—the heart and soul of NIMH—is to be terminated. Weinberger believes that support for these can and should, after a transitional period, come from states and communities, not from the federal government. More will be said about various effects of this decision later in this chapter, but it should be noted here that the organization implications of this policy include downgrading the NIMH and making it a component of the newly created Alcohol, Drug Abuse, and Mental Health Administration, the sixth health agency directly answerable to the assistant secretary for Health.

Meanwhile, the NIH lost the extensive health manpower functions that it had had since the Bureau of Health Manpower Education was transferred to it in 1968. The Bureau was moved into the newly created Health Resources Administration. Health manpower education has been a half-billion dollar program, one which Secretary Weinberger and President Nixon believe should be trimmed back materially.

Of no small importance in this reorganization is the direct line of comunications and responsibility from the ten regional health directors to the assistant secretary for Health, with the expectation that the health directors will have delegated to them many more operating decisions than they have made in the past. Under this arrangement, the reins of power are now held in the Office of the Secretary, and specifically in the assistant secretary for Health to a greater degree than ever before.

Under Assistant Secretary for Health Charles C. Edwards (he was elevated to this post in March, 1973, from his position as commissioner of Food and Drugs), there are now three organizations performing functions concerned with health services, health resources, and disease control. The Health Services Administration (HSA) oversees the work of five services: Community Health Service, Maternal and Child Health Service, National Center for Family Planning Services, Federal Health Programs Service (including the Public Health Service hospitals as long as they continue under federal operation), and the Indian Health Service. It is also intended to provide professional leadership in health service delivery. The HSA will seek to reduce its role in the direct provision of medical care to special groups of federal beneficiaries, and develop its leadership role in providing professional guidance to states and local communities in respect to health service delivery.

The Health Resources Administration (HRA) has the difficult assignment of improving the planning for, and distribution of, health resources, including professional and paraprofessional manpower, facilities, and knowledge of systems for the delivery of health care. It has nine subordinate units:

National Center for Health Statistics
National Center for Health Services Research and Development
Comprehensive Health Planning Service
National Health Service Corps
Health Maintenance Organization Service
Health Care Facilities Service
Regional Medical Programs Service
Emergency Medical Services Program
Bureau of Health Manpower Education

The Center for Disease Control is the residual legatee of traditional public health activities in preventing and controlling communicable diseases, directing foreign and interstate quarantine operations, and improving the performance of clinical laboratories. The center has also been requested by Secretary Weinberger to provide administrative direction for the National Institute of Occupational Safety and Health pending its possible transfer to a Department of Economic Affairs in line with the President's proposals for reorganization of the executive branch.

The scope and complexity of these health service and health resource functions are so great that it is possible within the scope of this book only to sketch a number of them. It may be useful to start with mental health activities. At the time of writing, the National Institute of Mental Health is about to be reorganized and partially split up. One NIMH official says that he and others feel like a goose being plucked. The Administration has made up its mind to try to move the alcohol and drug abuse programs out of NIMH if the Congress will agree. St. Elizabeths Hospital will be moved to the District of Columbia if Congress agrees. The present intent is to allow NIMH to continue to handle the community mental health center program for the present, perhaps as long as federal funds support those centers (until 1980), and to permit it to continue its responsibility for aiding in the support of mental health manpower education.

COMMUNITY MENTAL HEALTH CENTERS:
HAVE THEY SUCCEEDED TOO WELL?

When the National Institute of Mental Health was created in 1949, its director, Robert Felix, was dedicated to the proposition that most state mental hospitals built in the late nineteenth and early twentieth centuries were a blot on the national conscience, that they were custodial institutions where progressive therapy and hope were rarely to be found, and that they should simultaneously be upgraded in quality and replaced as rapidly as possible by community mental health centers and other similar forms of treatment. It took sixteen years for Dr. Felix's dream to be translated into the Community Mental Health Centers Act (1965) and still more years for the program to begin to show major results in terms of treating people near their homes. In the years from 1955 to 1967, state and county mental hospital loads declined at a snail's pace, but after 1967 the drop was much more rapid as the community mental health centers handled more and more of the burden. By 1973, there were 340 community mental health centers being operated with at least one in every state.

The cost of building and staffing community mental health centers has not been cheap—the federal subsidy in 1972–73 amounted to about $150 million—but the results, in the eyes of most participants and observers, have been well worth the cost. Although the program did not reach its fruition until after the colorful Dr. Felix had retired from the directorship of the National Institute of Mental Health, he and Mike Gorman deserve primary credit for laying the groundwork for the community mental health center program. (Gorman, it will be recalled, is the dedicated lobbyist associated with Mary Lasker and the one-man staff of the National Committee Against Mental Illness.)

To the consternation of mental health professionals and numerous others, President Nixon's 1974 budget recommendations gave the community mental health centers credit for having succeeded so well that it was possible to begin phasing out federal support. All funds to aid in the construction of centers were eliminated, and funds for the staffing of centers were reduced as the first step in a 6-year phase-out plan. Where substitute funds could be expected to come from to make up for the withdrawal of federal funds was not made clear. The implication was that if the communities felt them to be as successful as their articulate supporters claimed, the money should be forthcoming from somewhere, perhaps from revenue-sharing. The future of community mental health centers, at present writing, is very unclear.

THE WAR ON DRUG ABUSE: CALCULATED BY COST-BENEFIT ANALYSIS OR PUBLIC POPULARITY?

Largest of all of the programs of the National Institute of Mental Health in 1973 was the program to combat drug abuse, with appropriations of over $200 million in 1973. This program, operating principally through research, training, and community project grants and contracts for the treatment and rehabilitation of addicts, is neither succeeding so well that it can be "confidently" turned over to the states and cities—as the Administration has proposed for the community mental health program—nor is it failing so badly that it should be abolished entirely. It is somewhere in the vast "in-between." With the problem of drug abuse as serious as it is, it seems dubious that it would be decreased or terminated in any event, but there seem to be no good data by which to judge the degree of success or failure of this program. Public concern, especially as the parents of middle- and upper-class teenagers have become hooked on drugs, has pushed this to the forefront of NIMH responsibilities; it is the only program for which increased funds have been requested for 1974. All other mental health programs are, in effect, cut back. If anybody doubts that the "silent majority" influences budgeting, they need only look at the budgetary priorities within the NIMH programs.

ALCOHOLISM: THE PUBLIC DOESN'T LIKE TO BE "BUGGED"

Third largest among NIMH activities is the effort to combat alcoholism—a $90 million enterprise in 1973. Like the drug program, it operates through research, training, and community project grants and contracts. Demonstrably, alcoholism disables far more people than hard drugs, marijuana, barbiturates, and amphetamines combined, but since the great majority of the American public enjoys imbibing various amounts of alcohol, it adopts an attitude of self-conscious or amused tolerance toward those who drink too much. Rare is the person who feels outraged about the alcohol problem, as so many do about the drug problem. In consequence, much of the support for the program to combat alcoholism—as was true of the anticigarette "mini-crusade" of the surgeon general—comes from within the professional bureaucracy, which does its best to look at the issues objectively. Since budgeteers, especially the Number 1 Budgeteer, often pay more heed to outside than to inside influences, it is understandable that alcoholism did not receive the favored treatment that drug abuse did in the 1974 budget. It should be noted, however, that hard facts to show genuine success or failure are as hard to come by in this program as in the effort to conquer drug addiction.

HEALTH SERVICES FOR INDIANS: THE DOCTOR DRAFT HAS BEEN A BIG HELP

After long continuing difficulty on the part of the Bureau of Indian Affairs of the Department of the Interior in staffing and managing its health and hospital system, the President and Congress concluded in 1954 that the Public Health Service would be in a far better position to provide health services to Indians than the Bureau of Indian Affairs. Some fifty-seven hospitals—most of them with less than a hundred beds—and approximately 3,400 employees were transferred, and the Public Health Service was given a clear mandate to improve rapidly the facilities, the medical personnel, and the levels of service, both for those within hospitals and to Indians who never came to hospitals.

Especially for this kind of service, the Public Health Service had the advantage of its Commissioned Corps, paralleling in pay, ranks, and benefits the corresponding officer corps of the armed services. Young doctors could serve their military obligations in Indian hospitals as an alternative to doing their stint in the army, navy, or air force. This was attractive service for some, not only to improve the health of Indians—who are our least healthy citizens with the lowest life expectancy and highest incidence of communicable disease—but also to be able to see, recognize, and treat diseases that are now rare among the general American population, thus enhancing their medical education.

After nearly two decades of administration, the PHS can point to such dramatic changes as the decline in the incidence of tuberculosis among Indians by 70 per cent since 1955, but the tuberculosis death rate is still 3.5 times as high among Indians and Alaskan natives as among the U.S. general population. Among some groups of Indians, it is *eight* times as high. In fact death rates are down 48 per cent since 1955, but they are still 50 per cent higher than for the general U.S. population.

By 1972, the staff was about 6,500, nearly double the number that had been transferred to the PHS in 1955, serving 415,000 Indians and Alaskan natives. The physical plant has been greatly modernized, with a fine new 200-bed medical center in Phoenix, Arizona, being the latest and finest addition to the chain of what now numbers fifty-two hospitals.

With the military draft coming to an end, unless the doctor draft is extended, the Public Health Service may be hard put to entice and hold the number of doctors they need to assure decent medical care to reservation Indians and Alaskan natives. At current writing, the PHS is trying to devise some alternative personnel system that would be sufficiently attractive to keep their professional positions in these fifty-two hospitals filled. The availability of doctors in remote areas of the United States under a voluntary system is an extraordinarily knotty problem. The National Health Service Corps and its accompanying National Health Service Scholarship program (described later) may come to the rescue.

GRANTS TO STATES AND COMMUNITIES FOR HEALTH SERVICES

What started out in 1935 with the authorization in the Social Security Act of three types of health grants—support for improving state and local health departments, aid for maternal and child health programs, and grants for crippled children's services—evolved by 1973 into a half-billion dollar enterprise. Its emphases had adjusted to the times, and so had its funds.

Bloc grants are made to state health authorities to assist the states in attacking those health problems they consider of most immediate importance. State plans for carrying out these programs must be in accord with the over-all plans developed by the state comprehensive health planning agency. Project grants are awarded to public and nonprofit agencies, with particular emphasis on urban poverty neighborhoods and remote rural areas. Special funds are earmarked to provide health care to migrant agricultural workers and their families.

As nursing homes become more numerous and more important institutions, they also require more quality control and more technical assistance. Part of the Health Services and Mental Health Administration's most recent effort in respect to nursing homes is to stimulate the creation of "nursing home investigative ombudsmen" to hear and evaluate the complaints of those who suffer poor service, or the relatives of those who endure in Spartan silence.

The maternal and child health program seeks to reduce the infant mortality rate and promote the health of mothers during and after pregnancy; to promote the positive health, as well as the absence of disease, of young children through such means as "well-baby clinics"; and to locate, diagnose, and treat children who are suffering from crippling or handicapping illnesses.

By the mid-1960's, health grants were so numerous that HEW officials sought to get state and local officials to undertake some intelligent and comprehensive planning of health services. The result was the Partnership for Health program, enacted in 1966, a planning program that has served as a forerunner of Nixon's special revenue-sharing proposals. The objective of the Act was to provide financial support and moral encouragement for areawide health planning, including assessing needs, gaps, and overlaps, and producing action programs aimed at the highest priority needs. Funds were made available through project grants and were relatively modest, starting out at less than $5 million and moving gradually up to about $13 million in 1973. The degree of success has been spotty, depending almost entirely on the caliber, initiative, and cooperativeness of state and local health officials.

FAMILY PLANNING SERVICES: A RIGHT OR A PRIVILEGE?

In the 1950's and early 1960's, the idea of federal responsibility for making family planning services available to people who wanted but could not afford them was almost taboo. It was like the subject of venereal disease a few decades earlier. While he was President, Dwight Eisenhower would not touch the issue with a 10-foot pole, but the population crusader, General William Draper, converted Eisenhower after he left office. All but a few politicians found it an extremely prickly subject and avoided it as if it were a porcupine. Two senators, however, made the twin subjects of population and family planning a missionary enterprise and brought them into the limelight. One was Ernest Gruening of Alaska, and the other Joseph Tydings of Maryland. Gruening laid the groundwork by conducting a lengthy set of hearings in 1965 and 1966 on population and family planning, and Tydings was the Senate sponsor of the successful drive to enact the Family Planning Services and Population Research Act of 1970—his last effort before being defeated for re-election in November, 1970. Meanwhile, the Office of Economic Opportunity was using the flexibility that Congress had given it by establishing family planning clinics for the poor, and HEW Secretary Wilbur Cohen was using his power and influence to extend family planning services to public assistance recipients. The early 1970's put the federal government firmly in the business of supporting family planning services for those who seek them and could not otherwise afford them.

The Family Planning Services and Population Research Act (Title X of the Public Health Service Act) authorized federal grants that were intended, in conjunction with other available funds, in a 3-year period to reach a level that would provide services to most of the 5 million women who were estimated to want such services but not be able to afford them. Like a number of other health components of HEW, however, family planning services got caught in the 1973–74 budget squeeze. The President asked Congress to rescind $32 million of the $140 million appropriation for 1973, and, after transferring the residue of the Office of Economic Opportunity Family Planning Program to HEW, proposed to hold the entire program at the same level in 1974 as in 1973, far short of the goal set by the sponsors of the Tydings bill.

The National Center for Family Planning Services operates mainly through project grants to support public or voluntary non-profit clinics, with primary emphasis on services to people in low-income neighborhoods. It is far easier, of course, to organize such services in urban areas than in rural areas, although some of the most acute need is in small towns and rural areas. Partly because of the disproportionately high incidence of poverty among the blacks, and the correspondingly greater channeling of funds for

family planning services into black neighborhoods, cries of genocide were raised by some militant blacks, especially those who
believed most strongly in the adage, "there is safety in numbers."
But the blacks have their "women's equal rights" militants, too,
and they insisted that the services should be as much a right for
poor black women as for prosperous white women. Judging from
the decline in the cries of genocide, it would appear that the women
are winning.

St. Elizabeths Hospital: A White Elephant

Paralleling the Budget Bureau-OMB 2-decade crusade to close
out the Public Health Service hospital system has been a similar
effort to transfer HEW's second oldest activity—administering
St. Elizabeths Hospital, founded by Dorothea Dix in 1855—to
the District of Columbia. The stimulus came from the same source
—the second Hoover Commission. As of mid-spring, 1973, the
attempt at transfer had been no more successful than the persistent
drive to terminate the PHS hospitals.

After St. Elizabeths had operated for more than a century with
an intense sense of independence, first under the Secretary of the
Interior, then under the FSA administrator and the Secretary of
HEW, the latter decided that it was time to transfer this huge
mental hospital to the National Institute of Mental Health. This he
did in 1967, but with no great enthusiasm on the part of NIMH.
The hospital, with more than 3,000 in-patients (less than half the
number served in the 1950's), many of whom are senile, serves
primarily patients in the District of Columbia, but also has a substantial number of patients who are a federal responsibility. It
has about 4,000 employees and a budget of about $50 million (in-
cluding reimbursements from the District of Columbia).

HEW officials are not in disagreement with the objective of
transferring St. Elizabeths to the District of Columbia, but the
District of Columbia government has been reluctant to accept such
an expensive gift without assurance that the federal government
will continue to subsidize its operation and maintenance costs so
that the quality of hospital services will not rapidly deteriorate to
the level of many state hospitals. In the 1974 budget, the federal
government made an offer that on its face looks handsome, but
some District of Columbia officials, who are fairly expert at look-

ing gift horses in the mouth, are not so sure. The offer is for a $38 million subsidy for five years, followed by a gradual phase-out of the subsidy. It will be interesting to see how the District of Columbia government calculates its short-run versus its long-run interests, and to see what St. Elizabeths hospital will be like ten years hence if the proposal is accepted.

HILL-BURTON HOSPITAL CONSTRUCTION: IS IT NEAR ITS END?

For more than twenty-five years after the Hill-Burton program was passed by Congress in 1946, it was the principal stimulus for the construction of new hospitals, nursing homes, rehabilitation centers and other health facilities in all parts of the nation, but with initial emphasis on rural and other areas where the facilities were scarce. As mentioned earlier, Senator Robert Taft was particularly instrumental in seeing that the poorest states got maximum benefit from the program.

The Hill-Burton Act required each state, in order to be eligible for aid, to establish a state planning agency that would undertake to survey the degree to which there were hospital bed shortages in various parts of the state and establish a total plan with a priority listing, ranking community projects on an objective scale. This was the beginning of state planning in the health facility field. The federal government thus avoided becoming involved in making comparative judgments about the merits of individual projects, and confined itself to such roles as providing technical assistance in architectural planning to help avoid mistakes, reviewing plans to make sure that they met certain minimum requirements and yet were not too elaborate, and assuring that contractors met specified labor standards. Even though the states had an important planning role, they were not required to put up any of the matching funds. In fact, most of the Hill-Burton matching money over the last quarter century has come from local contributions, much of it from private contributors.

Without doubt, the Hill-Burton program has been one of the most popular and successful grant-in-aid programs ever devised. As the years have gone by, its emphasis has been changed from building new general hospitals to building chronic disease hospitals and nursing homes, rehabilitation centers, and modernizing existing hospitals. Most of the hospitals and other major facilities

built or modernized since World War II—some 11,000 of them—
have been aided by the $3.8 billion in Hill-Burton appropriations.
Even more important, in some respects, they have all been included in the over-all state planning done as a requirement of the
Hill-Burton Act.

Under the tight budgeting of 1973–74, the Administration took
a hard look at the figures showing increased bed vacancy ratios in
the nation as a whole and concluded that the nation was overbuilt
with general hospitals. It recommended complete termination of
the Hill-Burton program, not mentioning the extent and character
of need for modernization of the inner city hospitals, but asserting
that an increased share of the funds needed in the future by such
institutions should come from reserves built up from hospital insurance payments, or loan funds amortized from that source.
Whether or not the days of Hill-Burton are almost over, the
program can be labeled a great monument to Senator Lister Hill.
It was innovative and generally successful as a federal-state-local
planning and financing system for a quarter of a century. It has
been the central program of the Health Care Facilities Service.

REGIONAL MEDICAL PROGRAMS: GIVEN UP AS A FAILURE

Thrown together quickly in 1965 and given up as a bad job in
1973—that is the succinct story of the "Regional Medical Program." The 1974 budget puts it this way:

> Over a period of 8 years, the federal government, by means of
> grant awards and direct staff activities, promoted and developed 56
> RMP's, regional cooperative arrangements among the Nation's
> health care providers and institutions. Originally established to up-
> grade the health care of persons threatened by heart disease, cancer,
> stroke, kidney disease, and related diseases, the RMP's in recent
> years sought more to improve access to and generally strengthen
> the health care delivery system. Despite federal expenditures in
> excess of $500 million for these activities, however, there is little
> evidence that on a nationwide basis the RMP's have materially
> affected the health care delivery system. Further expenditures for
> scarce health resources cannot be justified on the basis of available
> evidence.

Regional medical programs were motivated by the idea that in
order to assure all citizens first-rate medical care, it would be
necessary to tie the nation's physicians and medical facilities into

a network of specialized centers and satellites, with clear channels of communication and referral from the most specialized and best-equipped medical centers to the most remote hospitals and doctors. When specialized treatment could not be provided in one of the outer rings of this network, either the patient would be moved to a facility in an inner ring or to the major medical center itself. The doctors in the outer rings would be given periodic refresher courses at the center and thereby both increase their diagnostic capabilities and learn to recognize what types of conditions could only be properly treated in highly specialized facilities. This concept was a pet idea of Dr. Michael DeBakey, the famous Texas heart specialist and surgeon.

That the program was developed too rapidly in 1965, without careful planning, there can be little doubt, but why the OMB concluded that it was a total failure is not clear. Essentially, the answer seems to be that there are no quantifiable measures to demonstrate that death rates or morbidity rates declined as a result of the half-billion dollars spent on the program. It was a lot of money, and in a tight budget period the budgeteers look for program weaklings to cull out. This was one that could not defend itself well. The abruptness of the proposed termination cannot fail to cause turmoil in the affected institutions and raise doubts about the dependability of the federal government as a business partner.

How Can Health Services Be Delivered More Efficiently?

One of the most important and complex problems for domestic policy-makers during the balance of the 1970's, at least, and probably far beyond, is how to keep the costs of health services and medical care from becoming prohibitive. How can first-rate health services be delivered to the public at reasonable cost? That is the central problem with which the National Center for Health Services Research and Development (NCHSRD) is grappling.

The NCHSRD makes grants for experimentation with and evaluation of various forms of health delivery mechanisms and practices. The work that has been done by NCHSRD so far has convinced the top policy officials of the government that they should encourage the development of health maintenance organizations (commonly referred to as "HMO's"). These are organizations that agree to provide a wide range of in-patient and out-patient services for a predetermined annual sum, like the Kaiser Permanente system on the West Coast and group health associations in various parts of the country. HMO's provide most services through salaried physicians and other professional personnel, rather than reimbursing them on a fee-for-service basis. HMO's had a boomlet two to three decades ago, but never gained national popularity. Whether governmental encouragement can make a difference remains to be seen. Their most conspicuous advantages are that there is a clear financial advantage to an HMO to keep its patients as healthy as possible, and the system also discourages unnecessary surgery. Their major disadvantage is the difficulty of attracting and holding enough first-rate doctors, since most doctors, especially surgeons, can earn a great deal more on a fee-for-service basis than on a salary.

So convinced has the Nixon Administration become that encouragement of HMO's is one of the best ways to provide good medical care at reasonable cost that it decided to set up a special organizational unit in 1973, the Health Maintenance Organization Service, to provide technical service and encouragement to the spread of this method of delivering health services.

The NCHSRD sponsors a wide variety of studies of health care delivery systems, including systems of cost accounting and reimbursement. The center has had more than $60 million annually for research and development contracts and some $35–40 million for the encouragement of comprehensive health planning—all told, a tidy sum. If it can make a significant contribution to the enormous problem of holding down the inflation of health costs, these sums may turn out to be well spent. But like so many HEW programs, the pay-off may be a long way off, and in the meantime, one has to operate on a combination of faith and best judgment.

The National Health Service Corps and National Health Service Scholarships

Thousands of small towns and rural areas in the country either have no doctors at all, or have totally inadequate health services. Others have single, dedicated doctors, and when they retire or die from overwork, the towns will be in desperate shape. To help overcome this problem, Senators Magnuson and Kennedy and Congressman Paul Rogers sponsored bills to create a National

Health Service Corps, a mobile group, somewhat like the Public Health Service Commissioned Corps, but not subject to the doctor draft. The Congress and President Nixon both approved the idea and it became law on December 31, 1970. In 1973–74, it is expected to provide health services to approximately 177 communities with a total population of some 1,770,000 people.

To assure that the National Health Service Corps would have a steady inflow of doctors and other health professionals, willing to put in a "tour of duty" in remote areas, Congress enacted in 1972 a National Health Service Scholarship Program, under which health professionals would be given scholarships in exchange for an agreement to devote specified periods of service to communities that are understaffed with doctors and allied professionals. The amount authorized was only $3 million per year, an amount which President Nixon considered inadequate to the purpose. In his 1973–74 budget, therefore, he announced that he would submit legislation to increase the authorization level and expand the authorities of the program to permit scholarship recipients to meet their obligations through a broad range of federal services. His budget included a projected expenditure of $22.5 million in the first year of operation.

HEALTH AND VITAL STATISTICS:
A SOURCE OF INFORMATION AND EMBARRASSMENT

Marriages, divorces, births, and deaths are recorded by state registrars of vital statistics and reported to the National Center for Health Statistics (NCHS), an expanded version of the National Office of Vital Statistics which was transferred by President Truman from the Census Bureau to the PHS in 1946. From their data, the NCHS produces reports on birth rates, death rates, fertility rates, and other vital data. At the end of 1972, they reported that the general fertility rate had dropped to the replacement level (2.11 children per married woman are needed for replacement). If this rate were to be maintained, the U.S. population would eventually stop growing, except for immigration. This is a condition that seems to be approved by an increasing share of American citizens, especially, judging from the figures, the younger generation.

The NCHS is also the source of regular reports on infant death rates and on the incidence of various reportable diseases. The former is a source of continuing embarrassment to the United States since this country stands fourteenth in its infant death rate.

The best source of information on the health of Americans is the National Health Survey, a periodic sample check like the special census samples. For policy-makers, the most disturbing of NCHS data are those that show a clear correlation between poor health and low socio-economic status. It may be arguable as to which causes which, but there can be little argument that improved medical care for the poor is essential not only on humanitarian grounds, but to help break the cycle of poverty.

HEALTH MANPOWER EDUCATION

The availability and cost of medical care are greatly influenced by an unusually inflexible supply of doctors, dentists, and other professional health manpower. It takes more than a decade to plan, design, build, and staff a new medical school and turn out its first graduating class. Long-term planning on a national basis is needed, therefore, to assure that enough health professional manpower is available to meet the steadily increasing demand for health services of a very wide variety. That is the role of the Bureau of Health Manpower Education, a bureau whose organizational location has been moved twice in the last five years. In 1967, it had an independent status within the Public Health Service; in 1968, it was moved by Secretary Wilbur Cohen to the National Institutes of Health; and in 1973, it was moved again by Secretary Weinberger to the newly created Health Resources Administration. When it was moved into NIH, one of the motivating factors was undoubtedly to aid the bureau in getting the added funds it needed. When it was moved out of NIH, it seems likely that one of the purposes was to reduce the appropriations for health manpower education. In any event, the organizational shift came on the heels of a sharply reduced budget for this program. Weinberger's 1974 budget called for expenditures of $370 million, as compared to estimated expenditures of $716 million in 1973.

The education of health professionals is extremely expensive, so expensive that without heavy state and federal subsidies, few such schools could survive. The argument now is whether more of the cost of such education cannot be borne by the health professionals themselves out of subsequent earnings, since they are among the highest paid of all professional groups. President Nixon's 1974 budget reflects the judgment that students should bear a higher share of the cost through long-term borrowing, and that states should bear a higher share of the cost of some types of professional education, such as schools of public health, and that the federal government should reduce its support of these programs. It is a difficult issue, since it involves a clash between the public need for an increased supply of health professional manpower and the equity of having high-income professionals pay for more of their highly subsidized education, which greatly enhances their earning power.

The 1974 budget recommended phasing out the general scholarship program for needy students seeking to become doctors and dentists, but asked for a continuation of the loan program at its previous level. To a limited degree, the elimination of new scholarships under the traditional program was to be offset by the new National Health Service scholarship program in which recipients agree to serve in the National Health Service Corps, which has already been mentioned. Similarly, there was an increase in funds requested to help disadvantaged and minority groups obtain better access to health education, a program for which $49 million was budgeted for 1974.

Federal funds have supported medical, osteopathic, and dental schools on a capitation basis—so much for each student enrolled—and also on a project basis to aid schools to expand their enrollments and experiment with programs designed to increase the quality of trained personnel. Grants are also available to relieve the acute distress of schools in serious financial straits. Grants are also available to enable 2-year schools to become degree-granting institutions. A sharp decrease in project grants is planned for 1974.

Schools of nursing, public health, and allied health professions (technical supporting personnel for hospitals, clinics, doctors, and dentists) received particularly disappointing news in the 1974 budget. The $115 million expenditure for nursing education in 1973 would drop to $47 million in 1974. Funds for educating students in graduate schools of public health would drop from $18 million to zero and funds for allied health education would drop from $33 million to zero. The rationale for so drastic a cut was that state, local, and private spending bears the main brunt of these costs and there seems to be no reason why it should not bear the entire cost. Such reasoning is alarming to the affected schools that have difficulty in obtaining even enough funds from these sources to continue programs at their current level. Making up for a federal withdrawal from the program seems well-nigh impossible. It remains to be seen whether Congress and the President can get together on some less traumatic budgetary plan.

Preventive Health Services: From Malaria Control to Rat Control

The core of public health is the prevention, rather than the cure, of disease. What was named for many years the Communicable Disease Center in Atlanta, Georgia, and what was renamed the Center for Disease Control (CDC) in 1967, is HEW's principal agency for preventing and controlling infectious diseases.

The greatest medical advances in all history have been those that have occurred in the last century through the control of a host of communicable and infectious diseases: malaria, typhoid, yellow fever, tuberculosis, syphilis, gonorrhea, small pox, diphtheria, poliomyelitis, and on and on. So effective has been the control of these diseases that the additional longevity it has brought has been a major contributing cause of the population explosion. Yet nobody is proposing that we reverse course and allow communicable diseases to solve the population problem. We are as bent on extending human life as ever.

The Center for Disease Control stands guardian at the gates to keep infectious diseases from being imported into the country and minimize their spread when they are brought in. Time was when the ports of entry, and holding facilities such as Ellis Island, were easily controllable gates, but with the coming of the air age the task of the CDC is like trying to monitor the comings and goings of a hundred million birds. The primary techniques have shifted from quarantine to extensive use of improved vaccines, quick identification of rare cases of lethal diseases, follow-up and inoculation of all contacts, and improved detection and diagnostic techniques and laboratory facilities.

Not only does CDC concern itself with communicable diseases, but it now has the more difficult task of trying to reduce mortality from health hazards that man inflicts upon himself, both deliberately and carelessly. CDC has within it the National Clearing House for Smoking and Health, which seeks to impress upon young people, especially, the decreased longevity they can expect if they spend their lives smoking cigarettes, while at the same time conducting a research program to learn more about the causal linkages between smoking and diseases of the lungs, heart, throat, and mouth. Despite their best efforts, they seem to have little, if any, influence on the consumption of cigarettes by the American public.

Since mid-1973, the Communicable Disease Center has also been given other responsibilities to aid communities to make their environments healthier. Two of the conditions that have turned the public spotlight on this need have been the attacks by rats on sleeping infants in poverty-stricken neighborhoods where trash is piled high, and the poisoning of children who have eaten lead-based paint peeling off the walls of poorly kept houses and apartments. The earmarking of federal funds for rat control has been pointed to as an extreme example of undesirable categorical specificity. It could as well be used as an example of the extent to which the public and Congress feel that if local and state governments do not properly take care of acute and shocking situations, the federal government should step in.

The Center for Disease Control is now also responsible for overseeing the work of the National Institute of Occupational Safety and Health. The high incidence of lung cancer among factory workers who have inhaled minute particles of asbestos, year after year, is one of many examples of the kinds of health hazard the institute is trying to avert. Preventing the contraction of "black lung" disease by underground coal miners is another example. The hazards of uranium mining have long been an object of analysis and protective regulations. The shielding of laboratory technicians and patients from unintended doses of radiation is still another of the numerous concerns of this institute. Like so many other adverse effects of technology, the pathologies may take years to show up, and when they do, they are usually irreversible.

The Center for Disease Control has for years been one of the outstanding international centers for the development and application of the most advanced techniques of immunization against communicable diseases. Its work in connection with tuberculosis, malaria, poliomyelitis, rubella, and a variety of other diseases has earned it well-justified international distinction.

IX

Health and Consumer Protection

The fourth profound change in the relationship between American citizens and their federal government has been the surprisingly sudden reversal of the policy and to some extent the practice of *caveat emptor*. No longer does the public think the buyer should have to beware; it wants him protected by the government from every form of hazard to his health, safety, and economic welfare— every form, that is, that can be handled through the regulation of interstate business (which covers most business) and some more besides. With occasional interruptions, free enterprise was in the saddle for most of American history until the 1960's, but "consumerism" is now shifting the balance of power between sellers and buyers, with the federal government acting as agent of the consumer.

The era of Ralph Nader has brought about an explosive increase in the expectations of the public for all manner of protective action—expectations that exceed the current capacity of government regulatory agencies to respond. But bureaucracies like to respond to opportunities and encouragement to expand their power, influence, and personnel, and, as we shall see, the Food and Drug Administration (FDA) has suddenly emerged as a major government function. It has grown in size from a Chihuahua to a foxhound, and may be headed toward that of a mastiff.

So great has been the swing in public expectation that the government should guarantee the purity and harmlessness of foods, drugs, vaccines, and other products, that aggrieved members of the public are now suing the federal government if it does not actually succeed in providing the public all the protection it seeks to provide. In January, 1973, a federal district court judge in Philadelphia, Clarence C. Newcomer, ordered the U.S. Government to pay Mary Jane Griffin $1,759,000 and $300,000 to her husband for loss of consort and for his own fate as her caretaker, following a case in which it was claimed that the polio vaccine Mrs. Griffin swallowed resulted in a severe case of paralytic polio, rendering her a largely paralyzed quadraplegic. Dr. Albert Sabin, developer of the vaccine, testified that the Division of Biologics Standards of the National Institutes of Health (NIH) (transferred in 1972 to the Food and Drug Administration) was not, in this case, negligent, but the judge thought otherwise. Dr. Sabin was skeptical of the diagnosis.

The more the government tries to protect the public against numerous hazards, the more the public believes it has a *right* to protection, and that the government has an obligation to assure that right. The more, too, government feels it must protect itself. It is no wonder that the FDA budget has moved upward from a measly $5.5 million in 1954 to $141 million in 1974, not counting another $30 million for a new, independent Consumer Product Safety Commission created in 1972 to perform a much enlarged set of functions—such as forbidding the sale of children's flammable nightgowns—which Congress thought FDA had not been handling adequately. But for the first five decades of its life, the Food and Drug Administration was afflicted with an acute case of poverty.

THE SLOW DEVELOPMENT OF FOOD AND DRUG PROTECTION

Federal laws to protect the American public against dangerous, adulterated, filthy and misbranded foods and drugs developed by spasms until the mid-1960's. Careful analysis by government scientists and other civil servants of serious health and safety hazards, and plans for regulation and control, often waited for years until a national tragedy claiming scores of lives or a dramatic exposé of scandalous hoodwinking of the public finally provided the marginal push needed to enact a newer and stronger law.

It took more than a century from the birth of the new nation for the U.S. Government to become significantly involved in health and consumer protection. By the last quarter of the nineteenth century, interstate traffic in patent medicines and in factory processed foods was becoming big business, and national magazines advertising these products were growing rapidly. With no controls whatsoever in most states, fakes and quacks had a field day. The fleecing of the public was bad enough, but the poisoning of untold thousands of people by the most irresponsible of these purveyors of nostrums was much worse. The stage was obviously set for a reaction. No small part of the governmental reform movement of the late nineteenth and early twentieth centuries developed from just this kind of situation.

In the twenty-six years from 1879 to 1905, more than 100 bills to protect the public from dangerous and improperly labeled drugs and food were introduced in the U.S. Congress, but none passed. Harvey Wiley was appointed chief chemist of the Bureau of Chemistry of the Department of Agriculture in 1883, and soon thereafter began a 20-year crusade to obtain enactment of effective federal legislation. Minor breakthroughs occurred in the 1890's and early 1900's, such as acts requiring the inspection of animals for disease before they were slaughtered, the inspection of teas entering U.S. ports, and the licensing and regulation of interstate sales of serums and vaccines used to prevent or treat diseases in humans. Finally, in the spring of 1906, Upton Sinclair's book, *The Jungle,* revealing with bloody vividness the cruel and unsanitary conditions in meat packing plants, and other shocking facts about the meat packing industry, was released to the public. For a time, the American reading public had a greater appetite for the book than for meat. Other muckraking journalists exposed the use of poisonous preservatives and dyes in foods, and the outlandish claims for worthless and dangerous patent medicines. The public mood and the political atmosphere were finally ready for Harvey Wiley's bill. Congress passed it in 1906, but not without some inevitable watering down. The Food and Drug Act and the Meat Inspection Act were passed on the same day, and promptly signed by President Theodore Roosevelt. The Food and Drug Act of 1906 was to stand for thirty-two years with comparatively little amendment.

The new law gave the Department of Agriculture the power to inspect and prohibit the movement in interstate commerce of misbranded and adulterated food and drugs. Dr. Wiley thought he was going to have a fairly free hand to administer the Act, but soon found himself hamstrung first by the Secretary of Agriculture and then by the courts. He was too much of a zealot to suit the cautious and conservative Secretary who became so concerned about Wiley's decisions and actions that he made him the minority member of a 3-man board that made all important policy and enforcement decisions. And the courts, all the way up to the Supreme Court, informed him that the new law did not prohibit false claims as to the efficacy of drugs, but only false and misleading claims as to the identity and composition of the drugs. Congress corrected the latter oversight fairly promptly with an amendment creating a new obstacle to enforcement: To prosecute a case, the government had to prove that fraud was intended. Nor did the Secretary of Agriculture restore Wiley's enforcement powers. Wiley resigned in 1912 to carry on his crusade from the pages of *Good Housekeeping* and from hundreds of lecture platforms.

From the days of Harvey Wiley until the creation of the Food, Drug, and Insecticide Administration in 1927 (renamed the Food and Drug Administration in 1931), progress was slow and arduous. Following the renaming of the agency, its chief, Walter G. Campbell, sought a complete rewriting of the original statute and its amendments, asserting that it was woefully inadequate. Nothing much happened for six years. Then, in 1933, following the inauguration of President Franklin Roosevelt, Walter Campbell found a sympathetic and strong supporter in the person of new Assistant Secretary of Agriculture Rexford Guy Tugwell. Roosevelt promptly gave Tugwell the green light for the development of a new charter for the Food and Drug Administration. In one major respect, Tugwell was an unfortunate ally. He was known as the most extreme left-winger of the New Deal "Brain Trust." And when the new Food and Drug measure was dubbed the "Tugwell Bill," it received the kiss of death. It remained for Senator Royal S. Copeland, a Democrat of New York, Commissioner Campbell, and others, to do what Tugwell could not. It was not until after Tugwell had left, and the elixir of sulfanilamide had killed more than a hundred people in the fall of 1937, that the time was again ripe for a major step-up in food and drug regulation.

Congress enacted what was, at the time, a rather comprehensive law—the Federal Food, Drug, and Cosmetic Act of 1938. It contained the following new features:

- Coverage of cosmetics and devices.
- Required clearance for safety of new drugs before distribution to the public.
- Elimination of the requirement to prove intent to defraud in criminal misbranding cases.
- Provision for the establishment of tolerance levels for unavoidable or required poisonous substances.
- Authorization to establish standards of identity, quality, and fill of containers, for foods.
- Authorization for factory inspections.
- Addition of the remedy of court injunction to previous remedies of seizure and prosecution.

The staff of the FDA in the year in which the new law was passed—1938—totaled 586 employees. Two years later it had increased to about 800. And there it stayed—except for the addition in 1945 of a unit to test and certify antibiotics—for fourteen years. The agency struggled under a doughty commissioner, Paul Dunbar, to meet its new responsibilities, but with little appreciation of the magnitude and difficulty of its task on the part of the Office of the Administrator of the Federal Security Agency (FSA), its new sponsor and superior, or on the part of the Bureau of the Budget. Its staff in 1953, when the FSA was converted into the Department of HEW, totaled less than a thousand.

BEET BALLS AND OTHER TRAUMAS FOR THE FDA

So weak was the public constituency of the Food and Drug Administration in the late 1940's and early 1950's, and so strong was the power of congressional antagonists, that the act of a single congressman could bring the FDA to its knees. In the spring of 1953, the chairman of the House Appropriations Committee, John Taber, vented his pent-up ire on the FDA by cutting its budget by about 10 per cent. The FDA had given an advisory opinion to a constituent of Taber's that it would be illegal to sell small beet balls, sculpted by machine from large beets, because they could be mistaken for baby beets. This was the proximate but not the only cause of Taber's wrath. The resulting budget cut caused the first "reduction in force" in FDA history and profoundly undermined morale. Even fifteen years later, the scars were still evident.

Nothing could better illustrate the contrast between the non-supportive atmosphere within which the Food and Drug Administration then lived and the political generosity that surrounded the activities of NIH and, in lesser degree, some other parts of HEW than this budget cut. It was not easy for HEW Secretaries and their staffs, or for Presidents and their staffs, to draw the sharp distinction that needed to be drawn at that time between their obligations toward regulatory agencies and those toward agencies with strong lobbies behind them. In seeking support for their regulatory functions, the FDA had hardly anywhere to turn except to the Secretary and the President, but neither FSA administrators, HEW Secretaries, or Presidents adequately understood that they, and only they, had the power and prestige to be the proper spokesmen for the American public in supporting the work of the FDA.

Until the recent upsurge of consumerism, the scales were heavily weighted against strong action by the federal government in the food, drug, and cosmetic fields. On the one side of the scale was the poorly expressed interest of 200 million Americans, which, like the air above the scale, was so diffuse as to have no weight. On the other side of the scale were some of the best-heeled lobbyists in the country, including the Pharmaceutical Manufacturers Association, the Proprietary Association and the American Medical Association (AMA). It was an uneven contest. The drug industry's interest in avoiding any more government regulation than it thought absolutely necessary was self-evident; the AMA's was less so. Organized medicine has long taken the position that doctors know better than the FDA what drugs are good for the patient and what ones are not; just so long as none are allowed on the market that are clearly dangerous. But what is dangerous? That is a complex question that is at the heart of the regulatory controversy.

What is not so widely understood about the AMA is that for most of its post-World War II existence, its principal income, in addition to membership dues, has been derived from drug advertising in the *Journal* of the American Medical Association. To what extent this has influenced the policies of the AMA will never be known; not even its own officials would know. But if the AMA were a public rather than a professional organization, this would be known as "conflict of interest" and would be forbidden by law. Whatever the wellsprings of its policy conclusions, the preponderance of the AMA's influence has been counterregulatory.

During its darkest days, some of FDA's strongest support came from producers of processed food and dairy products who were interested in standards to ensure consumer acceptance of their products and prevent misbranding and adulteration by competitors. One of FDA's legal responsibilities was to set food standards— definitions as to the required ingredients of bread and ice cream and strawberry jam and a hundred other foods shipped in interstate commerce. Old-timers at FDA still have a soft spot in their hearts for the support they got from food industry leaders at that time, but not, of course, from that part of the industry that wanted to make ice cream without milk, or imitation strawberry jam without strawberries.

TWO CITIZENS' ADVISORY COMMITTEES

As earlier mentioned, Commissioner Crawford and his successor, George Larrick, sought help after the Taber "baby beet debacle" from Under Secretary Nelson Rockefeller and Secretary Oveta Culp Hobby in the development of a bold plan to achieve broad public support. (See Chapter II.) They suggested the creation of a Citizens' Advisory Committee on the Food and Drug Administration. Although it took a year and a half for Crawford's proposal to be translated into action, such a committee was finally appointed in February of 1955. In five months, it produced a significant report recommending a three- to fourfold increase in five to ten years. This recommendation was promptly translated into a plan for increasing the staff by 15 per cent per year for ten years, but the increases came even faster. Congressman John Fogarty was highly sympathetic and overcame opposition from powerfully placed congressional octogenarians. A new $25 million laboratory in the HEW complex in southwest Washington was authorized, and a program of building new district laboratories was launched. The FDA entered on a new era of rapid expansion.

What none could foresee at the time was that public expectation for FDA services would increase at a much faster rate than 15 per cent per year, so that at the end of five years, the expression

of public concern about the inadequacy of food and drug protection would be much louder than half a decade earlier. Antibiotics, new drugs, pesticides, preservatives, color additives, and
other products sprang from the chemical laboratories onto the production lines and into the channels of trade during the 1950's at
such a rate that FDA could not possibly keep up with them. FDA
fell further behind each year, but far more so in terms of public
expectations than in absolute terms. Also, the psychological
bruises left by the negligence of their superiors in the executive
branch and by congressional mistreatment probably caused FDA
officials to move with greater caution in taking actions against
powerful segments of industry until they had unassailable cases.

As the expectation gap widened, the FDA thought that a second
citizens advisory committee might help them still more. This one,
appointed in 1961, was headed by George Y. Harvey, former top
staff man for the House Appropriations Committee. The report,
submitted a year later, stressed the need to upgrade the scientific
capabilities of the FDA, and especially emphasized—as did the
first citizens committee—the need to accomplish more through
industry and consumer education. In effect, the committee asked
for a major shift in emphasis from punitive enforcement to maximizing voluntary compliance. But George Larrick, only three years
away from retirement as commissioner of FDA, could not bring
himself to make such a shift. He established a Bureau of Education
and Voluntary Compliance but made no basic change of policy.

It is interesting to note that eight years later, when James S.
Turner wrote *The Chemical Feast* while serving in his role as
project director for the Nader study group on the FDA, he characterized the education-enforcement dichotomy as a phony formulation. "No idea has damaged the effectiveness of the FDA more
than the thought that law enforcement can be separated from
compliance with the law," asserted Turner. "It has divided industry, the FDA, and observers into vigorously warring camps
partisan to one side or the other—education or enforcement—
diverting energy and resources away from fundamental issues." If
properly formulated, the issue is one of the most fundamental of
American society. It is: Can regulatory agencies devise systems to
increase the incentives of industry to police themselves in the
interest of the consumer, or is it inescapable that the federal
government must become an ever larger regulatory force, making

and enforcing rules in ever greater detail? Grappling with such a dilemma, with notable lack of success, has been the unhappy fate of the FDA, with little help from Secretaries of HEW or their staffs, or from Presidents or their staffs.

THE KEFAUVER HEARINGS

Fortunately for unsophisticated citizens, a number of senators and congressmen, led by the late Senator Estes Kefauver of Tennessee, served as self-appointed spokesmen for the public interest in respect to food and drug matters, as watchdogs of the affected industries, and alternately as needlers and supporters of the FDA. Later, Senator Hubert Humphrey of Minnesota and three congressmen—John Blatnik of Minnesota, John Dingell of Michigan, and Lawrence Fountain of North Carolina—were to follow the Kefauver example. Kefauver, as chairman of the Senate Subcommittee on Antitrust and Monopoly, demonstrated that consumerism in the drug field was an attention-catching and politically popular outlet for his great energies. He was way ahead of Ralph Nader.

Kefauver's subcommittee held hearings from 1959 to 1962, beginning with the subject of extraordinary drug prices and profits, and moving to issues of drug safety and effectiveness and the internal management of the FDA. The hearings were a gold mine of publicity, and became both an embarrassment and an aid to the FDA. They revealed simultaneously weaknesses stemming from limited authority and resources and those stemming from human failure. In accordance with the first law of reporting, the human failures got the top billing and the dedicated lives of most of the FDA staff got none. But in the end, the hearings led to the landmark Kefauver-Harris Drug Amendments of 1962.

MER/29 AND THALIDOMIDE: A MISTAKE AND A TRIUMPH

The brief account of a serious mistake and a notable preventive action will help to illuminate the dilemma faced by food and drug officials in determining whether and when new drugs should be marketed. The mistake concerned a drug called MER/29 (triparanol) and the success story involves the drug thalidomide.

MER/29 was developed by Richardson-Merrell, Inc., and was

used primarily to reduce cholesterol levels in persons suffering from atherosclerosis. At the time the company filed its new-drug application in July, 1959, it was very widely believed by the medical profession and by the FDA that there was a causal relationship between high cholesterol levels and heart and artery diseases, even though it had not been clearly demonstrated. Since these diseases were hastening the deaths of millions of people, any drug that would reduce the cholesterol levels without severe side effects was believed to be an important medical advance (as well as a lucrative product for its manufacturer). Richardson-Merrell sought approval of its new drug, MER/29, based upon representations that it had been tested on animals without serious toxicity showing up.

As soon as the medical officer in charge of the review of the drug received the application, the company started contacting him about the drug, pressuring him for quick approval. The supporting data submitted by the company left a good deal to be desired, and the medical officer was resistant to a quick approval. He got conflicting reports from a variety of sources, including caution flags from the National Heart Institute. The drug company organized a conference at Princeton at which a number of physicians and scientists discussed the drug, with the preponderance of comment favorable to it. Still there was a paucity of test data.

By the spring of 1960, the medical officer decided to approve the drug, influenced, he said, by a paper given at a meeting of the American College of Physicians in which the author reviewed various drugs and said that MER/29 came out Number 1 in lowering cholesterol. He had the authority, as the lone reviewing officer, to approve the drug, and he did so in April, 1960, despite advice from an FDA pharmacologist that several years of testing would be highly desirable. The manufacturer then began a million-dollar promotional campaign for the product.

Even before marketing began, a Florida scientist noted that rats fed with MER/29 developed cataracts. A representative of the American Diabetes Association sought to get FDA to change its approval so that MER/29 could be used only experimentally, but it was to no avail. Eight months later, in January, 1961, a competing drug firm informed the manufacturer of MER/29 that a surprising percentage of dogs and rats fed with the drug went blind. Five months later, the AMA's Council on Drugs concluded that MER/29 had to be regarded as experimental and should not be prescribed for pregnant women, but its conclusions were not widely publicized. But the producer went right on promoting it, claiming few toxic or serious side effects.

Once the drug was cleared by the FDA, it became difficult for the medical officer who approved the drug to reverse the decision. Fortunately, in the case of MER/29, the key medical officer resigned in September, 1961, and his replacement required the company to provide strong cautionary labeling. When FDA determined that the animal test data provided by the company had been falsified, it clinched the case and MER/29 was withdrawn from the market in April, 1962. FDA then prosecuted the firm and three of its officials for submitting false information to the government. No contest pleas were accepted by the court and fines totaling $89,000 were imposed.

MER/29, according to the producer, was prescribed to some 418,000 persons, of whom, he estimated, less than 1 per cent were injured. Several hundred of the injured joined together and sued the manufacturer in thirty-six states for causing such injuries as cataracts, liver damage, ulcerative colitis, loss of hair, severe skin reactions, and impotence. Judgments amounting to millions of dollars were awarded to the plaintiffs.

In looking back on the case, Deputy FDA Commissioner John Harvey concluded that the drug should never have gone on the market in the first place. Senator Humphrey called it "a sharp indictment of the FDA." The case became one of the proximate causes of the enactment of the Kefauver-Harris Drug Amendments of 1962, increasing appreciably both the power and the responsibility of FDA for seeing that drugs were carefully tested before the army of "detail men" could take their free samples to the tens of thousands of busy but often unsophisticated doctors who prescribe widely advertised drugs to their patients on the assumption they are safe if allowed to be marketed.

Just how many drugs with greater or less side effects are kept off the market by the vigilance and deterrent effect of the FDA we can only surmise, but it must certainly be high. The most widely publicized success of the FDA as a preventive agent occurred about the same time as the MER/29 failure—the famous case of thalidomide.

Thalidomide was the American trade name of a sedative that

was extensively marketed in parts of Europe, particularly West Germany, under different trade names by European manufacturers. Its approval was held up in the United States by the Food and Drug Administration, and specifically by the medical officer, Dr. Frances O. Kelsey, to whom the new drug application was submitted. While Dr. Kelsey was demanding more adequate proof of safety, reports began coming out of West Germany that babies born to women who had been taking the drug were seriously deformed, often without arms or legs. When the full extent of the European tragedy—thousands of deformed babies—became known, Dr. Kelsey was given the highest Presidential award for having prevented a similar tragedy here, and Congress moved with dispatch to enact the pending Kefauver-Harris Drug Amendments of 1962, another milestone in FDA history.

The 1962 amendments gave the FDA a mandate for requiring the producers of new drugs to test them more carefully, more extensively, and longer than had the previous law. Even more important, in some ways, the FDA was directed to assure that drugs were not only safe, but effective for their intended use. The Kefauver hearings had brought out numerous cases of drugs that had both exorbitant price tags and dubious efficacy. Thus began a new era of enlarged activity by the FDA, entailing, among other things, a contract with the National Academy of Sciences–National Research Council to test some 3,700 drugs for effectiveness. The findings are now gradually being implemented.

THE BENEFIT-RISK DILEMMA

Although the FDA faces many dilemmas, its most difficult one, and the one that matters most to the American people, is the problem of where to strike the balance between the benefits and risks of drugs and other products. To much of the American public a drug is either safe or it is not, and if it is unsafe, it should not be allowed on the market. But, unfortunately, some of the most efficacious drugs are also very dangerous, if not properly used. If all drugs that were not "entirely safe" were removed from the market, doctors would be deprived of much of their power to defer death and reduce illness.

Penicillin is a good example of this. Over the years since its discovery, it has killed hundreds, probably thousands, of people because proper precautions were not taken to determine whether the patient was allergic to it before a massive dose was administered. Yet the amount of good that penicillin has done and can do is so great that it would be inconceivable to take it off the market because it is lethal when improperly administered to some people. Most drugs with sufficient potency to combat infections or systemic pathologies also have the power to upset the biological balance of some patients, causing toxic reactions. And some drugs have very slow time fuses, so that the adverse reactions do not show up for a long time, after irreversible damage has been done. To what extent should the FDA seek to ascertain the potential long-term safety of drugs before allowing them to go to market? In the case of drugs whose long-term adverse effect is genetic damage, it may take years—even generations—to obtain a solid scientific base for determining the degree of hazard that has to be weighed against efficacy.

The FDA is constantly battered from both sides in trying to find an appropriate middle ground between allowing new and potentially death-deferring or misery-reducing drugs to be merchandised, and keeping them off the market until FDA can be sure not only that the drugs can do what their producers say they can do, but also whether they have long-run adverse effects, and if so, whether the benefits outweigh the risks. And just how long is the long run? One thing is an absolute certainty: No commissioner of the FDA can ever satisfy both sides to this never-ending controversy over whether the FDA has made "the right judgment," in all cases.

The depth of this difference in point of view was well illustrated by a proposal recently advanced (1972) by an economist, Sam Peltzman, of the University of California at Los Angeles, and echoed widely by the more eminent Milton Friedman. Peltzman's analysis purported to demonstrate that the effect of the drug safety laws, especially the Kefauver-Harris Drug Amendments of 1962, was to deprive the American public of life-saving drugs— through the delays required by extensive testing that more than counterbalanced the good done by the testing. In other words, although some people would suffer and die prematurely if the new drugs were marketed before extensive testing, their value (everything was converted into dollar terms), according to Peltzman's "cost-benefit analysis," would be less than that of those whose deaths and illnesses would be deferred or prevented by the prompt introduction and use of the new drugs.

The Peltzman thesis presents in bold relief the contrasting viewpoints of Nader and Friedman. Nader is a "governmental protectionist" and Friedman an apostle of the efficiency of the free market. As Friedman points out, however, the Nader-supporters have an important political factor in their favor that is not likely to be overcome by any economist's "cost-benefit analysis." When drugs with lethal or permanently maiming effects on even a tiny minority of their users are marketed and used, their victims are identifiable people. If they are still alive, the sense of outrage they can create is potentially enormous, and if they are dead, their loved ones can develop a holy crusade against the "greedy drug manufacturers" and the "careless government" that allowed this to happen. But if the judgmental error is on the side of caution in the release of a new drug until its safety and efficacy are well proven, the nonusers of that drug or their surviving relatives may never be aware of the missed opportunity to use and be saved by a new miracle drug whose release was long postponed.

Friedman's conclusions were stated in extreme terms:

> The 1962 amendments to the Food, Drug, and Cosmetic Act should be repealed. They are doing vastly more harm than good. To comply with them, FDA officials must condemn innocent people to death. . . . Indeed, further studies may well justify the even more shocking conclusion that the FDA itself should be abolished.

Three weeks later, on January 29, 1973, President Nixon asked Congress for a $10 million increase in the FDA budget for 1974 to enable it to strengthen its drug testing and enforcement program. And after four days of special hearings, generated by the criticisms of the FDA, the Subcommittee on Antitrust and Monopoly of the Senate Committee on Small Business showed no sign of having been convinced that there was much merit in the Peltzman-Friedman thesis. FDA Commissioner Charles Edwards presented a counterattack, and the committee seemed satisfied that we have long passed the point where we can think seriously about returning to a policy of *caveat emptor*.

Food and Food Additives

The federal budget assures us that the "FDA is responsible for insuring the safety, quality, and nutritional adequacy of the Nation's food supply." It can do no such thing even with an annual budget of some $62 million for this purpose—a sum more than twenty times as great as twenty years ago. But it is a commentary on both the expectations of the general public and the sense of responsibility of FDA officials that they think that is a fair statement of their assignment. Actually, the assignment is shared by other agencies, but even so, it exceeds the realm of the possible.

The Department of Agriculture inspects meat and poultry while much of the checking on the sanitation of milk, bakery goods, and other products that are predominantly consumed in the states where they originate is done by state and city regulatory agencies. Nevertheless, the vast bulk of the fruits, vegetables, and prepackaged foods of all sorts consumed by the American public are shipped in interstate commerce and come under the eagle eye of the Food and Drug Administration. And the best the FDA can do is to sample a small fraction of the shipments, inspect the processing plants, interstate carriers, and distribution centers, at wide intervals test the samples to see that they do not contain hazardous pesticides or additives, and take action against indentified offenders. This procedure, coupled with the desire of the producers of nationally advertised brands and national chain store systems to hold on to their customers, results in giving the American public the greatest likelihood of food safety of any public in the world, but it is still far from a guarantee. A limited sampling system in relation to the more than $100 billion worth of food coming under the eye of the FDA cannot assure the purity, and especially not the nutritional adequacy, of all products.

The GRAS List: Is Salt Safe?

One of the FDA's central problems in dealing with the food supply is food additives. The Food Additives Amendment of 1958 required that all chemicals added to food had to be thoroughly tested for safety before being added to the food supply unless they were "generally recognized as safe." The FDA listed several hundred additives—beginning with such common items as salt, sugar, pepper, vinegar—on what quickly became known as the GRAS list. During the last decade, however, more and more of the items have come under suspicion and have been removed from the list, the most widely publicized being the artificial sweeteners used in diet colas and foods. The FDA is now committed to check out the whole list with meticulous care, not excluding salt itself.

Review of all the items on the GRAS list will take years. The FDA has a contract with the Federation of Experimental Biologists to do a good deal of work. Some idea of the magnitude of the undertaking can be gained from the fact that there are said to be some 14,000 scientific articles about just one item on the list— Vitamin A. Other common or uncommon additives may have had so little attention paid to them that most of the scientific testing will have to be done in the future (e.g., oil of nutmeg). Sodium nitrate and sodium nitrite, used to cure ham, bacon, and hot dogs (and with numerous other uses), will come under scrutiny, and a decision will be made on further use of saccharin. It is a very complex business.

ZERO TOLERANCE: DOES "ZERO" MEAN "ABSOLUTE ZERO"?

The Delaney clause of the Food Additives Amendment of 1958, named after its sponsor, Congressman James Delaney of New York, is one of the most famous in all food and drug law. It deems unsafe any additive "found to induce cancer when ingested by man or animal." It makes no difference how large an amount of the substance has to be ingested, nor how long a period of time it takes for an animal to develop the cancer. No trace of it, however minute, is permitted to show up in human food through additives, pesticide residue, or food processing methods. On its face, it may seem reasonable, but as technology progresses and detection instrumentation becomes more and more sophisticated, the concept of "zero tolerance" for carcinogens (cancer-producing substances) may prove impractical. It may turn out that massive doses of various items that might appear in very small quantities in human diets—and be well tolerated by humans in those amounts— may, after lengthy ingestion by rats or other laboratory animals, result in cancerous lesions. Should all questionable foods "in the commercial pipeline" suddenly be banned from sale under such circumstances, even though the risk is judged to be minuscule? The FDA and HEW Secretary Robert Finch decided, after cyclamates had been shown to cause bladder cancer in laboratory rats, that the risk to humans was so slight that they would allow the huge stocks of diet colas and other foods sweetened with cyclamates to be sold for a period, which was not an action that strictly adhered to the Delaney amendment.

The complexity of the issues involved in such questions is such that a number of concerned groups (including the Rockefeller Foundation, the Macy Foundation, the National Science Board, the Nutrition Foundation, Consumers' Union, and the Food and Drug Law Institute) banded together in February, 1973, to sponsor a new Citizens' Commission on Science, Law, and Food Supply to assist the public and the FDA in analyzing and understanding the options open to the American public in seeking to cope with these extremely difficult issues. The FDA should welcome all the aid it can get. It is to be hoped that one effect will be to help elevate the prestige of well-trained doctors and scientists who have an interest in going into the field of food and drug regulation.

How Much Filth Does It Take To Be Filthy?

The FDA has a responsiblity to prevent filthy food from being shipped in interstate commerce. Its officials have a never-ending problem of deciding just how much filth it takes to be filthy, especially since they are not able to establish any correlation between the absence of filth and the presence of health.

As noted in Chapter II, Mrs. Hobby was confronted with this problem soon after she was sworn in as HEW's first Secretary. Beginning in January, 1955, more than two rodent pellets of excreta per pint of raw wheat (on the average), or 2 per cent or more of insect-damaged kernels, made the grain filthy. The tolerance was reduced in 1956 to one or more pellets per pint, or 1 per cent or more of insect-damaged kernels. Lacking any clear evidence that there is a threshold of tolerance by the human body for a variety of forms of impurity, the subject becomes, in substantial degree, one of aesthetics.

Early in 1973, the Consumers' Union published a report critical of the FDA for its inadequate standards of cleanliness, using as one example what they considered to be an excessive allowance of rodent hair fragments in peanuts and peanut butter. Whatever level the FDA establishes, it cannot satisfy everyone. Since we live now in an era of "cost-benefit analysis," perhaps we should develop a system of polling the public and telling them that a given level of cleanliness would cost so and so much more, offering them several options. Or perhaps the problem should be solved through labeling, with producers permitted to label their products to show when they meet minimum standards of cleanliness and when they are superclean. Achieving agreed-upon levels of fastidiousness is no easy matter.

ANTIBIOTICS, BIOLOGICS, AND BLOOD

Ever since the end of World War II, the FDA has been operating, at no expense to the taxpayer, a system of testing and certifying every batch of penicillin and other antibiotics as to purity and potency. The producers of antibiotics pay a fee for such certification that is designed to cover all FDA expenses.

Biologics—the name used to cover vaccines, serums, and various other biological products—have been the responsibility of the FDA only since 1972 when the Division of Biologic Standards (DBS) was transferred from the National Institutes of Health to become a bureau of FDA. The transfer was no doubt hastened by a Senate committee inquiry by Senator Abraham Ribicoff into allegations of weak regulatory action by the DBS. What is now the Bureau of Biologics of FDA has an extremely well-equipped laboratory building on the NIH campus in Bethesda, Maryland.

In the case of widely used vaccines and other biologic products, FDA seeks to assure purity and potency by requiring that the producers submit "protocols" covering the numerous steps in the production process, including various tests for which precise methodology has been agreed upon. The producers certify that they have conducted the tests and provide the results to FDA's Bureau of Biologics. This procedure, supplemented by periodic inspection of the production laboratories, has been generally successful in assuring high quality vaccines.

Blood used for therapeutic purposes is legally a drug. Largely because some 1,500 to 3,000 hepatitis deaths occur each year from transfusions of contaminated blood, the FDA moved in 1972 to bring under its regulatory control some 3,000–5,000 blood banks and 200 processing centers not previously covered. (A major source of hepatitis infection has been the small commercial blood banks that pay vagrants for blood.) Previously, only 530 blood banks—those that shipped blood in interstate commerce—had been under FDA surveillance.

VETERINARY DRUGS AND ANIMAL FEED

The only way the FDA can adequately protect the food and drug supply for human beings is also to protect it for animals, especially animals used for human food. Drugs have become critically important in the prevention and treatment of devastating animal diseases, some of which are transmissable to man. Some idea of the size of the animal drug business may be gained from the fact that in a single year—1971—some 1,372 applications to market *new* animal drugs were received by the FDA, a jump of 25 per cent over the previous year.

It is estimated that in recent years 80 per cent of the animal protein consumed by Americans has originated from animals fed medicated feeds. The FDA must not only assure the safety of such drugs, but prescribe careful labeling to control the conditions of their use. All medicated feeds must be discontinued a specified period in advance of slaughter, so that meat and poultry products are free from harmful residues. The FDA inspects the feed mills periodically, but obviously they cannot be sure that all the animal growers and slaughterers follow the instructions on the labels. The Department of Agriculture maintains liaison with the FDA and monitors meat for excessive drug residues, whereupon the FDA takes appropriate follow-up action to prevent recurrence.

The greatest amount of publicity given any veterinary product has been focused on DES (diethylstilbestrol), used to accelerate the fattening of cattle, sheep, and poultry. It was purported to save the average consumer $3.85 per year in his or her food bill. But there was steadily increasing concern about its cancer-producing potential. A report appeared in the *New England Journal of Medicine* in 1971 showing a relationship between a rare vaginal cancer in teen-age girls and the treatment of their mothers with DES to prevent miscarriages. The FDA then strongly warned doctors against the use of DES for pregnant women. Next the Department of Agriculture came forward with information that DES residue had been showing up in meat to a greater extent than had theretofore been reported. A combination of external pressure —particularly from Senator William Proxmire of Wisconsin—and internal research finally caused the FDA to ban the manufacture of DES for use in feed, but the FDA regarded the hazard to health as being so slight that it permitted existing stocks of feed treated with DES to be used until January 1, 1973. But Congressman L. H. Fountain, a watchdog of FDA, would not allow the matter to rest there and secured a comptroller general's opinion that DES feed that should not be manufactured could not be sold. The FDA was not bound by this opinion and neither was it moved by it.

The case of DES is one of a number of evidences of FDA sensitivity to such considerations as possible temporary disruption of a major food industry with consequent decrease in supply and increase in prices, or possible losses to the producers, or both, when a ban is placed on a food additive whose hazard FDA believes to be insignificant. Many critics of the FDA feel that the chips should fall where they may when the decision has been reached that a food additive should be banned, but the FDA feels that it has an obligation to take into account a wide variety of considerations affecting the public good. The pendulum may have swung farther than the FDA realizes in the direction of congressional and public support for the avoidance of unnecessary risks through food additives, even to the point of paying less heed to the possibilities of market disruptions. This is part of the upsurge of public consciousness and concern for consumer safety and health.

PRODUCT SAFETY

Until 1973, FDA had responsibility for protecting the public against a large and growing number of hazardous consumer products—unsafe toys, flammable fabrics, detergents packaged in food cartons, fireworks, and all sorts of other products. In 1972, however, Congress decided to establish a National Commission on Product Safety and transfer to it many of the functions performed by the Bureau of Product Safety of the FDA. This was the compromise that occurred following a congressional move to take the Food and Drug Administration in its entirety out of HEW and set it up as an independent regulatory agency. (More will be said about this attempt in a moment.) Public concern about this field was understandably high in view of the fact that some 30,000 accidental deaths and 20 million injuries, a majority of them product-related, occur annually in or near homes.

Cosmetics, color additives, and man-made radiation sources constitute hazards for which the FDA has continuing responsibility for surveillance. Until comparatively recently, radiation hazards existed primarily in laboratories, industrial processes, and the healing arts, but with the advent of color television sets they moved into the home. Standards of shielding had to be established so that lengthy and continuing exposure to low-level radiation, especially in the case of children, did not occur. An entire FDA bureau is devoted to protecting people against radiological dangers.

ORGANIZATION AND MANAGEMENT OF THE FDA

The internal organization of the FDA is simple—a bureau is assigned to each major type of product or activity over which the FDA has surveillance: foods, drugs, veterinary medicine, radiological health, biologics, and toxicological research (a center rather than a bureau), plus an office that directs regional operations and a panoply of associate commissioners who act as staff officers in respect to science, medicine, planning and evaluation, compliance, and a number of other functions. District laboratories exist in nineteen cities strategically located throughout the country to create a reasonably balanced work load, and there is a fine central laboratory building located at the foot of Capitol Hill in Washington.

FDA's main organizational problem is establishing where it belongs within the executive branch. It has been housed in the Department of Agriculture, the Federal Security Agency, and HEW, but it has never really had a home. It has had no sympathetic parent who could take the time to understand it and assist it in coping with its fast-growing and fantastically complex set of problems. It has grown from a $5 million enterprise in 1954 to a $160 million enterprise in fiscal year 1973–74, and it is still expanding. It can no longer claim that it is starved for funds. The FDA is now like the adolescent son of a wealthy business executive who is so busy that he never pays any attention to his son except when he gets into trouble. The FDA is a headache to Secretaries of HEW, as it was, for example, to Robert Finch when he announced in October of 1969 that he was removing cyclamates from the accepted list of food additives and $100 million worth of diet colas and foods sweetened with cyclamates were affected. He could not have fully understood all he said about the subject at his press conference, but the announcement was so far-reaching that he felt he was the proper spokesman.

Three physicians whose backgrounds seemed to qualify them well for their terms as commissioner of Food and Drugs—James L. Goddard, Herbert L. Ley, Jr., and Charles C. Edwards— worked extremely hard to bring the FDA from adolescence to adulthood in the seven years from 1966 to 1973, and at least the first two men felt an acute sense of frustration as they left office. The FDA had outgrown the two generations of career chemists and inspectors who had dedicated their lives to it from 1906 to 1966, and its leadership had become a job for a tough scientist-administrator, with the capacity to handle himself well in the rough and tumble of politics and to communicate effectively with the public. FDA Commissioner Edwards had to testify frequently before various congressional committees during the years 1971 and 1972, sometimes trying to walk a tightrope between the views of the Secretary and the President, on the one hand, and those which he himself held, on the other. He was so busy, in fact, with high policy issues and external relations that he had too little time to devote to the internal overhaul of policies, procedures, and people that he recognized to be necessary.

The touchiest issue for Commissioner Edwards, in terms of his relationships with Secretary Richardson and President Nixon, was whether the FDA should be moved out of HEW entirely and made the principal component of a new independent Consumer Safety Agency, as proposed by a bill introduced by Senator Ribi-coff and supported by numerous members of Congress. The bill in fact passed the Senate in 1972, but Congressman Paul Rogers succeeded in defeating its main thrust by persuading the House and eventually the Senate to leave the bulk of FDA functions in HEW while agreeing to the Senate's recommendation for a new National Commission on Product Safety.

Richardson argued strongly to keep the FDA in HEW, while

Ralph Nader and others argued that it should become an independent agency. Former Secretary Wilbur Cohen sided with Ribicoff. Edwards, reflecting the feeling of all commissioners that nobody up the line had the time or interest to understand and give proper support to what he was trying to do, thought that it would feel good to share the burden with some full-time associate commissioners, as is customary in independent regulatory commissions and agencies, and to be able to manage the show as they thought best. It was a ticklish situation that he handled sufficiently well that he was promoted to the position of assistant secretary for Health in Caspar Weinberger's "HEW subcabinet" early in 1973. It seems highly likely that in his new position, Edwards will be a strong advocate of keeping FDA in HEW.

Three management problems have kept FDA in constant turmoil. The first is the rapid turnover of commissioners and their immediate staffs, Secretaries of HEW, and assistant secretaries for Health. Their tenure has averaged a little over two years each in recent years, much too brief a time to learn the complexities of FDA business and achieve policy continuity. Food and drug regulation is an area in which real understanding of issues is even more difficult than in most other parts of HEW.

Second, FDA has had an extraordinarily hard time in recruiting and holding able scientists and physicians. Good scientific work for the FDA does not seem to enhance an individual's reputation among the scientific community outside FDA; that community looks down on FDA science and some FDA scientists look down on themselves. It is a vicious circle from which it has so far been impossible to escape. Until that vicious circle is broken, FDA cannot become a first-rate scientific institution.

Third, and in a sense most difficult and important of all, is the lack of an adequate realization among virtually all segments of government and society that regulatory administration is a very special kind of administration, requiring special interests and dedication. It is unlike other forms of administration in numerous ways. The effects of the work of regulatory personnel of the U.S. Government are magnified many times, compared to that of most other managers, in terms of their effects for good or bad upon the American public. They require more training—and more sophisticated training—to perform their duties properly, necessitating an unusual kind of career service. They need a special code of behavior and special honors for adhering to it under the most trying circumstances. They are a tiny group compared to the rest of the U.S. officialdom, but their influence is enormous. They deserve far more attention, constructive criticism, encouragement, and recognition from political scientists, the public administration profession, Presidents, the Congress, and the public than they have received. If the public wants more and better protection of its food and drug supplies, it is going to have to devote more attention to the institution that does the protecting, the people who manage it, and the methods through which it seeks to serve the American consumer. The public cannot, unfortunately, depend on the President or the Secretary of HEW to do that for them.

X

Civil Rights

The fifth and most painful of the revolutionary changes in the relationship of American citizens to their government that has deeply involved HEW has been the enforcement of Title VI of the Civil Rights Act of 1964. That title of the law requires government departments and agencies to withhold grants from organizations and institutions that discriminate against individuals on the basis of race, color, or national origin. Next to the courts, HEW has been the government's foremost agent in changing the racial mores of the American people. Because of its ubiquity, HEW has borne the brunt of the animosity of those who have resisted that change. The Justice Department shares the onus of enforcement, but the representatives of HEW have had far more numerous negotiations and confrontations with school superintendents, school boards, county commissioners, and governors. For good reason, HEW became George Wallace's bête noire.

While it did not all begin, of course, with the *Brown* v. *the Board of Education* opinion of the Supreme Court in 1954, that opinion was such a landmark that it may be fairly labeled the beginning of twentieth-century federal legal action against segregation on the basis of race. Even though it had a slow fuse, it touched off the civil rights movement in the United States. The Supreme Court no doubt hoped that its 1954 opinion, coupled with another in 1955, would be followed by desegregation "with all deliberate speed," as they directed, but court decisions without active legisla-

244

tive and executive support are slow and inefficient instruments of social change.

For the seven remaining years of the Eisenhower Administration, and until after the escalation of civil rights protest in 1963, Congress and the President were inclined to act as if civil rights questions—including questions as to the propriety of making grants to school districts and universities that practiced segregation —were questions for the courts to decide. The courts continued to make case-by-case decisions, ultimately making some that required the backing of U.S. marshals and even the National Guard to make them stick. Hardly any action of President Eisenhower was more distasteful to him than calling out the National Guard to enforce the court order desegregating the Little Rock High School in 1957. But he was, above all, a good soldier and knew his duty under the Constitution.

Civil rights activists in Congress, led by Congressman Emanuel Celler of Brooklyn, managed in 1957 to gain enactment of a modest civil rights act that protected voting rights in all federal elections and established a temporary Commission on Civil Rights to study discrimination and report its findings to Congress. In retrospect it seems like a very limited advance, but at the time it was the most Congressman Celler could achieve.

During the 1950's, there was no organizational unit devoted to civil rights in HEW, and no individual assigned full-time to the subject. Beginning with the election of President John F. Kennedy, the interest in civil rights matters began to increase. James Quigley was appointed assistant secretary of HEW, with the odd assignment of concerning himself with civil rights and water pollution control, the two subjects that had interested him most as a congressman from Pennsylvania. He and his deputy, Lisle Carter, and Associate General Counsel Harold Horowitz searched for legal grounds on which HEW could base a threat to withhold funds from school districts that had taken no steps to desegregate. Except for a minor triumph in respect to school construction in federally affected areas, they did not succeed. Neither Secretary Ribicoff, nor his successor, Anthony Celebrezze, nor their superior, President Kennedy, thought it legal or politic to begin direct application of the principles embodied in the Supreme Court's decisions without congressional direction. Meanwhile, Congress continued to treat the whole matter as a very hot potato and kept its hands off.

But the pressure on the federal government to take major action to assure equality of treatment regardless of race in all public facilities, including schools, was steadily mounting. After the public outcry following the television broadcasts of police dogs attacking peaceful protesters in Birmingham, Alabama, on May 2, 1963, and the Medgar Evers murder a month later, President Kennedy decided that he had to ask Congress for a comprehensive federal civil rights law. His special message to Congress in June was followed two months later by the March on Washington, and Martin Luther King's "I have a dream" speech before 200,000 spiritually elated supporters surrounding the Lincoln Memorial. The psychological impact of these events on the nationwide television audience was to awaken the sleeping consciences of numerous people who had been preoccupied with their own concerns. Events of extraordinary drama were pushing the American people toward a splurge of nobility that some would later regret.

THE CIVIL RIGHTS ACT OF 1964

Then came a shock that had enormous indirect effect in accelerating the civil rights movement and converting protest into action: the assassination of President Kennedy. In the aftermath of the tragedy, President Lyndon Johnson moved with speed and firmness to capitalize on the mood and bad conscience of the country, especially in the matter of civil rights. President Kennedy's civil rights proposal was strengthened in a variety of ways. For HEW, the most important change was to make the withholding of federal grant funds *mandatory* from any and all recipient institutions that discriminated in the provision of services on the basis of race, color, or national origin. Kennedy's request had been to give federal granting agencies discretionary power to withhold funds. After Kennedy's death, President Johnson, the Congress, and the public swung rapidly to the conviction that the time for firmness had come.

The Civil Rights Act of 1964 was finally enacted on July 2, 1964, eight months after Kennedy's death. While many agencies had some share of enforcement responsibility, the major burdens were placed on the Departments of HEW and Justice. The courts had been the cutting edge for desegregation; HEW now became the bulldozer. Title VI of the Civil Rights Act was the machinery to carry out the desegregation, particularly in the South, and Title IV was to ease the pain of integration through special project grants.

Title VI of the Act stated: "No person in the United States shall, on the ground of race, color, or national origin, be excluded from participation in, be denied the benefits of, or be subjected to discrimination under any program or activity receiving federal financial assistance." Although it was a sweeping declaration of national policy, it needed to have some regulatory meat put on its legal bones in order to enable segregated school districts to know what they had to do and when. Even in the absence of such regulations, HEW was impatient to move and within a week after enactment of the law, teams of HEW representatives were touring the South, meeting with superintendents of schools to discuss voluntary compliance with the law. At that stage, no one knew what constituted an acceptable plan of desegregation, but it was a useful educational process for the federal participants, some of whom would later assist in the development of the much needed regulations.

Under Title IV, the commissioner of Education was directed to survey and report to the President and the Congress on the extent to which discrimination because of race, color, or national origin limited equal educational opportunities in public educational institutions. Title IV also authorized grants, training institutes, and technical assistance to help achieve integration with minimal trauma. Soon after its passage, the Office of Education commissioned a 2-year study conducted under the direction of James Coleman, which led to the report published in 1966 called *Equality of Educational Opportunity,* or, more popularly, the Coleman report, about which more will be said shortly.

Thus began, in the summer and fall of 1964, HEW's civil rights compliance program, which was to occupy more space in the public print, more Presidential attention, and more political controversy for the ensuing decade than any other HEW program.

HEW had little choice but to begin its compliance enforcement by using people who were trained for other purposes and who were career staff of the Office of Education, the Public Health Service, the Social Security Administration, and the Welfare Administration. A pragmatic decision was made to operate the program on a decentralized basis with a small leadership unit in the Office of the Secretary and the major compliance work conducted by HEW's program operating agencies. Subsequently, John Gardner, who became Secretary in 1965, a year after the Civil Rights Act became law, reversed the decentralized mode of administration at the behest of Congress.

The degree and pace of desegregation in the eleven Southern states in the decade before the Civil Rights Act was enacted can be judged from the fact that in 1963 only 1.17 per cent of Negro students were being educated in schools with white students, and in 1964 that figure had risen to 2.25 per cent. Those responsible for administering the new law wanted to see those figures accelerate very rapidly, but they were reluctant to take arbitrary action—such as requiring total desegregation of all school districts within a year or two—for fear that the disruption might defeat the purpose. They had, therefore, to move with a delicate mixture of caution and firmness—with more than a soupçon of bluff.

In the spring of 1965, HEW issued what were labeled "guidelines," a new type of instrument of administration. These guidelines fell short of being formal regulations and yet their sponsors sought to convey the impression that there was considerable force behind them. Their indeterminate status allowed a good deal of flexibility in their application. The commissioner of Education did not announce when he issued them that these were the "1965 model" guidelines, and that the 1966 guidelines would be much tougher. Many Southern school districts heaved a sigh of relief when they read the 1965 guidelines, feeling that they gave more elbow room than they had expected. The crunch was to come later.

By the summer and early fall of 1965, the attention of Commissioner of Education Francis Keppel and Assistant Secretary Quigley had begun to turn northward as complaints were being formally registered against such school systems as Boston, Philadelphia, and Chicago for discriminatory practices. Both Keppel and Quigley felt that in order to maintain credibility as to its evenhandedness, the Department could not seem to bear down on the South while letting the North go scot-free. The difficulty was that while Southern violations were relatively easy to establish as de jure segregation, the Northern violations were more subtle and far more difficult to prove. Unfortunately, Keppel moved before he had completely prepared the grounds and, almost incredibly, he took action against the strongest political empire in the country —the fiefdom of Mayor Richard Daley in Chicago.

Keppel sent a letter to the superintendent of Public Instruction of the state of Illinois informing him that funds under the new Elementary and Secondary Education Act—from which Chicago was due to get about $30 million—were being held pending a showing by the Chicago school authorities that the Chicago school system was not out of compliance with the Civil Rights Act. It was a political bombshell of the first magnitude. Keppel had let Assistant Secretary Quigley and the White House staff know what he was going to do and nobody had interposed objection, so he was completely unprepared when the roof caved in. Mayor Daley and Congressman Roman C. Pucinski were incensed, and the communication lines began to burn. Keppel was already in President Johnson's bad graces for having picked Henry Loomis—who was *persona non grata* to Johnson—as a deputy, and the Chicago episode was more than Johnson could stand. Under Secretary Wilbur Cohen was sent to Chicago to work out a compromise with Daley, a compromise that looked very much like a Daley victory. Keppel was quickly eased out. Gardner made him assistant secretary for Education—a new position not earmarked for education but which the Secretary so labeled. Keppel well knew that he had been "kicked upstairs" and soon left government. But he could do so with a quiet sense of satisfaction over one major success: He had had a key role in the enactment of the first general aid to education bill, the Elementary and Secondary Education Act.

The Chicago debacle, coming as it did only a month after Gardner had taken office, came as a deep shock. The Daley forces had won and the Department had had to back down—not all the way, but far enough to make it embarrassing. Where was the civil rights compliance program to go from here? Morale among the civil rights staff dropped, the civil rights organizations screamed "sell out," and the Southern school districts began to feel that they could achieve more through the application of political influence than they had previously thought possible. Gardner, a dedicated civil rights supporter, decided that a long-term strategy had to be worked out. In examining the causes of the Chicago fiasco, he also concluded, as did his staff, that the foremost lesson to be learned was that every case should be prepared thoroughly and carefully before federal action was taken.

Two appointments were key to Gardner's strategy and success in recouping his losses and moving ahead. One was Peter Libassi, who became special assistant to the Secretary and director of the Office for Civil Rights; the other was Harold Howe, who succeeded Francis Keppel as commissioner of Education. Both knew they had strong backing from Gardner and hoped they would get it from President Johnson. They did. But they tried no more power plays until they had their factual groundwork carefully laid.

In the spring of 1966, Commissioner Howe issued a revised set of guidelines that were considerably tighter than those issued a year earlier. They followed the principles that had been enunciated by the courts since the initial guidelines were set as to how "freedom of choice" plans had to operate to be acceptable, how the effectiveness of desegregation plans was to be determined, and how faculty desegregation was to be accomplished. These new guidelines were received bitterly by school officials who claimed that they had been led to believe that the 1965 issuance was the permanent policy.

In the fall of 1966, HEW received implied support for its desegregation efforts from the famous Coleman study and report (officially called *Equality of Educational Opportunity*, Government Printing Office, 1966), and the following spring the federal courts gave HEW an additional and larger boost. The Coleman study sought to determine the effects of segregated systems of education. The study came up with dramatic but ambiguous findings. At grade 12, black children were 3.9 grades behind white children in reading comprehension in the rural South, and 3.5 grades behind in the urban South. While it was impossible to determine how much of this shocking lag could be blamed on segregated schools *per se,* the findings were enough to give added impetus to HEW's desegregation efforts.

The principal bone of contention during this period between HEW and Southern school districts was over the "freedom of choice" method of desegregating schools. Under it, black children were to be permitted to attend predominantly white schools if they elected to do so. The problem, of course, was that when such "freedom of choice" plans were adopted they were ineffective because the psychological and economic pressures that were applied to black children and their parents were unbearable. Inevitably, therefore, HEW was forced to object to such plans. They were sustained by the courts in this. In the *United States* v. *Jefferson County Board of Education* (March, 1967), the Supreme Court said, "The only desegregation plan that meets constitutional standards is one that works."

Two months later, Justice William Brennan, speaking for the majority of the Supreme Court in the case of *Green* v. *County School Board of New Kent County,* gave "freedom of choice" its death knell. He said,

> The burden on the school board is to come forward with a plan that promises realistically to work and promises realistically to work *now.* . . . If there are reasonably available other ways, such for illustration as zoning, promising speedier conversion to a unitary non-racial system, freedom of choice must be held unacceptable.

Meanwhile Congressman John Fogarty had become increasingly restive over the decentralized administration of civil rights enforcement. From the original passage of the Civil Rights Act in 1964 until 1967, the Office of Education, the Public Health Service, the Social Security Administration, and the Welfare Administration had each developed enforcement staffs that operated under the policy guidance of a small Office for Civil Rights (OCR) in the Office of the Secretary. This office was headed by Peter Libassi. But there was uneven administration, and the Office of Education, in particular, had a bureaucracy that was extremely difficult to guide from the Office of the Secretary. Finally, under pressure from Congress, in May, 1967, Gardner ordered the centralization of all civil rights enforcement in the Office of the Secretary.

The years 1966 to 1970 were hard years for the South and very trying years for the Office for Civil Rights. The law was there and was not going to go away. The social system of the South had to be changed to comply with the law. Specific plans had to be drawn up, approved, and put into action to bring about desegregation. As the screw was tightened and as the 1968 Presidential election approached, many Southern school districts did their best to hold off action in the hope that the election would bring a change for the better. The OCR kept the pressure on, but they were not yet ready to set a date after which all schools had to be desegregated. On May 27, 1968, OCR issued a press release saying that approximately 14 per cent of the Negro students in eleven Southern states were enrolled in desegregated public schools. Progress had been slow, but close observers felt that the collapse of the segregation system was rapidly approaching, and, when it came, it would probably come with a rush.

Meanwhile, compliance efforts in other fields, especially in respect to health and medical facilities, had proceeded with astonishing rapidity and success. Medicare had been enacted only a year after the Civil Rights Act of 1964, with an effective date of July 1, 1966. To be eligible for reimbursement under Medicare, all health facilities had to operate on a nondiscriminatory, nonsegregated basis. To the delight of HEW, this economic pressure worked wonders. The vast majority of the 9,200 hospitals in the country, including those in the South, agreed to comply, and by 1968 HEW could report that 98 per cent of all the hospital and health facilities that had applied to receive Medicare payments were operating in compliance with the Civil Rights Act. Even assuming some exaggeration in the report, the result was surprisingly good.

THE NIXON ERA

When President Nixon took office in January of 1969, there was, as noted earlier, more than the normal degree of confusion as to what the new Administration's policy would be in the field of civil rights. The new President and the men around him began jockeying for policy and position with HEW Secretary Finch and his people, and with the Attorney General and his associates. Senator Strom Thurmond spearheaded the bloc of Southerners who had supported Nixon with the absolute conviction that his election would lead to a change of direction in the handling of civil rights issues. He and others were in frequent touch with the White House staff to express their opposition to the manner in which HEW's Office for Civil Rights was, in their view, being overzealous in enforcing the law. Basically, of course, they would have preferred to see Title VI of the Civil Rights Act repealed, but they realized that this was hardly likely. Essentially, therefore, the tactic they sought was minimal enforcement of the law, hoping that

Nixon would soon have the opportunity to appoint enough members of the Supreme Court to redirect the course of the majority decisions.

Into this floundering and rudderless situation came a young, liberal California Republican, Leon Panetta, who had served as an aide to California's erstwhile Senator Thomas Kuchel. No doubt bruised and defensive about the failure of the regular Republican organization to support Senator Kuchel in his primary election loss to George Murphy, Panetta was nonetheless hired by HEW Secretary Finch and Under Secretary Jack Veneman and assigned to head up civil rights activities for the Department. Hardly suited by perspective or experience to establish a durable working relationship among people of such widely differing viewpoints, Panetta was destined from the outset to tangle with the White House and eventually to get himself fired. It took less than a year. Panetta promptly wrote a book about what he considered a debacle, sarcastically titled *Bring Us Together,* a quote from Nixon's campaign oratory. In it he revealed himself as a man sincerely and strongly committed to civil rights but lacking any basic confidence in the Administration he was committed to serve and not above seeking confederates among the small bloc of liberal Republicans on Capitol Hill in opposing White House policies. The end, in his mind, justified the means, but it was an unforgivable sin so far as the White House was concerned.

Panetta may, unwittingly, have made a greater contribution to civil rights through his much publicized dismissal than he could have made in any other way. The White House finally faced up to the fact that it was necessary to arrive at a definite policy on the enforcement of the Civil Rights Act and stick to it. A month after Panetta's departure, a new set of guidelines was issued and a new director of the Office for Civil Rights was appointed. It was the beginning of an era of firmer enforcement of Title VI than many would have believed possible after observing the vacillation of the Administration's first year in office.

In March, 1970, J. Stanley Pottinger, thirty-year-old regional attorney for HEW in San Francisco, was called in to Washington to fill the post vacated by Panetta. From the outset, it became clear that he had an explicit understanding with the White House that they would support him and he would support them and that there was to be only one spokesman for President Nixon in dealing with the Secretary of HEW and Pottinger, namely, John Ehrlich-man. This was very different from Panetta's situation, in which he was told by a half dozen Presidential assistants what to do next or, more frequently, what not to do.

The new guidelines, issued on March 30, 1970, said, in effect, that time had run out, and that all schools had to have a desegrega-tion plan in operation by the time schools opened the following fall. The Justice Department and HEW collaborated in using their powers—Justice indicated that it was prepared to take any and all school districts that did not comply into court. The re-sistant school districts finally realized that the government really meant it this time and that the new rules applied to all of them. The end of *de jure* segregation was in sight.

In one of the great ironies of American society, in the period from 1969–70 to 1971–72, the South switched from having the most segregated school system in the nation to having a better record of bringing the races together in public schools than the North. Secretary Richardson announced on January 13, 1972, that the South had surpassed the North in the number of Negro pupils attending majority white public schools in the school year 1970–71 and that the gap was continuing to widen in 1971–72. The figures Richardson released showed an estimated 35.6 per cent Negro pupils in the United States in majority white schools— 27.8 per cent in the North and West, 43.9 per cent in the eleven states of the Deep South, and 30.5 per cent in the six border states and the District of Columbia. The issue of legal segregation had passed its contentious stage and was about to be converted into a new battle involving mostly Northern and border states over the problem of racial balance.

BUSING

The busing of school children to achieve racial balance became an issue of the first magnitude as the political campaign year 1972 began to loom ahead. It was much too big and hot an issue to be deftly managed by the Office for Civil Rights. Secretary Richardson, President Nixon and his White House aides, and numerous mem-bers of Congress became increasingly concerned as violence over busing erupted in widely scattered states, and in Michigan became an overriding political issue. But Richardson and the Office for

Civil Rights did not, in this instance, have open and clear lines of communication to the White House and the President.

For Richardson, the matter had its most embarrassing turn when President Nixon ordered the Justice Department, on August 3, 1971, to disavow in court a desegregation plan for Austin, Texas, which Pottinger and Richardson had proposed, involving substantial cross-town busing. Richardson was much put out at having the rug pulled out from under him and he took a month's vacation to think matters over. When he came back he had clearly made up his mind not to resign and to support Nixon's view that busing should not be used except to the minimum necessary extent. A few months later, he served as Nixon's principal spokesman before Congress in appealing for a one-year moratorium on busing. Congress did not enact the moratorium as such, but in its Education Amendments of 1972 it included, as Title VIII, a variety of prohibitions of and restrictions upon the use of federal funds for busing.

By 1973, the issue of busing had quieted down some, but was still smoldering with the potential of erupting again. The Supreme Court, in a Richmond, Virginia, case, decided in a 4 to 4 vote to uphold an appeals court decision that busing between the city of Richmond and its suburban area school systems to achieve racial balance was not required. It left very uncertain what would happen if and when other, somewhat similar cases reach the Supreme Court.

NONDISCRIMINATION IN EMPLOYMENT

In addition to its central role in enforcing Title VI of the Civil Rights Act of 1964, HEW's Office for Civil Rights has been named by the Department of Labor as its agent in respect to health and education institutions in the enforcement of Executive Order 11246 prohibiting discrimination in employment practices by any organization that enters into contract with the federal government.

The executive order, which was issued on September 24, 1965, and later amended by Executive Order 11375, dated October 13, 1967, states that in signing any contract with the federal government the contractor must agree that he "will not discriminate against any employee or applicant for employment because of race, color, religion, sex, or national origin," and that he "will take affirmative action to ensure that applicants are employed and that employees are treated during employment" without regard to these factors. The Office of Federal Contract Compliance (OFCC) in the Department of Labor, coordinating with the Equal Employment Opportunity Commission, was given basic responsibility for enforcement of the order with power to delegate such authority to other departments and agencies. Since the Office for Civil Rights in HEW seemed to be in a particularly good position to perform this role in respect to nonprofit institutions and insurance companies (because it had so many other dealings with them), a delegation was made to HEW's Office for Civil Rights to assure compliance by the following groups of contractors: insurance organizations; medical, legal, and educational services; museums and art galleries; nonprofit organizations; and construction contractors involved in work financed through HEW.

The executive orders are supplemented by a set of federal regulations issued by the OFCC in the Department of Labor and by further elaboration in the form of guidelines issued by HEW's Office for Civil Rights. The OFCC regulations require each contracting institution to conduct a "utilization analysis," followed by the establishment of goals and timetables for overcoming identified deficiencies. The goals are supposed to be based on a variety of factors spelled out in the OFCC regulations, such as the availability within the labor market area of unemployed members of minority groups and women having requisite skills although they are underrepresented in the employer's work force. In establishing timetables to meet goals, the contractor is supposed to consider the expansion, contraction, and turnover of the work force, but under no circumstances is the contractor to fire or lay off any employee to bring about better balance of minority employees or women.

Since HEW is the agent of the whole government—including the Department of Defense—in spearheading the enforcement of this program in all institutions of higher learning that have federal contracts, which means most of the nation's universities and a good many of its colleges, it is widely assumed that the regulations on implementation come from HEW. But HEW's role is to try to work out a suitable adaptation of the executive order, which was framed primarily for industrial and commercial employers who enter into procurement contracts. University employment presents a case sufficiently different to create difficult problems.

This program has created resentment in various universities. The requirement for the establishment of employment goals and timetables is especially troublesome since it frequently tends to be considered quota setting. Nothing engenders backlash and charges of discrimination in reverse quite so quickly as the notion that quotas, based on an assumption of equal distribution of skills throughout the population, are to be imposed by law. President Nixon has made it clear that he opposes such quotas.

Universities complain that they have no way of determining the size of the professional labor pools of women and minorities from which they might draw, nor of ascertaining the relative qualifications of the members of those pools as compared with others. How, then, does it make sense to set goals and timetables without having the essential information on which to base them? Further exacerbating the situation for the universities was the increased pressure on them in 1971 and 1972, at the very time when the financial squeeze became particularly acute and low turnover of faculty and other staff gave them little latitude to take much "affirmative action" in redressing any imbalances that existed.

Adding to the tension, universities have been confronted with demands from the Office for Civil Rights, which some regard as bureaucratic invasion of institutional privacy. The OCR has requested such information as the names, job classifications, date of hire, salary, grade, sex, race, and source of referral of all employees hired in the previous twelve months, and a master list of all employees currently on the universities' payrolls, by department, showing job classification, date hired, salary grade, current rate of pay, race, sex, age, and date of tenure. Additionally, it has asked for assurance that universities will permit OCR representatives access to all personnel files it deems necessary to investigate complaints of employment discrimination. While OCR undertakes to guarantee the universities that it will exercise the utmost care in maintaining the confidentiality of personnel records made available to it, the universities may be excused for worrying about the dependability of such assurances from one administration to the next.

Stanley Pottinger, director of the Office for Civil Rights from 1970 to early 1973, tried to alleviate the concerns of the universities and other institutions by assuring them that the goals and timetables required by the Labor Department's regulations are not quotas, but that they are devices to help the institutions monitor themselves as to whether they are trying to overcome identified discriminatory practices. If an institution makes a "good faith effort" to end such discriminatory practices, they will not be called to account for failing to meet their own goals. They must, however, be able to document the good faith effort. Nevertheless, the confusion over the difference between goals and quotas seems inescapable.

The sanctions available to the Office for Civil Rights in enforcing its decisions in respect to discriminatory employment practices may include the termination, suspension, or cancellation of existing contracts and subcontracts held by an institution, and debarment from future receipt of such contracts. Institutions are permitted, of course, to request and receive a public hearing on the issues before a final decision is made in any case.

Some institutions have been so upset by what seems to them undue demands upon them from an all-seeing bureaucracy that they have even considered terminating all federal contracts and subcontracts. Columbia University reportedly came very close to making such a decision but, in the end, its officials decided that the amount of money the university would lose would be so great that they simply could not afford to do it. The City University of New York, with substantially smaller sums involved, was similarly tempted but after an ultimatum to provide the required information and open its personnel files to OCR representatives or face a fund cutoff, the City University gave in. Money talks. As of the end of July, 1972, the Office for Civil Rights had delayed the award of contracts totaling $23 million to twelve colleges.

In theory, the Office for Civil Rights could examine individual complaints of discrimination and decide that a decision made, for example, by a particular faculty committee in appointing a male WASP (white, Anglo-Saxon Protestant) to an assistant professorship was discriminatory because, *in their judgment,* there was an equally qualified Catholic woman of Mexican origin—a minority underrepresented on the faculty—available for the job. It is the specter of OCR field representatives substituting their judgment for that of faculty committees as to who is best qualified, or equally qualified, for specific appointments that has worried the administrators of universities. This kind of decision-making in individual cases by an overzealous bureaucracy could cause a backlash of the first order. If the OCR sticks to the identification of *patterns of discrimination* and the elimination of those patterns, the likelihood of public and university acceptance of their purposes will be much enhanced.

OTHER FORMS OF DISCRIMINATION

Title VI of the Civil Rights Act of 1964 says that no person shall, on the ground of race, color, or national origin, be excluded from participation in or otherwise subjected to discrimination under any program or activity receiving federal financial assistance. For HEW, this language is so inclusive as to encompass virtually every one of its grant, loan, and contract programs. The Office for Civil Rights with its staff of 700 people could not possibly check to see that this provision is carried out by all states, subdivisions, and institutions in the United States. It has to operate on the basis of complaints, paying particular heed to those that appear to affect large numbers of people. One recent action by the OCR illustrates the kind of case that calls for enforcement action.

On June 22, 1972, OCR Director Pottinger informed the Sonoma County, California, Social Services Department that it was in probable noncompliance with the Civil Rights Act. He said that a review had indicated that 800 to 950 Spanish-surnamed clients were excluded from receiving public assistance as a direct result of the county department's failure to communicate with them in a language they understood. The county employed no Spanish-speaking telephone operators or receptionists, so that Spanish-speaking people were turned away without a chance to explain their needs. The OCR gave Sonoma County thirty days in which to inform it of specific steps it would take to correct the violations. Simultaneously, OCR announced that it was working with the California Department of Social Welfare to determine where other similar deficiencies might exist elsewhere in the state.

The language problem, which comes under the heading of discrimination because of national origin, is one to which relatively little attention has been paid during the long years of the black-white confrontation. Since the public school systems of the South have been desegregated to the point that they are more integrated than those in the North, some of the manpower of the OCR has been shifted to deal with these other, less publicized forms of discrimination. Despite the fact that the Presidential election was less than four months away, OCR announced on July 19, 1972, that it planned to undertake a year-long investigation to see whether the New York school system was discriminating against minority children, particularly Spanish-speaking children. Involved in the issue was the number of Spanish-speaking teachers in relation to the number of Spanish-speaking students.

Albert Shanker, head of the United Federation of Teachers, became much disturbed at the suggestion that potential teachers from the Spanish-speaking community should bear some preconceived percentage relationship to the ethnic composition of the community. "Teaching staff in large cities," he was quoted as saying, "has practically never reflected the ethnic balance of students because teachers generally come from the previous generation of immigrants. . . ." He asserted that he and his organization were unalterably opposed to quotas. So, too, is the Office for Civil Rights, according to its statements. If both parties to the issue mean what they have publicly stated, they should be able to get together. This issue will be interesting to watch in 1973 and 1974.

APPEALS

Decisions by the Office for Civil Rights are always appealable. The first step in the appeals process is to a hearing examiner, appointed by HEW but not from within the OCR which made the decision. The examiner is like a one-judge court, without all the formalities. All hearings are public. The OCR first presents its case and the aggrieved institution follows with its defense. If the finding is against the defendant, a second appeal may be made to a panel of five citizens from outside the government, appointed by the Secretary. The administrative appeal of last resort is to the Secretary himself. The Secretary is not required to review the case if he has reason to believe the lower appeals have been properly handled. Secretaries rarely do review such decisions; if they did, they would have time to do little else.

THE FUTURE OF CIVIL RIGHTS

In the Brown case of 1954, the Supreme Court stated that "to separate [black children] from others of similar age and qualifications solely because of their race generates a feeling of inferiority as to their status in the community that may affect their hearts and minds in a way unlikely ever to be undone." In arriving at its conclusion and expressing its judgment, the Court invoked social science research findings that seemed to indicate that prejudice could be reduced, in the words of Gordon Allport, "by equal status contact between majority and minority groups in the pursuit of common goals. The effect is greatly enhanced if this contact is sanctioned by institutional supports (i.e., by law, custom, or local atmosphere), and if it is of a sort that leads to the perception of common interests and common humanity between members of the two groups."

The continuous line of court decisions and the civil rights acts have assumed the soundness of the research on which the conclusions were based, and with comparatively few exceptions social scientists suspended study of the subject, treating it rather as a closed issue. In recent years, however, since the Coleman report of 1966—which revealed, among other things, much greater academic achievement differences between the races, even in integrated school systems, than had been realized—social scientists began to restudy the premises on which some of the court decisions had been based. The preliminary results of some of the research, summarized by Professor David Armor, who was then of Harvard and who was himself deeply involved in one such study, were disconcerting, to say the least, to those who had placed complete faith in the soundness of the premises.

The Armor report focused on those aspects of the previously accepted behavior model that postulated "positive effects of school integration for black students; namely, that school integration enhances black achievement, aspirations, self-esteem, race relations, and opportunities for higher education." To the surprise of many social scientists and others, none of the studies, according to Armor, was able to demonstrate conclusively that integration has had an effect on academic achievement as measured by standardized tests, nor did integration raise aspiration or self-esteem levels. Most startling of all was the finding that, under the circumstances in the limited number of studies, "integration heightens racial identity and consciousness, enhances ideologies that promote racial segregation, and reduces opportunities for actual contact between the races."

Armor cautions against unwarranted generalizations from the data, and his associate at Harvard, Thomas F. Pettigrew, as well as some others have taken strong issue with Armor's analyses. Nevertheless, the results raise questions that deserve better answers than any provided thus far. Above all, the report highlights the lack of any continuing, adequately financed research program to provide the kind of information on which sound public policy decisions can be based.

The Office for Civil Rights of HEW does not have such a research program. Its officials regard themselves as an enforcement arm of the federal government. Theirs is not to question why. They are dedicated to integration as the foremost means of improving race relations and opportunities for minorities. They see no point in questioning the premises on which their operation is founded. Who, then, should have responsibility for examining such questions? The assistant secretary for Evaluation and Planning. But he has neither a research program nor, at last reports, any plans for developing one in this area. It is a research and public policy void, so far as the federal government is concerned. The data in the Armor report and other available studies are not sufficient in themselves to base conclusions on, and it would take substantial sums of money, which probably means government support, to conduct studies that might be sufficient in size and duration and scientific care to enlist widespread respect, especially from those whose preconceptions were not supported by the results.

What the future will bring in the field of civil rights and to HEW is impossible to forecast with any confidence. The ethnic variety of the people of the United States, when combined with the blot of slavery, which has marred their consciences and character and, most of all, has scarred its victims, has generated a set of problems in human relationships unlike that of any other country. We have no successful model to look to; we can find no historical analogies that will help guide us. We will simply have to work our way out of this most difficult of all domestic problems in our society. And in the forefront of this profound social change will be the Department of Health, Education, and Welfare and its Office for Civil Rights.

XI

Managing So Complex an Enterprise

When HEW was thirteen years old, in 1966, Secretary John Gardner used to speak confidently of its manageability by comparing its number of employees—then roughly 100,000—with the more than 500,000 of General Motors and assure his listeners that size was no problem. No one thought of General Motors as unmanageable, at least not then. The Defense Department had more than two million employees, he asserted, but no one talked about dismembering it. Why talk about HEW as being unmanageable? These were the defensive words of a new Secretary who had been hearing much talk about HEW's excessive size and complexity. He had not yet learned enough about the Department to realize the inappropriateness of any comparison with General Motors, or even with the Department of Defense.

First of all, General Motors and much of the Department of Defense are primarily "hardware organizations." They produce or procure large numbers of physically identical products to which quality testing and control can be applied. The managers of the organizations usually have agreed-upon measures of success and failure. This is not true of HEW. Most of HEW's two hundred programs relate to various aspects of improving the human condition, but frequently there is no agreement as to how to determine whether improvement is occurring or not. How does one measure the effectiveness of thousands of medical research grants, of funds to supplement the programs of thousands of local school districts for educationally deprived students, of the various public assistance programs, of Social Security, of loans to needy college students? In these and nearly two hundred other programs, HEW has been called upon to administer what seem to the President, the Congress, and the public to be humane programs, with the faith that they will do some good, but with no agreed-upon measures of success or failure.

Second, General Motors and the Department of Defense have a much higher degree of control over their management environment. They can hire and fire managers. They can enter into contracts and subcontracts that have a high level of specificity as to what product is to be delivered and when. Despite unforeseen delays and cost overruns, they have the legal and practical capacity to hold their employees and contractors responsible for producing certain products at certain times. The officials of HEW do not have this power, even in theory, and as a practical matter their ability to control their management environment is unavoidably low. They operate most of their programs through grants-in-aid to state and local governments and institutions that are not under their direction. Only in limited degree can they control their end products except by the means of advance agreement as to how money is to be spent and the threat of withholding grants if the agreement is not adhered to. Under grants-in-aid, unless there are flagrant violations of the legal conditions, the money has to be paid whether or not the end product is considered satisfactory. This is a fundamental difference between procurement contracts and grants-in-aid.

Third, the board of directors of General Motors allows its top management to make most management decisions. Similarly, Congress allows the Department of Defense to make the vast majority of key management decisions. In contrast, HEW's "board of directors"—the Congress—makes a very large number of its management decisions. The very fact that Congress has legally authorized and mandated over two hundred grant, loan, and contract programs, and decides for the most part how much shall be spent each year on each program, is a clear indication as to how deeply involved the Congress has become in making the kinds of decisions that lie at the very heart of management.

The fact must be faced that HEW is not the kind of organization that is subject to "good management" by a good manager. It is, first and foremost, a political organization, not political in the invidious sense, but in the sense that the elected representatives of the people—the Congress—have intense interest in participating in the policy and management decisions of the Department. "Politics," according to Harold Lasswell, is "who gets what, when, and how." In those terms, HEW has an inseparable combination of political and managerial problems that make both General Motors and the Department of Defense look like simple enterprises. Its programs touch every person in the United States, whether he knows it or not, and most of them know it. And they are the judges, on a subjective basis, as to how satisfactorily these programs are being administered. How then, could their elected representatives fail to seek a strong voice in making the key program decisions of the Department with the largest supply of money the world has ever seen?

The Social Security program should be exempt from some of these generalizations. While Congress is as intensely interested in the policy decisions in respect to Social Security as any other program in the Department—if not more so—once the policy decisions have been made, the management decisions are left to the Social Security Administration (SSA). Congress makes a lump sum appropriation of more than $1 billion for SSA's 55,000 employees, and the determination of their deployment and use and the vast majority of other management decisions are left to the recognized professional managers. This half of HEW can control its management environment and, compared to other mass paper and electronic data processing mills, public and private, does so very well.

Because of the difficulty of providing income maintenance for the poor through a federal-state-local partnership on a reasonably efficient and equitable basis, the welfare reformers of the Nixon Administration concluded that the only way to make the system work was to take it out of the hands of state and local governments and establish a new, fully federal organization that, it was hoped, might reach the level of efficiency of the Social Security Administration. This decision again emphasizes the relative advantage of direct control by federal managers of the personnel, the processes, and the other elements of administration. But, as stressed elsewhere, no one should be misled into believing that federal administration of welfare will solve the welfare problem.

THE SECRETARY'S ROLE

To any but the rare individual who thrives on decision-making in a maelstrom of conflicting pressures and differing judgments, a typical week in the life of a Secretary of HEW is nothing short of grueling. He is at the beck and call of Congress to testify on all manner of matters. The White House staff and the Office of Management and Budget constantly have their fingers in many of his pies, and on selected issues—not necessarily the biggest issues —the President brings his own special perspective and style to bear. The press is constantly after him for interpretation of the crosscurrents of politics, seeking always to highlight conflict, while he does his best to minimize it. The pressure groups, euphemistically called "public interest groups" when they are noncommercial and nonprofit, rarely let up their efforts to obtain preferential treatment—meaning more money, or less regulation. When the subordinate units of the Department fail to satisfy the special pleaders' myopic sense of equity, many of them will not be appeased until they have pulled out all the stops to see the Secretary about their unique and misunderstood problems. It is never feasible for the Secretary to turn down all such requests, and therefore it is doubly difficult and awkward to select some and turn down others.

If the Secretary were the ultimate decider of executive branch policy in respect to all issues that come within the purview of his Department, life would be simpler, but he is not. He is not at the top of a pyramid-shaped hierarchy, but at the narrow neck of an hourglass. In the upper glass, in addition to the President, the Congress, and the Office of Management and Budget, there is the White House staff, whose members in almost every administration develop a skill for conveying the impression they are representing the President's views whether or not they have discussed the matter with the President. It sometimes seems as though the Secretary has as many bosses and would-be bosses as subordinates.

There is a never-ending queue of issues in search of decision lining up at the Secretary's door. Some of the issues will be patient and wait for his decision, but others are impatient, and if he keeps them waiting too long without attention, they go elsewhere for resolution. The traditional management problems are all there too:

attracting and holding first-rate people, adjusting the organization to fit changing circumstances, dealing with issues that involve other Cabinet officers and agency heads, long-range planning, short-range planning, deciding on the tough issues of resource allocation among intensely competitive claimants, and on and on. Some of these, the Secretary can partially delegate to others, but the most difficult issues wind up on his desk. It takes enormous strength of character for the Secretary not to fall complete victim to Gresham's Law of Public Administration: "The pressure of day-to-day operations with short deadlines tends to drive out long-range planning" or "The urgent is the deadly enemy of the important."

One of the most difficult roles of a Secretary—and this is especially true of the Secretary of HEW—is to be the advocate and spokesman before the Congress and the public for positions that have been decided by the President on grounds that may be different from those perceived by the Secretary to be relevant to the issues. In some cases the Secretary may have a significant disagreement with a Presidential decision, yet be called upon to be the Administration's spokesman. He shifts from being the spokesman of his own views to being the advocate of the President's views. He cannot say, "These are the President's views with which I disagree." He can only make up his mind whether the difference over the issue is one of such significance that he must resign, or whether he will be able to find a way to become a good salesman of the President's program of action. Rarely do Cabinet officers resign over single issues of this kind.

Some Cabinet officers, by virtue of their backgrounds and training, can manage the role of advocate of Presidential decisions much more easily than others. John Gardner's background made the role a particularly distasteful one to him. He had had the luxury during all of his prior professional career of being able to create an identity between himself as a public person and himself as a private person. He had been able to say what he thought, and he had not had to say publicly what he did not firmly believe. Elliot Richardson's background, on the other hand, was from the beginning that of a lawyer who is trained to put forward the best case he can construct on behalf of the client he represents. With a brilliant legal mind and with full understanding of not only the propriety but the necessity of having key officials of government carry out with good grace the decisions of their superiors, unless they are in very deep and irreconcilable disagreement with them, Elliot Richardson was an example of the superb advocate.

At HEW the burden of spokesmanship to Congress falls with particular force and persistence on the brain and tongue of the Secretary. Congress is continually asking for his considered opinions on bills before them and not infrequently for his personal appearance and direct testimony. The number of requests for reports on pending bills has gone up rather steadily from 660 during the Eighty-third Congress in 1953–54 to 2,321 in the Ninety-first Congress in 1969–70. Many of these apply to bills whose chances of enactment seem so unlikely that the Department can manage to avoid detailed analysis and reply unless they are moved from the back to a front burner. But in a fairly typical period, 1969–70, the Department made 668 reports covering 883 requests. Most of these reports are drafted in the Legislative Division of the Office of the General Counsel and are routed to the Secretary for his consideration and signature. The range of the subject matter is tremendous, and he must be careful to be familiar with what he has signed as he appears before Congress to testify on related subjects.

In the 4-month period from mid-January to mid-May, 1972, a not atypical period in terms of the demands upon the Secretary, Secretary Richardson appeared before Congress on twelve occasions and testified on a wide variety of subjects.

The fact hardly needs emphasizing that to be effective the Secretary must be extremely well informed concerning the subjects on which he is testifying and on the relationship of the subjects to specific concerns of key congressmen and senators.

HEW Secretaries have varied considerably in the extent to which they have regarded their testimony before committees as sufficient communication of the rationale for their position. Secretaries with considerable direct personal acquaintance with numerous senators and congressmen have often felt that courteous private calls upon them were at least as important as logically reasoned presentations before the relevant committees. But with the size of the portfolio of responsibilities of the Secretary of HEW, there are sharp limits to this kind of personal contact. The Secretary has no choice but to have much of it done by his under secretary, his assistant secretary for Legislation, and others.

THE BUDGET

The Department of HEW offers its Secretary a difficult and frustrating challenge in the field of budgeting. Most Secretaries come to their jobs without any realization of how small a proportion of the total budget of the Department is classified as controllable. About 85 per cent of the budget is generally classified as "noncontrollable." Noncontrollable items are those that are prescribed by law and become federal obligations with the force of contracts. They include, first and foremost, the benefit payments and the Medicare payments under Social Security. They include the grants to states where the government has committed itself by law to pay states according to specified matching formulas. The programs of financial aid and social services for the aged, the blind, the disabled, and for families with dependent children, and the program of assistance for the medically indigent are by far the most costly of these noncontrollable grant programs. Out of its total appropriations for 1972–73 in excess of $80 billion, all but about $13 billion fell in the so-called noncontrollable category.

This common use of the term "noncontrollable" (often used interchangeably with "uncontrollable") is misleading in one important respect. Except for Social Security, the contractual nature of the vast majority of HEW's noncontrollable programs is not of a long-term character. If Congress is persuaded of the desirability of changing any of the laws so as to limit or modify the obligations, it is at liberty to do so. Presidents have often recommended that one or more of them should be so changed. But once on the books, and after states or school districts or other institutions become accustomed to thinking of them as continuing federal commitments, it becomes very hard to persuade Congress to constrict them without an extremely persuasive set of reasons. Few Secretaries, or their staffs, have given much time to intensive analyses of possible ways of revising and improving the laws governing noncontrollable programs. Secretary Richardson recognized that this may be the most important and productive role that the Secretary's analytical staff might undertake and was concentrating his efforts in this area at the time President Nixon asked him to take over the reins of the Department of Defense. Secretary

Weinberger shares this view and is pursuing a like course. Similarly, when new programs are designed, they deserve, but frequently do not get, intensive and painstaking care to assure that they have no hidden flaws that will later make effective and economic management difficult or even impossible. The social services "Treasury raid" described in Chapter V was just such a flaw—a multibillion dollar flaw—which could have been avoided by more careful design of the Social Security Act Amendments of 1967 and the regulations implementing them.

Some people, both in and out of government, have the impression that considerable money could be saved by judicious pruning of HEW's staff, which exceeds 100,000 people. As in all other departments, economies from improved management are certainly possible and desirable. Yet staff salaries and expenses constitute such a small percentage of the total HEW outlays that opportunities for economies by reducing personnel are comparatively few. Even though nearly a third of federal expenditures is handled by HEW employees, only a thirtieth of the total federal civilian work force is located in HEW. The staff responsible for administering all of HEW's grant, contract, and loan programs—more than 200 programs dispensing over $20 billion—is less than 15,000 people, far less than the 23,000 employed at a single air base such as Kelly Field, near San Antonio, Texas. Scrimping on the number of employees overseeing such grant programs as public assistance has cost the federal government many, many millions of dollars, rather than saving anything.

Over half of HEW's employees are administering Social Security (they are paid from payroll taxes rather than general taxes), and another sixth (at least up until early 1973) are involved in providing hospital and health services to American Indians, merchant seamen, coastguardsmen, and federal mental patients. Savings in these areas come gradually from steady application of improved management practices. Across-the-board cuts unconnected with improvements in productivity simply reduce service to the public. Long delays in processing Social Security benefit claims would not be popular. Therefore, major savings from sweeping reductions in personnel are not feasible.

Of the 15–20 per cent of the budget that is theoretically controllable, much of it has a built-in momentum that is either difficult or unwise to arrest. For example, the $2 billion budget of the

National Institutes of Health (NIH) is included in the controllable category and is therefore subject to discretionary decreases as well as increases. But in 1968, when the Budget Bureau recommended and the President approved substantial cutbacks in medical research and training funds, both financial crises and crises of faith in the government's implied promises were created. Medical schools and other institutions all over the country had come to depend on what both NIH and the grant recipients regarded as "moral commitments" to continue multiple-year research grants without reduction. They had no cushion to absorb the shock of totally unexpected cutbacks. They suffered.

Most of the controllable part of the budget is in the form of grant programs, small and large, that can be used for a very wide variety of purposes. Like the NIH grants, these are part of the financial lifeblood of the recipient institutions and adjustment to any reduction in flow is painful. The cries of anguish from these institutions when President Nixon recommended in his 1973–74 budget the substitution of special revenue-sharing for earmarked special purpose funds—especially when there was any budgetary reduction in "their" funds—provided a gauge of the institutions' financial uncertainty and concern. Even the same amount of money as in the preceding year will not sustain the same level of operations for these institutions; an increase of at least 6 per cent is needed just to stay in the same place.

In periods of very tight budgets, the President, the Office of Management and Budget, and the Secretary are faced with the question of whether there may be programs that could be cut out entirely. The 1974 budget was the first in memory in which a President decided to "bite the bullet" and recommend termination of federal aid for a number of programs. As of current writing, it appears that what is happening is exactly what one might have expected—the beneficiaries of the federal programs and their congressional supporters are fighting back with all their might. HEW is now in the center of the fight between the President and Congress as to who has the power to set program priorities.

In three of the four years of President Nixon's first term, the HEW budget that Nixon proposed seemed to Congress too low, so it added substantial funds, and the President vetoed the bills. No other department has had this problem. It complicates the relationships between HEW and Congress considerably. Congress feels that it has the constitutional power to appropriate funds and that if it wishes to cut $2 billion from defense and foreign aid appropriations and add that amount to HEW funds, it should have the right to do so. The Office of Management and Budget and the White House take a different view. Although they would never voice it in quite this way, they feel that the President's budget is the "correct" budget and that anything the Congress does to it is a poorly considered action. Perhaps unconsciously they feel the President should have essentially the same power in respect to the budget that the prime minister has in a parliamentary form of government. A prime minister balances all considerations in his preparation of his national budget, and then his government is prepared to stand or fall on the soundness or wisdom of that budget. The parliament is not permitted to tinker with it; their role is to ratify it. Many members of Congress feel quite strongly that each President has taken one more step toward putting them in the role of a parliament instead of a legislative body with explicit constitutional powers over the appropriation of funds—a parliament without the power to force a national election when they vote "no confidence" in the executive.

HEW has been in the middle of the cross fire between Congress and the President on this matter during all the years when there has been a Republican President and a Democratic Congress. In some ways it is a very awkward position, but the embarrassment of having more money pressed upon HEW than it has asked for is envied by many another department. Eventually after each veto of the HEW bill, an accommodation has usually been reached, with appropriations at a somewhat higher level than the President's original budget, but lower than the vetoed bill. But in fiscal year 1973, after two Presidential vetoes, HEW went through the entire year on a hand-to-mouth basis with no regular appropriation act.

This tension between the Congress and the President over the HEW budget has inevitably, over the years, created a counterpart tension between the Office of Management and Budget (formerly the Bureau of the Budget) and HEW, and to some extent between the White House and HEW. Inevitably, the triangular relationship described in Chapter VII on NIH, linking special-interest pressure groups, congressional supporters, and program administrators into a mutual alliance, exists in various degrees in HEW. Many members of the President's staff—both career people in the Office of

Management and Budget and politically appointed White House staff (it matters not which party)—seem to expect, both consciously and unconsciously, that the Secretary ought to stamp out these unholy alliances. They fail to comprehend that this would be an extremely unwise use of the Secretary's time and power. He must work with the men in Congress who control one angle of this triangular relationship, and he has no control over the second angle of the triangle—the outside pressure groups. If he were to try to develop a litmus test of the loyalty of the third party to the triangle—the program administrators and their staffs—to the precise policies of the President, he would find himself in an utter quagmire. Flagrant violations of loyalty surely deserve to be punished, but these are infrequent. What makes the White House and the Office of Management and Budget edgy is something they can't quite put their fingers on—but they know it is there. Their suspicions usually exceed the facts, but there is no question that to an unmeasurable extent what they suspect does go on. Wise Secretaries seek to create an atmosphere of mutual trust and loyalty that will minimize "end runs" rather than creating an espionage system for "getting the goods" on persons suspected of disloyalty.

THE OPERATIONAL PLANNING SYSTEM

For the Secretary to elbow aside other pressing matters and devote a significant segment of his time to managing the Department, in the sense in which business executives manage their enterprises, is a real test of his interest in, and concern for, the processes of management. The mere listing of HEW's nearly 200 grant, contract, and loan programs (see Appendix A) shows the impossibility of personal oversight of each program. As the number of programs has become so large, and as the external demands on the Secretary's time have escalated, it has seemed to some Secretaries that it would be almost hopeless to try to perform the role of "general manager" of HEW. They have, in consequence, tended to leave most of the managerial duties to the under secretary, the heads of the operating agencies, the assistant secretary for Health (until 1972, the only line assistant secretary), and to the other assistant secretaries even though they are theoretically staff officials. But Secretary Richardson demonstrated the possibility of giving personal oversight to assessing the operational performance of

HEW's agencies in respect to the managerial objectives of highest priority. Secretary Caspar Weinberger intends to continue this practice, but it is difficult to do so without shortchanging some other key part of his job.

Two men who are Harvard Business School products—former Deputy Under Secretary Fred Malek who served with Secretary Robert Finch and Richardson's Assistant Secretary for Administration and Management Rodney Brady—were responsible for initiating and developing a system of "management by objectives," which they labeled the Operational Planning System. It was specifically designed to involve the Secretary in regular meetings with the heads of the seven operating agencies and their key staffs to report progress, or lack of progress, on an agreed-on set of high-priority program objectives. It is an adaptation of business monitoring practices to HEW's needs.

The keys to the success of such a monitoring system are the degree of personal involvement of the Secretary or his deputy, the choice of objectives, the method of measuring progress, and the degree to which the operating agencies regard the process as a collaborative and useful one. To the extent the agencies treat their meetings with the Secretary defensively, seeking to cover up any bad spots and embellish apparent successes, their utility is correspondingly diminished. Under Richardson, there seemed to be little doubt that operating agencies felt that better communication existed, in substantial part through this system, than had existed in HEW for most of its previous history, and that they, as well as he, profited from the exchange. Richardson's unusual knowledge of departmental activities, coupled with his incisive questioning, also made it difficult for operating agencies to give him a "snow job." (Secretary Weinberger, too, has the reputation of being a sharp questioner.)

Even under the best conceivable conditions, it is obviously not possible for the Secretary of HEW to do more than monitor what he thinks are the most important and the most vulnerable points of his stewardship. In so vast a Department, it is inevitable that serious misjudgments, or the appearance of grave fault, will suddenly come to the surface in the most unexpected places and in respect to matters that nobody would ever have thought to include in a secretarial monitoring system. In the fall of 1971, for example, Senator Abraham Ribicoff, in his capacity as a subcommittee chairman of the Senate Committee on Government Operations, received complaints from a scientific employee of the Division of Biologics Standards of NIH alleging that the division had been approving the release of influenza vaccine that was totally ineffective. Other allegations were included. Ribicoff promptly asked Comptroller General Elmer Staats to look into these allegations and submit a report to him. Thus began a series of events that ended nine months later in the transfer of the Division of Biologics Standards out of NIH into the Food and Drug Administration, and the replacement of the director of the division. Despite the admission by the General Accounting Office that most of the questionable practices had been corrected and despite stout support from the top officials of NIH and from a special *ad hoc* committee of outside consultants that reviewed the work of the division, the adverse publicity generated by the charges and replies was highly embarrassing to HEW. Finally Secretary Richardson, perhaps influenced by the threat of congressional action if he did not move, ordered the regulatory functions covering vaccines and other biological products transferred to the Food and Drug Administration (FDA). This occurred in June, 1972, and was followed soon after by an order to transfer the whole Division of Biologics Standards to FDA because of the difficulty of separating the regulatory from the research functions.

The publicity about the Division of Biologics Standards had hardly quieted when another flare-up occurred. As is not uncommon in an enormous enterprise, the news media picked up a story about which the Secretary had no knowledge concerning a research project on the treatment of syphilis that had been going on since the early 1930's. The project began when arsenical treatment was the best available, and its long-term efficacy and side effects were not known. The Public Health Service launched a research study to compare two groups in Tuskegee, Alabama—one of treated and the other of untreated syphilitics, in both the latent and active stages, all of whom were black—as to long-term health and longevity. The shocking part of the story was that after penicillin replaced the arsenicals as the accepted means of treatment, it was withheld from the control group. Public Health Service officials asserted that the members of the control group from whom penicillin was withheld had latent, rather than active, syphilis, and for an extended time after the use of penicillin became prevalent, there was no medical consensus that the new miracle drug should be prescribed for latent syphilitics. But even so, it was quickly admitted that the standards used by the Venereal Disease Division of the Center for Disease Control for protecting human beings during research work had not been carefully reviewed. They were much less rigorous than the standards promulgated by HEW's principal medical research arm—the National Institutes of Health—for all medical research conducted either directly by NIH or by NIH grantees. A special group of consultants from outside the Department was immediately assigned to determine whether and to what degree the control group suffered as a result of this research project.

These two cases illustrate well the monitoring problem in a Department with some two hundred programs. Neither the Secretary nor his assistant secretary for Health had any knowledge of the circumstances that suddenly blew up into front-page stories. Nor did heads of the operating agencies within which the events occurred have any system for bringing to their attention potential trouble spots of this kind. Nor would any existing audit system or other review system currently in use have spotted these problems in a timely fashion. To what extent such problems result from the sheer bulk and complexity of HEW, it is difficult to say, but that the Department's enormous size is a major contributing element, there seems little doubt. To put it another way, if HEW is to increase its chances of heading off such embarrassing situations in the future, it must develop and apply some new managerial techniques. Valuable as the Operational Planning System may be for some purposes, it cannot be an effective early warning system for all trouble spots.

The Operational Planning System makes no attempt to assess the performance of the various important units in the Office of the Secretary. This appears to be an unfair exemption for the Secretary's staff arms, some with numerous employees. But, as one official remarked, "If the system is extended to include all assistant secretaries, the Secretary will collapse from the amount of time he must devote to it."

Secretary Weinberger and Under Secretary Frank Carlucci have supplemented the Operational Planning System with a new Departmental Management Council, chaired by the under secretary. It includes the assistant secretaries for Administration and for Planning Evaluation, the comptroller, the deputy under secretary for Regional Affairs, the special adviser to the under secretary, and the executive secretary. The council meets weekly to discuss organizational and management matters, including such problems as the flow of communications within the Department—always difficult in complex organizations—and the need for clarifying the relationship between audit and program evaluation.

PROFESSIONALS VS. GENERALISTS

Underlying many of the management problems of HEW is the struggle—both conscious and subliminal—between the professionals and the generalists. It is a struggle that has been ebbing and flowing within government at all levels for many decades. The reform movement of the late nineteenth and early twentieth centuries laid great stress on professionalism in government and sought to ensconce professional educators and doctors in key administrative posts with protection against interference from politicians. School boards, separate school districts, and boards of health were the means of sheltering superintendents of schools and directors of public health from the crudities of politics. Educational and public health administrators became defenders of a faith that such professional separatism was in the highest public good.

The history of HEW's first two decades could be written as a chronicle of the struggle for power between these professional elites and their competitors: the Secretary, the short-term appointees around the Secretary, the economic analysts, the career budgeteers and lawyers, the regional directors, and others, all of whom might be grouped under the rubric of generalists. The struggle might also be characterized as one between the power and capacities of the operating agencies and those of the Office of the Secretary to control the management of the Department. The two competitions are not precisely the same, but they are close enough to be discussed as one.

The operating agencies—the main bailiwicks of the professional elites—have been steadily losing this power struggle. The ascendancy of the Office of the Secretary gained momentum during the regime of John Gardner with the addition of several new assistant secretaries and a much enlarged Office of the Secretary staff, and gained comparative strength under each succeeding Secretary. John Gardner used to say, only half in jest, that the function of intelligence is to enable one to eat his cake and have it too. This is what he and his successors have sought to do in simultaneously centralizing and decentralizing decision-making. They have wanted decisions made according to the policies that they prescribed, but at the same time they wanted strong, able operating agency heads and regional directors to whom major delegations of decision-making power could confidently be made. It is hard to have it both ways, but, as Gardner implied, perhaps not completely impossible.

John Gardner centralized civil rights enforcement in the Office of the Secretary partly because Congress asked him to, and partly to speed up the slow and inadequate action of HEW's professional program managers. As mentioned, Secretary Wilbur Cohen transferred the authority for the planning and direction of the health programs of the Public Health Service to the Office of the Secretary, together with staff to carry them out, an action that essentially was a vote of no confidence in the Public Health Service professional leadership. Robert Finch put the Office of Child Development in the Office of the Secretary to prevent the Head Start program from being submerged under what he felt were tradition-bound educators in the Office of Education. Secretary Richardson, following both his own convictions and the "New Federalism" policies of President Nixon, made substantial shifts of power and responsibility from the professional operating agency officials to the generalist regional directors who are part of the office of the Secretary. And Secretary Weinberger has placed even greater emphasis than Richardson on shifting power from professionals to generalist regional directors. Weinberger has also shifted two program units into the Office of the Secretary: the Administration on Aging and the Youth Development and Delinquency Prevention Agency.

The trend toward centralization of power and people in the Office of the Secretary is illustrated, in an oversimplified but still significant way, by the growth in the number and percentage of HEW employees in the Office of the Secretary. In 1954, HEW's first full year, there were 900 employees in the Office of the Secretary, less than 3 per cent of total employment in the Department. By August, 1973, its twentieth year, there were more than 7,500 employees, some 7 per cent of total employment. How much further this trend is likely to go is difficult to predict. But one thing is very clear: if one stands off and takes a long-range view, HEW's major internal management problem is not now the problem that has for so long been ascribed to it. It is not the need for a further extensive build-up in the power and staff of the Secretary to enable him to bring the professional program administrators into line. Rather it is a two-edged problem. First, there is a need to aid the professional managers in improving their own eroded capability to do well what they are supposed to be doing. Simultaneously, there is the need to build up the capacity of regional offices to knit together the disparate but related HEW programs and other federal programs so they can be meshed at the point of delivery to the public for whom the programs were created. This is a management problem requiring extraordinary insight and capacity to inspire subordinates to try new, imaginative and cooperative approaches.

The contest for power between health administrators, educators, and other professional program managers on the one hand and the regional directors on the other is a reflection of a larger contest extending down through the states to every community. It is the competition between the professional specialists, who are supported by their own clientele groups, and the governors, city managers, and mayors, who are supposed to be coordinating and integrating the programs of the professional specialists. To illustrate: Assume that a governor should decide to support a plan for one-stop multiservice centers where people with multiple personal and family problems could find advice and help without being shunted around from one agency to another in a totally disconnected and frustrating way. This was the central purpose of Secretary Richardson's proposed "Allied Services Act," introduced but not enacted in 1972. If and when such an act is passed, the governor will have to overcome numerous obstacles, many of which stem from the parochial professionalism of the doctors, educators, social workers, employment service specialists, and other program administrators, each with a specialized empire to protect. All the professional administrators at the Washington level have their counterparts at state and local levels. There are, therefore, vertical lines of communication, money, and organizational pride running from the educators at one level to those at another and another; and from social workers, from public health administrators, and on and on, up and down the federal, state, and local lines of professionalism. This is a fact of life with both good and bad consequences. Professionalism is needed to achieve high levels of expertise, but it gets in the way of the kind of coordinated administration that deals with people as whole human beings rather than as confused clients of numerous specialized and uncoordinated services.

Strong regional directors, working together with similar regional directors from other departments and agencies in the newly constructed Federal Regional Councils, are supposed to be the answer to the centrifugal forces of professional specialization. Under this concept, power will be progressively transferred from the professional program managers to the regional directors and used by the regional directors in a group decision-making process in the Federal Regional Councils. Unless professionals in education, public health, and social work are more imaginative and cooperative than they have been in the past in learning how to provide integrated services to people who clearly need them, this trend toward administration by region and by generalist administrators of professional functions may become the wave of the future.

But generalist administrators, personified by regional directors, have their problems and limitations, too. Most regional directors have an unquenchable thirst to administer all the departmental grant-in-aid programs that give money, with strings, to the states, cities, school districts, and institutions of their regions. If there is one single, sure method of ruining the capacity of the regional directors, and the Federal Regional Councils in which they are key participants, to perform their coordinative roles effectively, it is to overload them with the final decision-making power and the total administrative headaches of the hundreds of grant-in-aid programs that pump funds through the fiscal arteries of their regions. Unless Secretaries and regional directors have the wisdom and restraint to be highly selective about delegations of power and responsibility to the regional directors, administrative constipation will quickly become a serious regional affliction.

MANAGEMENT IN PERSPECTIVE

Although it was earlier asserted that HEW is not the kind of organization that is subject to "good management" by a good manager, this should be put in proper perspective. Two-thirds of the Department, in personnel terms, is subject to good management by competent people. As mentioned earlier, half of the employees of HEW are engaged in the administration of the Social Security programs, and this is done well and economically. Impartial studies of Social Security Administration (SSA) management by experts from the private insurance field have given most of the administration of this largest component of HEW high marks. Certainly the record of having performed all administrative functions of SSA—from maintaining lifetime earnings records to paying the 30 million monthly benefit checks, and from adjudicating complicated disability cases, to the administration of Medicare —for only two and a half cents per dollar of benefits paid belies the slurs of those who claim that large federal bureaucracies are inherently far less efficient than large private bureaucracies.

Another sixth of HEW's employees are engaged in the operation of hospitals, a field in which good administration is not easy but not impossible either. This includes the old-line Public Health Service hospital system, primarily for merchant seamen and coastguardmen, the hospital system for American Indians, the largest federal mental hospital—St. Elizabeths Hospital in the District of Columbia—and the Clinical Center of NIH. While the efficiency of administration and management of these hospitals is difficult to measure because of the unusual or unique character of many of the units, where it is possible to compare them with community or other hospitals, they seem to be as well managed as their counterparts.

Credit for the good to excellent management of these direct operations of HEW, involving two-thirds of all its employees, is very rarely accorded by the press or electronic media, and probably not even well understood by Presidents. It is the other programs of HEW—mostly those that operate through grants-in-aid to state and local governments and institutions—that generate most of the widespread impression of HEW's acute difficulties in achieving effective management, and correctly so. The regulatory functions, too, are inherently controversial for very different reasons. Food and drug regulation and the enforcement of civil rights may seem to have little in common, but both apply sanctions where it hurts, and one measure of that hurt is the frequency of resort to the courts for determination as to whether the regulatory agencies have overstepped their proper bounds. The effectiveness of management in the regulatory field is not easy to measure. It is certainly not possible to use the criteria used by competent managers in private business.

It is the grant programs that present the most baffling management problem, largely because they present a profound philosophical dilemma. On the one hand, Presidents of both parties, but especially President Nixon, have espoused a concept of federalism which emphasizes the importance of state and local government capable of initiative and adaption to the widely diverse conditions of an enormously varied nation. Under this concept, state and local governments and school systems and educational institutions are supposed to "do their own thing," and the federal government stands ready to help them become innovative, achieve institutional change (but not all in one direction), and maintain a healthy and imaginative diversity throughout the nation.

On the other hand, Presidents, Secretaries, and congressmen are under the political gun to assure the public that the program funds appropriated by Congress are well spent. What does "well spent" mean? Are funds supposed to achieve some set of agreed-upon national objectives? Or are the states and local communities entitled to define differing objectives, chosen according to their widely varying ethnic constituencies? If it is the latter, how is it possible to have any national measures of success or failure? If the federal government is to set national measures of progress, does not this vitiate the commitment to diverse federalism with its accompanying local freedom?

Here we find one of the most profound political issues of this or any generation underlying the problem of how to manage the grant-in-aid programs of HEW. To what degree should HEW try to establish national measures of progress—which also implies setting objectives against which progress can be measured—for each of its 200-odd grant programs? How can a federal department do anything about management that is very meaningful if it does not have defined objectives? Or, to put it more bluntly, how can a manager manage if he is not told what he is supposed to achieve?

Who shall set the objectives and the criteria of progress in respect to functions that have traditionally been state and local provinces, but which now require large infusions of federal funds? President Johnson and especially the Eighty-ninth Congress answered the question one way, and President Nixon is attempting to answer it another. The enactment during the 1960's of many federal programs of narrowly focused categorical aid to states, communities, and institutions was an unwitting assumption of federal responsibility for the determination of state and local priorities. President Nixon's recommendations for Special Revenue-Sharing (as well as his already adopted general revenue-sharing plan) seek to hand the determinative power, in large degree, back to the states and communities. But, simultaneously, many of Nixon's appointees are seeking to improve the management of federal grant programs by insisting on quantifiable objectives, common to the nation as a whole, and measurement of performance in relation to those objectives. Federally established objectives and performance measurement to determine efficiency of operation are not consistent with promotion of state and local initiative and with delegation of power to adapt programs to significantly varying local needs.

We have, therefore, an insoluble dilemma. We cannot have, much as we might like it, uniformly applicable national goals, objectives, and performance standards administered with efficiency and economy by state and local governments exercising initiative and imagination to adapt programs to the needs of widely varying constituencies and circumstances. We have a case of national schizophrenia. The unfolding of the events of the 1970's and 1980's will reveal whether the trend toward greater and greater federal establishment of goals, objectives, and performance criteria in respect to health, education, welfare, and other functions is the inexorable wave of the future, or whether it will recede. If it is to be the wave of the future, HEW will need more program administrators trained in the techniques of quantitative analysis and contract management. If the tide should turn, HEW will need a different kind of program manager and administrator, one who encourages state and local goal-setting and who offers a wide variety of aids to promote their achievement. Effectiveness and efficiency could not then be measured by any common national norms. Such program managers would be harder to find.

XII

Whither HEW?

As President Nixon said, with surprising pride, in his 1972 State of the Union address, the Department of Health, Education, and Welfare is now the largest department, in budgetary terms, in the U.S. Government—even larger than the Department of Defense. He might well have called it the largest department the world has even seen. Its expenditures are greater than all other domestic departments and agencies of the federal government combined. In 1973, expenditures exceeded $83 billion, and they will top $100 billion in the fiscal year 1974–75. (See Chart IV.)

Before the year 1972 was over, Nixon's brief pride in the fact that HEW's budget had surpassed that of the Department of Defense had vanished and in its place was deep concern, bordering on alarm, that HEW's voracious appetite for funds had become Gargantuan. Not once, but twice he vetoed the HEW appropriation bill, an unprecedented action. His second veto was timed so that Congress did not have an opportunity to override his veto before adjournment. In each case he had stern words about irresponsible additions by Congress in respect to his carefully considered fiscal plan. So keen was his distress over the inflationary effect of congressional additions to HEW appropriations that President Nixon decided to send his most eagle-eyed budget cutter, Caspar W. Weinberger, to HEW to do what no previous Secretary had been able to do—rein in the burgeoning HEW budget.

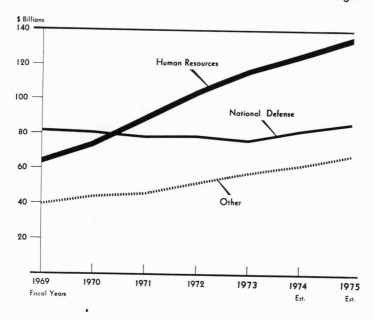

CHART IV.
HEW Expenditures Represent Three-Fourths of the Rapidly Rising Human Resource Component of the Federal Budget

RICHARDSON'S "MEGA PROPOSAL"

Secretary Elliot Richardson made little attempt to hide his disappointment at not being able to continue at the helm of HEW. In the fall of 1972, he had been working on a radical plan, proposed by his Assistant Secretary Laurence Lynn, called the Comprehensive HEW Simplification and Reform Plan, or, to those who worked with it, the "Mega Proposal." It was much too sweeping to be included in its entirety in the 1973–74 budget, but Richardson hoped that it would become the basis for a more far-reaching application of President Nixon's New Federalism than anything previously proposed. Some of the consolidations and retrenchments in the new budget did, in fact, reflect a blend of the new Richardson plan and the Weinberger economy drive.

The intent of the Mega Proposal was to reduce sharply the number of federal programs in health, education, and welfare, so as to simplify the choices of government officials and congressmen, and to generate consensus on needed retrenchment—not an easy thing to do when numerous vested interests would likely be gored in the process. The plan was intended to appeal to many of the ultimate beneficiaries of government programs by channeling more cash to them and letting them procure their own services, thus reducing the number of federally-aided service programs. The plan was intended to increase the use of the private sector (including nonprofit institutions) and the free market mechanism to provide services selected by individuals in need of them.

In briefest outline, the Mega Proposal would:

- Establish three special revenue-sharing packages, consolidating scores of existing categorical programs.
- Create a new national maximum liability health insurance plan, financed from an income tax surcharge, superseding Medicare and Medicaid, but covering only catastrophic costs, leaving smaller bills to be paid by individuals, either directly or through voluntary insurance. The definition of "catastrophic" would vary from the poor to the well-to-do, covering most of the costs of the former group and few of the costs of the latter, statistically speaking.
- Revamp Nixon's welfare reform plan in several ways, one of which would reduce the pressures on "welfare mothers" to take jobs, thus reducing the need for day-care services.
- Consolidate college student-aid programs, encourage the use of insured loans, and cut back sharply on direct aid to professional schools.
- Intensify efforts to help state, local, and private agencies build their capacity to provide services, but with less federal money, the magic formula for which was not spelled out.

Richardson's Mega Proposal made clear that he had concluded that categorical programs, especially service programs, had proliferated beyond the point of manageability. Some system of simplifying them had to be worked out.

Whatever Secretary Weinberger and President Nixon may decide to do with Richardson's proposal, it will almost certainly not be submitted as a package plan to Congress. Some aspects of it are too radical to be acceptable in a country with long-standing traditions of incremental political change. Nevertheless, its philosophy did have a significant impact in shaping the 1973–74 budget. President Nixon proposed three special revenue-sharing bills—in education, health, and social services, as Richardson had—consolidating scores of categorical programs. He recommended complete termination of some programs that he felt were outmoded or should be financed without federal aid. And he recommended increased emphasis on cash loans or scholarships to college students and less direct aid to colleges and universities.

THE END OF AN ERA

The 1973–74 budget and the appointment of Caspar Weinberger as Secretary signify that HEW is approaching or has reached the end of an era. It has been an era in which, for two decades, HEW has absorbed an increasing percentage of the federal budget. At the beginning—in 1954, HEW's first full year—its budget outlays represented 7.5 per cent of the federal budget. In 1972–73, it reached 33 per cent, and despite intense economy efforts, Nixon's 1973–74 budget showed HEW with 35 per cent of the federal budget outlays—$94 billion. In 1975, HEW's expenditures will exceed $100 billion. If defense expenditures and interest on the public debt are set aside, HEW's 1973–74 budget represents 58 per cent of all remaining federal outlays.

This trend obviously cannot continue much longer. HEW would soon monopolize the federal budget. The crunch had to come, and the time seems now to have arrived. What is not well appreciated, however, even by many top policy-makers, is the extent to which Social Security has generated the crunch. Following the 20 per cent increase in Social Security benefit levels enacted in 1972, Social Security outlays increased $10 billion in 1973 and will increase an additional $8 billion in 1974. Social Security taxes were likewise increased to cover these additional expenditures, which now represent 70 per cent of all HEW expenditures. While Social Security expenditures do not contribute to inflationary pressures, since income is sufficient to cover outgo with a little margin, they do add to the tax burden of John Q. Citizen.

In June, 1972, President Nixon signed the bill giving a 20 per cent increase in monthly payments to Social Security beneficiaries —requiring $7 billion more in expenditures than he had recommended. Twice in the next four months he vetoed the HEW appropriation bill because it authorized outlays for education and health programs amounting to less than $2 billion over his budget request. The new Social Security taxes had put an extra squeeze on him to avoid, if possible, increasing federal income taxes. (It seems ironic that the Social Security tax hike that the Congress, the President, and the public accepted with hardly a murmur is a tax that bears most heavily on workers with less than average income; the working poor pay a much higher percentage of their income in Social Security taxes than do the rich.) The effect of the large outlays for Social Security benefits is to make it appear to budgeteers at the top level of government that HEW's total budget is mammoth and out of control. When the education lobbies fully comprehend the extent to which they are tarred with the HEW label of "Gargantuanism," even while federal expenditures for public elementary and secondary education amount to only 8 per cent of total federal-state-local outlays for that purpose, they are likely to begin a much more concerted drive than previously for an organizational separation from the omnivorous income maintenance programs.

The rapidity with which perspectives can change on the American political scene is evidenced by the appearance of two books that either advocated or foresaw further large increases in the HEW budget, apart from Social Security. One was *Counterbudget* (Praeger, 1971) written by the staff of the National Urban Coalition, urging a human resource component of the federal budget (most of which would be for HEW) of $212 billion in 1976. The other—*Setting National Priorities—The 1973 Budget* (Brookings, 1972)—made no long-range projections but discussed the human resource programs in such a way as to leave the strong impression that the public demand for day care, education, welfare, and health services would be strong enough, when added to defense and other requirements, to make income tax increases unavoidable in the near future. Whether such an increase turns out to be necessary or not, there exists the prospect of a deeply felt and loudly expressed contention between the President and Congress over how much the federal government should spend to help people and how much they should rely on themselves. And HEW lies squarely in the center of this controversy.

Solving major social problems of American society without substantial additional amounts of money would be no easy trick. Nixon's welfare reform plan would have made some 11 million working poor the recipients of monthly federal checks to supplement their low wages. The $4 billion first-full-year price tag on that program was probably a serious underestimate, as were the predicted costs of Medicare and Medicaid. When the inequities in the availability of health care, and its high cost, push the issue of health insurance close to the top of the list of social issues, it seems inconceivable that any solution to that problem can be devised that will not cost multiple billions. And President Nixon's oft-repeated goal of relieving the local real estate taxpayer from the rising costs of government, especially the educational burdens of local government, seems unlikely to be achieved without substantially more federal funds.

Secretaries of HEW are confronted with an incredible number of tough issues and challenges. These are but three of a dozen important social policy issues that will confront future Secretaries for the balance of the 1970's.

THE PROPOSAL FOR A DEPARTMENT OF HUMAN RESOURCES

If he is to exercise leadership rather than merely keep the lid on a social kettle with a big head of steam, the Secretary must not only become deeply involved in the design and redesign of basic policy, he must also concern himself with important issues of organizational change and improvement. The Congress will not let him do otherwise, since congressmen have their own ideas about organization—so much so, in fact, that the Secretary is constantly on the defensive. To carve out sufficient time in the Secretary's busy schedule to deal thoughtfully and affirmatively with organizational issues is extremely difficult. Even the redoubtable John Gardner, apostle of institutional change, said of his experience in HEW:

I've been concerned about institutional change for the last 20 years, and I don't think there was a time when I thought less about it than when I was Secretary of HEW. I had to try to gain yards in terms of the way the game is played. I couldn't think about some other way of doing it. I had to get my appropriations. I had to get my bills passed—and fight, fight, fight. . . .

With society and government in the midst of dynamic change, HEW is caught between two powerful, contending organizational currents. The President seeks to create an even larger version of HEW—the previously mentioned Department of Human Resources—while the dominant forces of Congress and the numerous organizations and associations that ally themselves with the subdivisions of HEW, or at least with their programs, are gathering strength to dismember it.

In his State of the Union message of January, 1971, President Nixon recommended the consolidation of most domestic functions of the federal government into four superdepartments: Community Development, Human Resources, Natural Resources, and Economic Affairs. Under his original plan, the President would have abolished four departments—Agriculture, Labor, Commerce, and Transportation—but with a sudden flash of insight he decided, as election year approached, that it would be wise to keep at least a slimmed-down version of the Department of Agriculture. All of the functions of the abolished departments, and many of those of the Department of Agriculture even under the revised plan, would be distributed among the four broad-purpose superdepartments.

Under the President's Departmental Reorganization Program, the Department of Human Resources would encompass virtually everything HEW now has in it, plus the manpower and unemployment insurance functions of the Department of Labor (including the network of state employment services), the food and nutrition service and the meat and poultry inspection services from the Department of Agriculture, the college housing program from the Department of Housing and Urban Development (HEW would exchange this for the library construction program it now sponsors), a few functions from the Office of Economic Opportunity, and the whole of the Railroad Retirement Board.

What the Department of Health, Education, and Welfare has been requested by President Nixon to do, in addition to changing its name, is to assume enormous new duties and to digest, within the next several years, some 25–30 thousand additional employees, and to provide leadership, coordination, and surveillance over

70,000 state employees engaged in unemployment compensation and employment service functions. Simultaneously, the Department would be asked to furnish greatly strengthened analytic and policy aid to the President in dealing with the kinds of profound social issues sketched briefly above.

While handling this deluge of management responsibilities, the new Department of Human Resources would undergo a radical internal reorganization, according to the plan President Nixon presented to Congress in support of his Department Reorganization Program. The new Department would be organized into three major administrations and would have a much enlarged field staff operating under major new delegations of power. There would be a Health Administration, a Human Development Administration, and an Income Security Administration.

The administrator for Income Security would have under him the Social Security Administration, the previously independent Railroad Retirement Board, and the newly transferred Unemployment Compensation Service from the Department of Labor, under the label "Social Insurance." He would have, initially, the Medicare and Medicaid programs under the heading "Health Benefits," and, in due course, either the Nixon-style health insurance standards program or the Kennedy-style national health insurance program (see Chapter IV). And he would have, under the heading "Assistance Benefits," the current public assistance program, or, if some version of the Family Assistance Plan were ever to be enacted, a wholly federal operation larger than the Social Security Administration.

The administrator for Health would have responsibility for the biomedical research, communications, and training programs administered by the National Institutes of Health, regulatory functions of the Food and Drug Administration, and all the numerous health programs now grouped together under the Health Services Administration, the Health Resources Administration, and the Center for Disease Control.

The third agency head, the administrator for Human Development, would have the 100+ programs administered by the Office of Education and the new National Institute of Education, the manpower and training programs of the Department of Labor, as well as its chain of employment service offices (administered through the states). He would also have the Vocational Rehabilitation Program, grants to the states for social services, and the programs for aging, for juvenile delinquency prevention, for "Head Start," and for child care. Just where the Department of Agriculture's food and nutrition programs would be placed remains to be determined.

President Nixon's Departmental Reorganization Plan was in large measure the product of the Ash Council, a commission composed of private business executives who had had some opportunity to observe governmental operations, plus one political executive—John Connally. Its chairman was Roy Ash, then president of Litton Industries, later appointed by President Nixon to head the Office of Management and Budget beginning in January, 1973. The Ash Council, appointed by Nixon in 1969, was asked to work without fanfare. It was itself a kind of successor to a similar body appointed by President Johnson in 1966, chaired by Ben Heineman, then president of the Chicago and Northwestern Railroad. The Heineman Commission was so secret that its existence was never revealed by President Johnson, nor were its recommendations ever declassified by the late President, though they were made available to the Ash Council. The study was completed in 1967 when Johnson was deeply preoccupied with Vietnam, and he did nothing with it.

Although the backgrounds of the members of the two groups were significantly different (the Heineman Commission had fewer business executives and more top-level government executives), their basic conclusions were remarkably similar. Both the Ash Council and the Heineman Commission viewed the problem of how best to organize the U.S. Government as a managerial problem. They looked upon the role of the President as that of chief executive of the world's largest corporation and asked themselves how they would structure it if they were in his postion. They were not particularly concerned with how the "board of directors"— the Congress—might view the organization of the federal government, nor how stable any organization plan might be in the context of congressional interests and realities. None of the men on the two commissions had ever served in Congress, nor had any served in top positions in any of the departments they sought to consolidate. One had served as Secretary of Defense and naturally extrapolated his experience to recommend organization changes in other departments even though the departments were fundamentally dissimilar.

What the members of these two commissions sought to do was to make the President's job as manageable as possible in classical organization terms: group like functions together, narrow the President's overextended span of control by reducing the number of departments, and delegate operating decisions to the regional officials in each department who are closer to the problems than headquarters officials can be. But above all, what they sought to accomplish was to insulate the President from the pleas and pressures of Cabinet officers with narrow points of view, each constantly seeking a larger chunk of the fiscal pie for their constituencies. The larger the portfolio of responsibilities of a Cabinet officer, they reasoned, the more likely he would be to take a very broad view as to where the public interest lies. Thus, the larger the scope of related responsibilities given a Secretary, the more nearly he will approximate the perspective of the President and the more he will be able to relieve the President of his onerous burdens. It was a compelling line of reasoning to the members of the two commissions, and it was persuasive to President Nixon.

THE POLITICAL INSTABILITY OF AN ENORMOUS DEPARTMENT

Secretary Richardson and former Secretaries Marion Folsom, John Gardner, and Wilbur Cohen have publicly supported the concept of an enlarged Department of Human Resources. Of the former Secretaries, only Abraham Ribicoff has publicly thrown up his hands at what he regards as an administrative monster. But however important the narrowing of the President's span of control may seem to some Presidents and some Secretaries, this consideration is not likely to be as decisive in the long run as the political acceptability to Congress of continuing to crowd so many rapidly growing functions into a single organization. Major reorganizations are rarely perceived as completely positive or even neutral in their political effect. Some groups in the society lose, while others gain.

The problem of overcrowding was well illustrated by the strong effort of Congress in 1971 to remove the National Cancer Institute from HEW and establish it as an independent National Cancer

Agency. (See Chapter VII.) The argument was that the subject was too important to be located eight layers down (a slight exaggeration, but the point was clear) from the President, and that in the competition for funds this kind of submergence was almost sure to mean an inadequate budget to wage total war on cancer. So persuasive was the argument, or so powerful were the political forces behind the proposal for an independent, NASA-like agency, with the mission to conquer cancer, that the President felt he had no choice except to compromise sound organizational principles to head off the removal of the Cancer Institute from HEW. He agreed to—in fact lent his support to—the design of an organizational deformity in which the institute remains in the National Institutes of Health (NIH) and in HEW, but its director, who is now appointed by the President, submits his budget directly to the President (although the Secretary of HEW is given the courtesy of comment on it). A special 3-man President's National Cancer Panel reviews the National Cancer Institute's budget and otherwise oversees and evaluates the work of the agency. It is one of the strangest organizational designs ever concocted. (See pp. 183–85.)

The Ash Council and the Heineman Commission would have been deeply shocked by such an anomalous arrangement if it had been presented to them and would almost certainly have recommended that the President veto such a bill. It was the first high price that the Administration has paid for having a very large number of very important functions performed several layers down within an immense department. More will follow.

Reduced to its simplest terms, the problem is this: The President, the Heineman Commission, the Ash Council, and the Office of Management and Budget *want* the Secretary of HEW or the Secretary of the Department of Human Resources to help keep the lid on the NIH budget. The proponents of a big budget for cancer research (and for many other purposes) know that is what the President wants, and they believe that the only way they can get around that is to have the director of the National Cancer Institute in a position to submit his budget directly to the President. That is what they now have. Organization, as earlier mentioned, does not have a neutral effect on "who gets what, when, and how."

For somewhat similar reasons, Congress seems bent on removing various other functions from HEW and elevating their status so they are directly answerable to the President. Just before adjournment in 1972, it created an independent National Commission on Product Safety, transferring the product safety functions from the Food and Drug Administration to it. The Senate even voted to remove the entire Food and Drug Administration from HEW, but the House did not concur. Still another bill to remove all the health functions from the Department and put them in a new Department of Health has been introduced by Senator Abraham Ribicoff and Congressman Paul Rogers. Rogers obtained a hundred co-sponsors in the House. This bill will probably get considerable attention in the Ninety-third Congress. Other bills with less firepower would establish a separate Department of Education.

AN ALTERNATIVE TO SUPERDEPARTMENTS

The natural and proper query is: If giant departments, such as a Department of Human Resources, are not the solution to the problems inherent in the President's unusually broad span of control and are not a durable method of lightening the President's work load, what alternative is there? Without spelling it out at length, the principal other option open to the President would involve two complementary steps: first, the appointment of several first-rate special assistants with substantial coordinating and decision-making power, and, second, the establishment of an Office of Special Studies—a euphemism for an office to do long-range planning.

The special assistants need not have the "passion for anonymity," which the Brownlow Committee prescribed for the six Presidential assistants it recommended to President Roosevelt. Assignment of responsibility to them by the President for resolving all but the most major *interdepartmental* issues could properly become public knowledge. Their authority, when necessary, to knock heads with Presidential backing would be correspondingly clear to all concerned. They would not be administrators, in the sense of being line officers, but resolvers of interagency conflict that now either goes unresolved, or waits much too long for resolution.

The Office of Special Studies would be assigned a role that the Domestic Council staff does not now have time, nor is it appropriately staffed, to do—namely, it would make in-depth analyses of problems that represent the most difficult social policy issues of the time and produce recommendations for Presidential initiatives. Imaginative social architecture takes an enormous amount of analysis and thought and cannot be accomplished by administrative and political firefighters. For this reason, such an office has long been needed, entirely apart from considerations of the necessity of narrowing the President's span of control.

WHAT ARE THE PRESIDENT'S PRIORITIES?

This issue of whether a Department of Human Resources will ever come into being—or, indeed, whether the Department of Health, Education, and Welfare can be held together—will hinge upon the amount of political capital the President is willing to expend to achieve and sustain such an objective. He and his staff are the principal proponents of this form of organization. He must face the fact, however, that it is an inherently unstable organizational arrangement and only by a considerable expenditure of his valuable political capital can he either persuade the Congress to enact it or keep it in existence after enactment. The pressure from those who want more departments and independent agencies is politically stronger in Congress, and much more insistent than from those who like a small number of very large departments. The more gigantic and out of balance with the rest of government any single department becomes, the greater the political pressure to dismember it.

The subject of "political capital" is often misunderstood. To many people, the term connotes patronage, or dams, or post offices. To the purists, therefore, it seems at least slightly sinister. But in its deeper and proper meaning, it should convey the idea that leaders in a democracy have to be negotiators and compromisers and cannot always have their way. Otherwise they would be dictators. Presidents have programs and Congress has the constitutional power to legislate. The members of Congress have their own perceptions as to where the interests of their constituencies lie, and their perceptions understandably differ from that of the President with his larger constituency. If he is to achieve a substantial share of his purposes, the President must be selective about those things he tries to get Congress to do against its natural inclinations. And when the situation is reversed, he must be willing to yield to Congress on issues that do not seem to him to be crucial.

The President's political capital is the strength from which he negotiates. It includes patronage, which becomes less and less important as the years go by, and it includes some public works and other types of fund allocations. But in the current era, the most significant components of his political capital are the President's extraordinary access to the public media and the general presumption on the part of much of the public and Congress—at least in the years up to 1973—that the President should be given the benefit of the doubt. If Congress feels that the President respects its role and is negotiating in good faith with it, it is prepared to reciprocate. But if he refuses to "give and take," he is bound for trouble. Selectivity in picking the critical issues is the key to success in this political bargaining process.

In this meaning of the term "political capital," it cannot be presumed that all Presidents will feel that the corporation-style organizational pattern proposed by the Ash Council need be one of their critical issues. If Congress keeps presenting successive Presidents with bills that represent its view that one department —HEW—has become so big that it is out of balance with the rest of government and should be split up, Presidents may veto one, or even conceivably two, but they are unlikely to go on and on with an unproductive organizational war. As indicated above, the first battles of such an organizational war have already begun. And President Nixon has vetoed neither of the two recent bills that Congress has sent him dismembering or distorting HEW's health agencies and enlarging rather than narrowing the President's span of control.

In Conclusion

Careful analysis of other options open to the President to improve upon the current organizational arrangement of domestic functions would exceed the scope of this book. Two final points, however, deserve brief comment.

First, it should be emphasized that the skepticism here expressed about the political acceptability and durability of a Department of Human Resources as proposed by President Nixon is not intended to apply to two of the three other major components of his Departmental Reorganization Program, namely, the Department of Community Development and the Department of Natural Resources. Neither of these departments would begin to approach the Department of Human Resources in size and complexity, and the arguments for putting these related functions together, especially for planning and operational coordination, seem much more persuasive.

Second, an outstanding feature of the proposal for a Department of Human Resources—the merger of manpower and education functions within a single department—should not be ignored or buried in the event that the proposed Department is found unacceptable by Congress. Eventually, the United States Employment Service, now financed with federal funds but managed and staffed by state employees, should be federalized as it was during World War II, and become the catalytic agent for building far better bridges from the school rooms to the world of work, especially for those for whom academic study is unsuitable. With the peak of the postwar baby boom reaching the labor market beginning in 1975, no social need is greater than to find or provide satisfactory and satisfying occupations and vocational preparation for this largest of all younger generations. Grouping manpower and education together in a single department might contribute much to this end.

Epilogue

The five revolutions described in this book have carried the United States far along the road toward the "welfare state." To some, this is a pejorative term. To others, it represents an upward step in the evolution of society. The late W. L. Mackenzie King, former Prime Minister of Canada, observed that, "The era of freedom will be achieved only as social security and human welfare become the main concern of men and nations." However beneficial or perilous it may seem, the chances seem better than even that we shall continue to move in this direction.

The Department of Health, Education, and Welfare struggles in the center of these swirling currents of revolutionary change. Government departments have never, heretofore, been consciously designed to assist Presidents to guide the nation through what are recognized as necessary reconstructions of social policy, in addition to the departments' normal duties of carrying out all the laws whose administration is assigned to them. It is an open question whether this is a manageable combination. It seems likely, however, that the Heineman Commission that advised President Lyndon Johnson and the Ash Council that advised President Nixon had this at least in the back of their minds when they recommended that the Department of Health, Education, and Welfare be expanded into a Department of Human Resources. Yet it seems very doubtful that these advisers had anything like an adequate realization of the overwhelming load that was being placed on a single department by this organizational design.

Administering some 200 programs costing some $85–100

billion would be difficult enough if all the programs were under
the control of the Department. But with the conspicuous exception
of Social Security, most of them are under the control of states,
local communities, and institutions. The problem of determining
whether each such program is accomplishing anything, and if so,
what and how much, is enormously more complex than evaluating
the performance of a C-5A military transport plane. Evaluation of
relative success or failure of HEW's numerous grant-in-aid programs will require almost a quantum jump in the sophistication of
social science research and evaluation techniques. If we wish to
preserve diversity and avoid enforced uniformity, we may not
even be able to establish quantifiable national objectives against
which all communities and institutions must measure their progress, as the operations research analysts would have us do.

While all this is going on, HEW, and the proposed Department
of Human Resources a fortiori, will be expected to guide us through
the maelstrom of political forces and counterforces as we develop
a new system for the distribution, delivery, and payment for medical care in this country, and the trained manpower to make it
effective. It will also be expected to continue to wrestle with the
dilemma of civil rights and racial tension, especially as reflected
in the public schools; to work on the refinancing of public education in the light of recent court opinions; to get us out of our
extraordinarily complicated "welfare mess"; to help determine
whether we should, in effect, develop a new cultural pattern for
caring for children in their preschool years; and to take leadership in overcoming the alarming and growing misfit between the
jobs available in our technico-service society and the qualifications
of those in the work force.

Is this not asking too much of a single department? One is
impelled to ask, "Why pile on one department so large a proportion of the major problems of our society?" Surely other alternatives that would balance the load deserve careful consideration.

Appendix A
List of HEW Programs Included in the *1973 Federal Catalog of Federal Domestic Assistance**

FOOD AND DRUG ADMINISTRATION
Food Research Grants
Radiological Health Research Grants

HEALTH SERVICES AND MENTAL HEALTH ADMINISTRATION
Disease Control—Consultation and Technical Assistance
Disease Control—Laboratory Improvement
Disease Control—Tuberculosis
Disease Control—Venereal Disease
Comprehensive Health Planning—Areawide Grants
Comprehensive Health Planning—Grants to States
Comprehensive Public Health Services—Formula Grants

* Produced by the Office of Management and Budget, Executive Office of the President, and for sale by the Superintendent of Documents, U.S. Government Printing Office, Washington, D.C. 20402. The catalog contains a detailed description of each program. HEW produces its own version of the catalog, called *HEW Catalog of Assistance,* limited to a description of its own programs, also for sale by the Government Printing Office.
This list covers all programs of direct interest to state and local officials. It does not include a number of programs that are operated exclusively by federal personnel with no direct relation to state and local government, such as the Public Health Service hospital system, various food and drug enforcement activities, the clinical center programs of the National Institutes of Health, and a variety of others, the most important of which have been described in the text of this book.

Crippled Children's Services
Family Planning Projects
Health Facilities Construction—Grants
Health Facilities Construction—Technical Assistance
Health Services Development—Project Grants
Health Services Research and Development Grants and Contracts
Health Statistics Training and Technical Assistance
Indian Health Services
Indian Sanitation Facilities
Maternal and Child Health Research
Maternal and Child Health Services
Maternal and Child Health Training
Mental Health—Community Assistance Grants for Narcotic Addiction
   and Drug Abuse
Mental Health—Hospital Improvement Grants
Mental Health—Hospital Staff Development Grants
Mental Health—Narcotic Addict Treatment
Mental Health—Community Mental Health Centers
Mental Health Fellowships
Mental Health Research Grants
Mental Health Scientific Communications and Public Education
Mental Health Training Grants
Migrant Health Grants
Disease Control—Smoking and Health
Mental Health—Community Assistance Grants for Comprehensive
   Alcoholism Services
Mental Health—Direct Grants for Special Projects (Alcoholism)
Health Facilities Construction—Loans and Loan Guarantees
Mental Health—Direct Grants for Special Projects (Narcotic Addic-
   tion and Drug Abuse)
Health Maintenance Organization Service
Mental Health—Alcohol Formula Grants
National Health Service Corps
Mental Health—Children's Services
Family Planning Services—Training Grants
Family Health Centers
Occupational Safety and Health—Research Grants
Occupational Safety and Health—Training Grants
Childhood Lead-Based Paint Poisoning Control
Urban Rat Control
Disease Control—Project Grants
Mental Health—Drug Abuse Formula Grants

NATIONAL INSTITUTE OF EDUCATION
Educational Research and Development

NATIONAL INSTITUTES OF HEALTH
Allergy and Infectious Diseases—Research Grants

Animal Resources
Arthritis and Metabolic Diseases—Research Grants
Cancer—Research Centers
Cancer—Research Grants
Child Health and Human Development—Research Grants
Training in Expanded Auxiliary Management
Dental Health Continuing Education Training Grants
Environmental Health Sciences—Fellowships
Environmental Health Sciences—Research Grants
Environmental Health Sciences—Training Grants
Eye Research—Research Grants
General Clinical Research Centers
General Medical Sciences—Research Grants
General Research Support Grants
Health Professions—Capitation Grants
Health Professions—Student Loans
Heart and Lung Research—Research Grants
Medical Library Assistance—Library Resources Grants
Biomedical Scientific Publications Grants
Medical Library Assistance—Regional Medical Libraries
Medical Library Assistance—Research Grants
Neurological Diseases and Stroke—Research Grants
Nurse Training Improvement—Special Projects
Nursing Student Loans
Nursing School Construction—Loan Guarantees and Interest Subsidies
Biotechnology Resources
Heart and Lung Research—Specialized Research Centers
Minority Schools Biomedical Support
Health Professions Teaching Facilities—Loan Guarantees and Interest
    Subsidies
Family Medicine—Training Grants
Health Manpower Education Initiative Awards
Health Professions—Financial Distress Grants
Health Professions—Special Projects
Health Professions—Start-Up Assistance
Cancer—Task Forces
Cancer—Construction

OFFICE OF EDUCATION

Adult Education—Grants to States
Adult Education—Special Projects
Adult Education—Teacher Education
Bilingual Education
Civil Rights Technical Assistance and Training
College Teacher Graduate Fellowships
Cuban Education—Student Loans
Dropout Prevention
Educational Broadcasting Facilities

Educational Personnel Training Grants—Career Opportunities
Educationally Deprived Children—Handicapped
Educationally Deprived Children—Local Educational Agencies
Educationally Deprived Children—Migrants
Educationally Deprived Children—State Administration
Educationally Deprived Children in State Administered Institutions Serving Neglected or Delinquent Children
Follow Through
Teacher Exchange
Fulbright-Hays Training Grants—Faculty Research Abroad
Fulbright-Hays Training Grants—Foreign Curriculum Consultants
Fulbright-Hays Training Grants—Group Projects Abroad
Fulbright-Hays Training Grants—Doctoral Dissertation Research Abroad
Handicapped—Research and Demonstration
Handicapped Early Childhood Assistance
Handicapped Innovative Programs—Deaf-Blind Centers
Handicapped Media Services and Captioned Films
Handicapped Physical Education and Recreation Research
Handicapped Physical Education and Recreation Training
Handicapped Preschool and School Programs
Handicapped Regional Resource Centers
Handicapped Teacher Education
Handicapped Teacher Recruitment and Information
Higher Education—Land-Grant Colleges and Universities
Higher Education—Strengthening Developing Institutions
Higher Education Act Insured Loans
Higher Education Personnel Fellowships
Higher Education Work-Study
National Defense Student Loan Cancellations
National Direct Student Loans
School Assistance in Federally Affected Areas—Construction
School Assistance in Federally Affected Areas—Maintenance and Operation
Educational Activities Overseas—Inter-Institutional Cooperative Research
Special Services for Disadvantaged Students in Institutions of Higher Education
Talent Search
Teacher Corps—Operations and Training
Upward Bound
Vocational Education—Basic Grants to States
Vocational Education—Consumer and Homemaking
Vocational Education—Cooperative Education
Vocational Education—Curriculum Development
Vocational Education—Special Needs
Vocational Education—State Advisory Councils
Vocational Education—Work Study

Vocational Education—Innovation
Educational Personnel Development—Urban/Rural School Development
Higher Education—Cooperative Education
Educationally Deprived Children—Special Grants for Urban and Rural Schools
Educationally Deprived Children—Special Incentive Grants
Preschool, Elementary, and Secondary Education—Special Programs and Projects
Supplementary Educational Centers and Services, Guidance, Counseling, and Testing
Special Programs for Children with Specific Learning Disabilities
Emergency School Aid Act—Basic Grants to Local Educational Agencies
Emergency School Aid Act—Pilot Programs
Emergency School Aid Act—Metropolitan Area Projects
Emergency School Aid Act—Bilingual Education Projects
Emergency School Aid Act—Special Programs and Projects
Emergency School Aid Act—Educational Television
Emergency School Aid Act—Special Programs
Right to Read—Elimination of Illiteracy

OFFICE OF THE SECRETARY

Child Development—Head Start
Child Development—Technical Assistance
Civil Rights Compliance Activities
Mental Retardation Coordination and Information
Surplus Property Utilization
Facilities Engineering and Construction Activities—Technical Assistance
Child Development—Child Welfare Research and Demonstration Grants

SOCIAL AND REHABILITATION SERVICE

Child Welfare Services
Medical Assistance Program
Public Assistance—State and Local Training
Rehabilitation Services and Facilities—Basic Support
Vocational Rehabilitation Services for Social Security Disability Beneficiaries
Work Incentives Program—Child Care—Employment Related Supportive Services
Developmental Disabilities—Basic Support
Public Assistance—Social Services
Special Program for the Aging
Comprehensive Social Rehabilitation Research
Developmental Disabilities—Special Projects
Developmental Disabilities—Demonstration Facilities and Training

Public Assistance—Maintenance Assistance (State Aid)
Refugee Assistance—Cuban Refugees
Rehabilitation Services and Facilities—Special Projects
Youth—Development and Delinquency Prevention

SOCIAL SECURITY ADMINISTRATION

Medicare—Hospital Insurance
Medicare—Supplementary Medical Insurance
Social Security—Disability Insurance
Social Security—Retirement Insurance
Social Security—Special Benefits for Persons Aged 72 and Over
Social Security—Survivors Insurance
Special Benefits for Disabled Coal Miners

Appendix B
Careers in HEW

HEW offers an enormous variety of career opportunities, with the broadest range being in health and allied professions, but with numerous other career ladders in the fields of education, Social Security, welfare, and all the supporting service and management professions.

In the health field, the Department operates numerous hospitals —fifty-one for the care of American Indians, eight for the care of merchant seamen, coast guard personnel and others, St. Elizabeths (a large mental hospital in the District of Columbia), and the largest clinical research hospital in the world at the National Institutes of Health in Bethesda, Maryland, employing more than 1,500 people, with all the different occupations and professions one would expect in a hospital setting. Almost every specialty in the biomedical research field is represented among the 13,000 employees of NIH, or in the additional research units of the Health Services and Mental Health Administration or the Food and Drug Administration. Every subdivision of the public health professions is also represented in HEW.

In the Social Security Administration (SSA) with its 55,000 people, more than 99 per cent of the employees in the middle and upper grades are career people. The opportunity exists for those who demonstrate competence and promise to move up from claims examiners and claims reviewers to office managers and field supervisors, and on up to the headquarters staff in Baltimore. Computer programmers, console operators, and other computer specialists are used in both the payment centers and headquarters. Actuaries and social scientists play an important role on the SSA staff, as do all the supporting management professionals needed to manage any mammoth organization.

Social workers, behavioral scientists, economists, and technical specialists in all aspects of physical and vocational rehabilitation, social services, and income maintenance can find careers in the various parts of the Social and Rehabilitation Service.

The Office of Education and the new National Institute of Education, with more than 100 programs, review project proposals from, and offer technical assistance to, thousands of school systems and institutions, and thus require persons with a wide variety of backgrounds and skills. The list of programs in Appendix A gives a good insight into the range of skills needed and used by HEW in the education field.

Career opportunities for lawyers, accountants, auditors, civil rights program representatives, budget analysts, personnel officers, purchasing and contracting officers, and scores of other occupations exist in what is called the Office of the Secretary, but what might better be described as the central headquarters staff, serving all of HEW.

The vast majority of employees are recruited competitively through Civil Service examinations and serve exclusively under that system. In the health field, another option is available in the filling of particular kinds of positions—the Commissioned Corps of the Public Health Service, which parallels in pay and retirement benefits the similar system for military officers. HEW has been seeking to gain congressional approval for a new personnel system for health professionals, but as of mid-1973 had not succeeded.

In-service training is extensively available, and persons who show promise and dedication may have their tuition paid to take courses related to their occupations so as to put them in line for promotion. Special programs even assist students to gain college degrees while working for HEW, using part of their working time for classroom work at nearby universities. For unusually promising employees with a number of years of service, the government pays full tuition and salary during a year of study in residence at the nation's leading universities.

HEW is making a special effort to make sure that representatives of minorities and of the majority—women—are given every possible chance to demonstrate their capacities and be fully considered for jobs in which they have been seriously underrepresented heretofore. Two offices in the Office of the Secretary—the Office of Equal Opportunity and the Office of Upward Mobility—have been created specifically for this purpose.

Of HEW's employment of over 100,000, approximately 39 per cent are in GS grades 1–5, with starting salaries ranging from about $4,300 to $7,300. About 36 per cent are in the next five grades, GS 6–10, with starting salaries from $8,100 to $12,100. Nearly 25 per cent are in the professional, technical, and managerial grades GS 11–15, with starting salaries from $13,300 to $25,600. About 400—just under a half per cent—are in the supergrades, GS 16–18, with salaries of $30,000 to $36,000. This distribution is indicative of a surprisingly high proportion of positions in the middle and upper brackets, a good sign for a person with talent and ambition.

Appendix C
Principal Officials of HEW and
Predecessor Organizations, 1867-1973

FEDERAL SECURITY AGENCY ADMINISTRATOR

Paul V. McNutt	1939–45
Watson B. Miller	1945–47
Oscar R. Ewing	1947–53
Oveta Culp Hobby	1953

SECRETARY OF HEALTH, EDUCATION, AND WELFARE

Oveta Culp Hobby	1953–55
Marion B. Folsom	1955–58
Arthur S. Flemming	1958–61
Abraham Ribicoff	1961–62
Anthony J. Celebrezze	1962–65
John W. Gardner	1965–68
Wilbur J. Cohen	1968–69
Robert H. Finch	1969–70
Elliot L. Richardson	1970–73
Caspar W. Weinberger	1973–

UNDER SECRETARY

Nelson A. Rockefeller	1953–54
Herold C. Hunt	1955–57
John A. Perkins	1957–58
Bertha S. Adkins	1958–61
Ivan A. Nestingen	1961–65
Wilbur J. Cohen	1965–68

James H. McCrocklin 1968–69
John G. Veneman 1969–73
Frank C. Carlucci 1973–

DEPUTY UNDER SECRETARY
Dean W. Coston 1966–68
Frederick V. Malek 1969–70

DEPUTY UNDER SECRETARY FOR POLICY COORDINATION
Robert E. Patricelli 1970–71

DEPUTY UNDER SECRETARY FOR WELFARE REFORM PLANNING
Richard P. Nathan 1971–72

GENERAL COUNSEL
Parke M. Banta 1954–57
Alanson W. Willcox 1961–69
Robert C. Mardian 1969–70
Wilmot R. Hastings 1970–73
John Rhinelander 1973–

COUNSELOR TO THE DEPARTMENT
Jonathan Moore 1970–73

ASSISTANT SECRETARY FOR PROGRAM ANALYSIS
Roswell B. Perkins 1954–57

ASSISTANT TO THE SECRETARY FOR PROGRAM ANALYSIS
Willis D. Gradison 1957
Robert H. Hamlin 1958–60
Jarold A. Kieffer 1960–61

ASSISTANT SECRETARY FOR LEGISLATION
Elliot L. Richardson 1957–59
Robert A. Forsythe 1960–61
Wilbur J. Cohen 1961–65
Ralph K. Huitt 1965–69
Creed C. Black 1969–70
Stephen Kurzman 1971–

ASSISTANT SECRETARY FOR PROGRAM COORDINATION
William Gorham 1965–68

ASSISTANT SECRETARY FOR PLANNING AND EVALUATION
Alice M. Rivlin 1968–69
Lewis M. Butler 1969–71
Laurence E. Lynn, Jr. 1971–73
William A. Morrill 1973–

ASSISTANT SECRETARY

Russell R. Larmon	1953–55
Bradshaw Mintener	1955–57
Edward Foss Wilson	1957–60
James M. Quigley	1961–66

ASSISTANT SECRETARY FOR INDIVIDUAL AND FAMILY SERVICES

| Lisle C. Carter, Jr. | 1966–68 |

ASSISTANT SECRETARY FOR COMMUNITY AND FIELD SERVICES

Edward C. Sylvester	1968–69
Patricia Reilly Hitt	1969–73
(Office retired, 1973)	

ASSISTANT SECRETARY FOR HUMAN DEVELOPMENT

| Stanley Thomas | 1973– |

SPECIAL ASSISTANT FOR HEALTH AND MEDICAL AFFAIRS

Dr. Chester S. Keefer	1953–56
Lowell T. Coggeshall	1956–57
Aims C. McGuinness	1957–60
Boisfeuillet Jones	1961–64
Edward Dempsey	1964–65

ASSISTANT SECRETARY FOR HEALTH AND SCIENTIFIC AFFAIRS

Dr. Philip R. Lee	1965–69
Dr. Roger O. Egeberg	1969–71
Dr. Merlin K. DuVal	1971–73
Dr. Charles Edwards*	1973–

ASSISTANT SECRETARY FOR PUBLIC AFFAIRS

Robert O. Beatty	1971–73
Sanford H. Winston (Acting)	1973
Lewis M. Helm	1973–

DIRECTOR OF ADMINISTRATION

Rufus E. Miles, Jr.	1953–55
Fordyce Luikart	1955–56
Rufus E. Miles, Jr.	1956–61

ADMINISTRATIVE ASSISTANT SECRETARY

| Rufus E. Miles, Jr. | 1961–64 |

ASSISTANT SECRETARY FOR ADMINISTRATION

Rufus E. Miles, Jr.	1964–65
Donald F. Simpson	1966–69
James Farmer	1969–70

* Title changed to Assistant Secretary for Health in 1973.

Rodney H. Brady   1971–72
Robert H. Marik   1973–

COMPTROLLER
Rufus E. Miles, Jr.   1955–56
(Office retired, 1956–61)

DEPUTY ASSISTANT SECRETARY, COMPTROLLER
James F. Kelly   1961–66

ASSISTANT SECRETARY, COMPTROLLER
James F. Kelly   1966–70
James B. Cardwell   1970–73
John D. Young   1973–

ASSISTANT SECRETARY FOR EDUCATION
Paul A. Miller   1966–68
Lynn M. Bartlett   1968–69
James E. Allen, Jr.   1969–70
(Office retired, 1970–72)
Sidney P. Marland   1972–73

DIRECTOR, OFFICE FOR CIVIL RIGHTS
Peter Libassi   1966–68
Ruby Martin   1968–69
Leon Panetta   1969–70
J. Stanley Pottinger   1970–73
Peter E. Holmes   1973–

DIRECTOR, OFFICE OF CONSUMER AFFAIRS
Virginia H. Knauer   1973–

DIRECTOR OF PUBLIC INFORMATION
J. Stewart Hunter (Acting)   1953–57
Harvey A. Bush   1957–66
Carleton E. Spitzer   1966–68
George L. Brand   1969
Baxter H. Omohundro   1969–71

DIRECTOR, NATIONAL INSTITUTE OF HEALTH
Dr. George W. McCoy   1930–37
Dr. Lewis R. Thompson   1937–42
Dr. Rolla E. Dyer   1942–48

DIRECTOR, NATIONAL INSTITUTES OF HEALTH
Dr. Rolla E. Dyer   1948–50
Dr. William H. Sebrell, Jr.   1950–55

Dr. James A. Shannon	1955–68
Dr. Robert Q. Marston	1968–73
Dr. Robert Stone	1973–

ADMINISTRATOR, HEALTH SERVICES AND
MENTAL HEALTH ADMINISTRATION

Dr. Robert Q. Marston	1968
Dr. Joseph T. English	1969–70
Dr. Vernon E. Wilson	1970–73
(Administration abolished, 1973)	

ADMINISTRATOR, HEALTH SERVICES ADMINISTRATION

| Harold Buzzell | 1973– |

ADMINISTRATOR, HEALTH RESOURCES ADMINISTRATION

| Dr. Kenneth M. Endicott | 1973– |

CENTER FOR DISEASE CONTROL

| Dr. David J. Sencer | 1966– |

ALCOHOL, DRUG ABUSE, AND MENTAL HEALTH ADMINISTRATION

| Dr. Roger O. Egeberg (Interim) | 1973– |

SURGEON GENERAL, PUBLIC HEALTH SERVICE

Dr. John M. Woodworth	1871–79
Dr. John B. Hammond	1879–81
Dr. Walter Wyman	1891–1911
Dr. Rupert Blue	1912–20
Dr. Hugh Cumming	1920–36
Dr. Thomas Parran	1936–48
Dr. Leonard Scheele	1948–56
Dr. Leroy E. Burney	1956–61
Dr. Luther L. Terry	1961–65
Dr. William H. Stewart	1965–69
Dr. Jesse L. Steinfeld	1969–73

COMMISSIONER OF EDUCATION

Henry Barnard	1867–70
John Eaton	1870–86
N. H. R. Dawson	1886–89
William T. Harris	1889–1906
Elmer E. Brown	1906–11
Philander P. Claxton	1911–21
John James Tigert	1921–28
William John Cooper	1929–33
George F. Zook	1933–34
John W. Studebaker	1934–48
Earl James McGrath	1949–53

Lee M. Thurston	1953
Samuel Miller Brownell	1953–56
Lawrence G. Derthick	1956–61
Sterling M. McMurrin	1961–62
Francis Keppel	1962–66
Harold Howe, II	1966–68
James E. Allen, Jr.	1969–70
Sidney P. Marland	1970–72
John R. Ottina	1973–

DIRECTOR, NATIONAL INSTITUTE OF EDUCATION

Thomas K. Glennan	1973–

ADMINISTRATOR OF FEDERAL FOOD AND DRUG LAW

CHIEF, BUREAU OF CHEMISTRY, U.S. DEPARTMENT OF AGRICULTURE

Harvey W. Wiley, M.D.	1883–1912
Carl L. Alsberg, M.D.	1912–21
Walter G. Campbell (Acting)	1921–23
C. A. Browne, Ph.D.	1923–27

DIRECTOR OF REGULATORY WORK, U.S. DEPARTMENT OF AGRICULTURE

Walter G. Campbell	1927–40

COMMISSIONER OF FOOD AND DRUGS (FSA AND HEW)

Walter G. Campbell	1940–44
Paul B. Dunbar, Ph.D.	1944–51
Charles W. Crawford	1951–54
George P. Larrick	1954–65
James L. Goddard, M.D.	1966–68
Herbert L. Ley, Jr., M.D.	1968–69
Charles C. Edwards, M.D.	1969–73
Sherwin Gardner (Acting)	1973
Alexander Schmidt	1973–

COMMISSIONER OF SOCIAL SECURITY

Arthur J. Altmeyer	1946–53
John W. Tramburg	1953–54
Charles I. Schottland	1954–58
William L. Mitchell	1959–62
Robert M. Ball	1962–73
Arthur Hess (Acting)	1973
James B. Cardwell	1973–

COMMISSIONER OF WELFARE

Ellen Winston	1963–67
(Office retired)	

COMMISSIONER ON AGING
William D. Bechill   1965–69
John B. Martin   1969–73
Arthur S. Flemming   1973–

DIRECTOR, OFFICE OF VOCATIONAL REHABILITATION
Mary E. Switzer   1953–63

COMMISSIONER, VOCATIONAL REHABILITATION ADMINISTRATION
Mary E. Switzer   1963–67

ADMINISTRATOR, SOCIAL AND REHABILITATION SERVICE
Mary E. Switzer   1967–70
John D. Twiname   1970–73
James Dwight   1973–

Bibliography

BOOKS AND ARTICLES

ABBOTT, GRACE. *From Relief to Social Security: The Development of the New Public Welfare Services and Their Administration.* Chicago: University of Chicago Press, 1941.

ALTMEYER, ARTHUR. *The Formative Years of Social Security.* Madison: University of Wisconsin Press, 1966.

ARMOR, DAVID. "The Evidence on Busing," *The Public Interest,* No. 28, pp. 90–126, Summer, 1972.

BAILEY, STEPHEN K. *The Office of Education and the Education Act of 1965.* Inter-University Case Program Report No. 100. Indianapolis: Bobbs-Merrill.

BAILEY, STEPHEN K., and EDITH K. MOSHER. *ESEA: The Office of Education Administers a Law.* Syracuse: Syracuse University Press, 1968.

BELL, WINIFRED. *Aid to Dependent Children.* New York: Columbia University Press, 1965.

BOWEN, WILLIAM, FREDERICK HARBISON, RICHARD LESTER, and HERMAN SOMERS. *The American System of Social Insurance: Its Philosophy, Impact and Future Development.* The Princeton Symposium. New York: McGraw-Hill, 1968.

BROWN, J. DOUGLAS. *An American Philosophy of Social Security.* Princeton: Princeton University Press, 1972.

BROWNLOW, LOUIS. *A Passion for Anonymity.* Chicago: University of Chicago Press, 1958.

BURNS, EVELINE M. *The American Social Security System.* Boston: Houghton Mifflin, 1951.

CAMPBELL, ROALD, et al. *The Organization and Control of American Schools.* New York: Merrill, 1965.

CUBBERLY, ELWOOD P. *Public Education in the United States.* Boston: Houghton Mifflin, 1919, 1934.

317

GARDNER, JUDY. "FDA's Existence Threatened by Product Safety Battle," *National Journal*, Vol. 4, No. 24, pp. 987–997, June 10, 1972.

HABER, WILLIAM, and WILBUR J. COHEN. *Social Security; Programs, Problems, and Policies: Selected Readings*. Homewood, Ill.: Irwin, 1960.

IGLEHART, JOHN K. "Welfare Report/HEW program doubles in size as officials scramble to check its growth," *National Journal*, Vol. 4, No. 25, June 17, 1972.

MILES, RUFUS E., JR. "The Case for a Federal Department of Education," *Public Administration Review*, Vol. XXVII, No. 1, pp. 1–9, March, 1967.

MINTZ, MORTON. *The Therapeutic Nightmare*. Boston: Houghton Mifflin, 1965.

MOYNIHAN, DANIEL P. *The Politics of a Guaranteed Income*. New York: Random House, 1972.

MYERS, ROBERT J. *Social Insurance and Allied Government Programs*. Homewood, Ill.: Irwin, 1965.

NEAL, HARRY E. *The Protectors: The Story of the Food and Drug Administration*. New York: Messner, 1968.

OBERMAN, C. ESCO. *A History of Vocational Rehabilitation in America*. Minneapolis: Dennison, 1965.

ORFIELD, GARY. *The Reconstruction of Southern Education*. New York: John Wiley, 1969.

PANETTA, LEON, and PETER GALL. *Bring Us Together*. Philadelphia: Lippincott, 1971.

PECHMAN, JOSEPH, HENRY AARON, and MICHAEL TAUSSIG. *Social Security, Perspectives for Reform*. Washington, D.C.: Brookings, 1968.

PETTIGREW, THOMAS F., et al. "Busing: A Review of 'The Evidence,' " *The Public Interest*, No. 30, pp. 88–118, Winter, 1973.

SCHLESINGER, ARTHUR M., JR. *The Crisis of the Old Order, 1919–1933*. Boston: Houghton Mifflin, 1957.

SCHMECKEBIER, LAWRENCE F. *The Public Health Service, Its History, Activities, and Organization*. Baltimore: Johns Hopkins Press, 1923.

SCHOTTLAND, CHARLES I. *The Social Security Program in the United States*. New York: Appleton-Century-Crofts, 1963.

SCHULTZE, CHARLES, EDWARD FRIED, ALICE RIVLIN, and NANCY TEETERS. *Setting National Priorities, The 1973 Budget*. Washington, D.C.: Brookings, 1972.

SEIDMAN, HAROLD. *Politics, Position, and Power: The Dynamics of Federal Organization*. New York: Oxford University Press, 1970.

SMITH, DARRELL H. *The Bureau of Education: Its History, Activities and Organization*. Baltimore: Johns Hopkins Press, 1923.

SMITH, GLENN. *History of the U.S. Office of Education, 1867–1967*. Doctoral dissertation, University of Oklahoma, 1968.

STEIN, HAROLD, ed. *Public Administration and Policy Development:*

A Case Book. New York: Harcourt, 1952 ("The Transfer of the Children's Bureau," p. 15; "The Office of Education Library," p. 31).

STEINER, GILBERT Y. *Social Insecurity: The Politics of Welfare.* Chicago: Rand McNally, 1966.

STRICKLAND, STEPHEN P. *Politics, Science, and Dread Disease: A Short History of United States Medical Research Policy.* Cambridge: Harvard University Press, 1972.

TURNER, JAMES S., et al. *The Chemical Feast: The Ralph Nader Study Group Report on Food Protection and the Food and Drug Administration.* New York: Grossman, 1970.

WEBER, GUSTAVUS A. *The Food, Drug, and Insecticide Administration; Its History, Activities, and Organization.* Baltimore: Johns Hopkins Press, 1928.

WILLIAMS, RALPH C. *The United States Public Health Service 1798–1950.* Richmond, Va.: Whittet and Shepperson, 1951.

WITTE, EDWIN E. *The Development of the Social Security Act: A Memorandum on the History of the Committee on Economic Security and Drafting and Legislative History of the Social Security Act.* Madison: University of Wisconsin Press, 1962.

U.S. GOVERNMENT PUBLICATIONS

The following publications are published by the United States Government Printing Office, Washington, D.C.

ADVISORY COUNCIL ON PUBLIC WELFARE. *Having the Power, We Have the Duty.* A report to the Secretary of Health, Education, and Welfare. 1966.

ADVISORY COUNCIL ON SOCIAL SECURITY. *Permanent and Total Disability Insurance.* A report to the Senate Committee on Finance. 1948.

The Budget of the United States Government. 1930–74.

COLEMAN, JAMES S., et al. *Equality of Educational Opportunity.* 1966.

COLL, BLANCHE D. *Perspectives in Public Welfare—A History.* 1969.

CORNING, PETER A. *The Evolution of Medicare: From Idea to Law.* 1969.

COMMISSION ON ORGANIZATION OF THE EXECUTIVE BRANCH OF THE GOVERNMENT (1st Hoover Commission). *Reports* and *Task Force Reports.* 1949.

——— (2nd Hoover Commission). *Reports* and *Task Force Reports.* 1955.

COMMITTEE ON ECONOMIC SECURITY. *Report to the President.* 1935.

CONGRESS. HOUSE OF REPRESENTATIVES. COMMITTEE ON GOVERNMENT OPERATIONS. "Creating a Department of Health, Education, and Welfare," *Report* (to accompany H.J. Res. 223). 83rd Cong., 1st Sess., House Report 166. 1953.

DEPARTMENT OF HEALTH, EDUCATION, AND WELFARE. *Annual Reports*

320   BIBLIOGRAPHY

—A Common Thread of Service: An Historical Guide to HEW.
1972.
PRESIDENT OF THE UNITED STATES. *First Plan on Government Reorganization.* Message from the President (76th Cong., 1st Sess.,
House Doc. 262). 1939.
————. *Proposals for Welfare Reform.* Message from the President
of the United States relative to welfare reform (91st Cong., 1st
Sess., House Doc. 91-146).
PRESIDENT'S PANEL ON MENTAL RETARDATION. *A Proposed Program
for National Action to Combat Mental Retardation: Report to
the President.* 1962.
RICHARDSON, ELLIOT L. *Responsibility and Responsiveness.* A speech
published in pamphlet form. Department of Health, Education,
and Welfare. 1970.
————. *Responsibility and Responsiveness (II): A Report on the
HEW Potential for the Seventies.* Department of Health, Educa-
tion, and Welfare, January 18, 1973.
VOCATIONAL REHABILITATION ADMINISTRATION. *Restoring Disabled
People to Jobs and Useful Living* (89th Cong., 1st Sess.). House
Committee on Education and Labor, Committee Print. 1965.
WHEALEN, JOHN J. "A History of Federal Aid to Education, 1785–
1965." A mimeographed publication of the Office of Education,
Department of Health, Education, and Welfare. Undated.

Index

321

Brownlow Committee, 22, 31, 295
Budget, HEW, 269
Budget, U.S. Domestic, 8
Bureau of Federal Credit Unions, 58
Bureau of Health Manpower Education, 53, 172, 181, 202, 216
Bureau of Public Assistance, 113
Bureau of the Budget, 28, 31, 149, 175, 196, 197, 224, 271, 272
Burns, Arthur, 57

Campbell, Walter G., 223
Cardozo, Benjamin N., 14
Cardwell, James Bruce, 79
Carlucci, Frank, 67, 74, 276
Carter, Lisle, 245
Celebrezze, Anthony J., 43, 44–46, 128
Celler, Emanuel, 245
Children's Bureau, 22, 57, 194
Citizens' Advisory Committees (FDA), 226, 227
Citizens' Commission on Science, Law, and Food Supply, 236
City University of New York, 258
Civil Rights Act of 1964, 2, 55, 56, 143, 155, 246–262
Civil Works Administration, 11
Civilian Conservation Corps, 10, 16, 21
Claxton, Philander P., 141
Clinical Center, NIH, 169, 171
Cohen, Wilbur J., 41, 42, 52–54, 71, 117, 147, 200, 209, 216, 242, 278, 293
Coleman Report, 247, 261
Coll, Blanche C., 112
Columbia University, 258
Commissioned corps, PHS, 192, 196, 199
Committee on Economic Security, 13
Committee on Education Beyond the High School, 152
Commons, John R., 12
Community Development, Department of, 290
Community health services, 207
Community mental health centers, 58, 204, 205
Connally, John, 292

Consumer Product Safety Commission, 221
Copeland, Royal S., 223
Corson, John, 106
Cotton, Norris, 177
Council of Chief State School Officers, 163
Cranberries, 37, 38
Crawford, Charles, 226
Curtis, Carl, 88
Cyclamates, 58

Daley, Richard J., 249
Davey, Martin L., 16
DeBakey, Dr. Michael E., 176, 213
Defense, Department of, 48, 49, 263, 264, 265
Delaney, James, 235
Delaney Amendment, 37, 235
Derthick, Lawrence, 159
Dingell, John, 23
Division of Biologics Standards, 221, 237, 274
Downey, Herman, 187
Dunbar, Paul B., 224
Dyer, Rolla, 169, 185, 187

Economic Affairs, Department of, 290
Education, Bureau of, 8
Education Amendments of 1962, 154
Educational renewal, 156
Educational television, 76, 77, 156
Edwards, Charles C., 202, 233, 241, 242
Ehrlichman, John, 254
Eisenhower, Dwight D., 25, 36
Elementary and Secondary Education Act, 35
Emergency Medical Services Program, 203
Epstein, Abraham, 83
Equal Employment Opportunity Commission, 256
Evers, Medgar, 246
Ewing, Oscar R., 20, 23, 168

Falk, I. S., 108
Family Assistance Plan, 57, 124–26, 291
Family planning, 208, 209

Federal Coal Mine Health and Safety Act, 58
Federal Emergency Relief Administration, 11
Federal Regional Councils, 280
Federal Security Agency, 18–25, 28, 29, 68, 223, 240
Finch, Robert H., 55–59, 67, 252, 253, 278
Flemming, Arthur S., 36–41
Flood, Daniel J., 100, 177
Fogarty, John E., 50, 170, 175, 182, 188, 189, 251
Folsom, Marion B., 33–36, 49, 60, 83, 98, 108, 145, 293
Food additives, 234, 235
Food and Drug Administration, 3, 30, 31, 37, 38, 64, 220–43
Fountain, Lawrence H., 228
Friedman, Milton, 125, 232, 233

Gallaudet College, 161
Gardner, John W., 46–51, 128, 248, 249, 250, 263, 277, 278, 289, 293
Garner, John Nance, 19, 26
General Motors, 263, 264, 265
Goddard, James L., 241
Goodrich, William W., 37
Gorham, William, 72
Gorman, Mike, 175, 182, 204
"GRAS" List, 234, 235
Green, Edith, 148
Gresham's Law of Public Administration, 267
Gruening, Ernest, 209
Gulick, Luther H., 17

Harding, Warren G., 141, 142
Harlow, Bryce, 80
Harvey, John, 230
Head Start, 57, 76, 77
Health Care Facilities Service, 203
Health Education Facilities Act of 1963, 152
Health Maintenance Organization Service, 203, 214
Health Resources Administration, 65, 203, 216
Health Services Administration, 65, 202
Health Services and Mental Health Administration, 53, 54, 191, 200, 201

Heineman Commission, 292, 294
Helm, Lewis M., 72
Hill, Lister, 170, 175, 182, 188, 195
Hill-Burton program, 23, 191, 195, 211, 212
Hobby, Oveta Culp, 25–33, 88, 226
Hollings, Ernest F., 118
Hoover, Herbert, 9, 10
Hoover Commission, Second, 197, 198
Hopkins, Harry, 16
Horowitz, Harold, 245
Housing and Urban Development, Department of, 68
Howard University, 162
Howe, Harold, 250
Human Resources, Department of, 3, 4, 290–300
Humphrey, George, 34
Humphrey, Hubert, 228

Indian Health Service, 202, 206, 207
Ink, Dwight, 159

Johnson, Lyndon B., 45, 48, 147, 148, 149, 152, 246, 250, 292, 299
Justice, Department of, 56, 143

Kefauver, Estes, 228
Kefauver-Harris Drug Amendments, 230, 231
Kellogg, Paul, 7
Kelly, James F., 79, 80, 81
Kelsey, Frances O., 231
Kendall School, 162
Kennedy, Edward M., 107, 108
Kennedy, John F., 40, 41, 146, 152, 245, 246
Keppel, Francis, 146, 147, 159, 248, 249
Kerr-Mills Bill, 133
Keynes, John M., 1, 10
King, Martin Luther, Jr., 2, 246
King, W. L. Mackenzie, 299

Labor, Department of, 120, 256, 257
Laird, Melvin, 188
Lasker, Mary, 174–77, 182
Lasswell, Harold, 265
Lee, Philip R., 52